A DOUGHBOY
== WITH THE ==
FIGHTING 69th

A REMEMBRANCE OF WORLD WAR I

Albert M. Ettinger & A. Churchill Ettinger

POCKET BOOKS

New York   London   Toronto   Sydney   Tokyo   Singapore

All photographs marked with an asterisk are from the collections of Lieutenant Colonel Kenneth H. Powers, Historian of the Sixty-Ninth Regiment of New York, or from the collection of the regimental association. All photographs not otherwise credited are from the U.S. Army Signal Corps collection now in the collections of the National Archives and Records Administration.

The author appreciates permission to reprint a paragraph of a letter from William J. Donovan to his wife, as contained in *The Last Hero* by Anthony Cave Brown, copyright © 1982, Times Books, a Division of Random House, Inc.

POCKET BOOKS, a division of Simon & Schuster Inc.
1230 Avenue of the Americas, New York, NY 10020

This book is dedicated to the footsoldiers of the 69th New York National Guard (165th United States Infantry) and to their comrades of the 42nd Rainbow Division that they might enjoy a doughboy's perspective of their World War I compatriots.

As one who has observed with pride and delight the spirit and enhanced color of today's regiment, a pride that my father would fully have shared, I am confident that it will not only uphold the regimental traditions of yesteryear, but forge its own out of the great humanity that is ever renewed in the City of New York.

Acknowledgments

Concerning those in the United States who facilitated the production of *Doughboy,* I am primarily indebted to ma femme, Yen Ettinger, resident French-English translator, who also, amid tears and laughter, transcribed these stories from tape; to David Einhorn, friend and fellow history buff, who constantly prodded me to undertake this venture; to Annemarie Albaugh, first-cut editor of the manuscript; to Fred Pernell, currently assistant manager of the still photos branch at the National Archives, for his invaluable assistance in researching court-martial records; to Lieutenant Colonel Kenneth Powers (Ret), the 69th's Regimental Historian, who provided access to documents, photographs, and personnel; to Colonel Robert J. T. Joy, M.D., who, by reviewing Chapter 9 on the Allerey Hospital Complex, brought several items of importance to the author's attention; and by no means least, to my publisher, Dr. Martin Gordon, whose cross appears to be a redoubtable effort to reconcile perceived historic value to an amoral balance column and the hysteric protestations of this writer at the deletion of an opinionated footnote or photograph . . . or two . . . or three . . . or . . .

Over There . . . I should particularly like to acknowledge the assistance of Jean-Claude Dupuis, chief of the documentary mapping unit of the National Geographic Institute of France, who, by providing access to World War I period maps, demonstrated that the location of today's road system in that country, sans the few Autoroutes, is virtually identical with that trod by 1917–18 Doughboys. My gratitude and deep affection also to Monique Harris of Angomont, Jules Legras of Croismare, Alain Bene of Baccarat, Francois de Vaux of Bourg, Mayor Maurice Jacquin of Mouacourt, Jean Morisot of Longeau-Percey, to Monsieur and Madame

Acknowledgments

Albert Dorey of Allerey, to Mayor Jean Nouvier and Antoine Humbert of Badonviller, to Antonin Guillot of Chalon-sur-Saone, and to my precious French brothers-in-law, Vu Ngoc Tranh and Yves Billot, all kindred spirits and guides extraordinaires.

A. C. Ettinger
Arlington, VA
October 1990

viii

Contents

Contents

Contents

Contents

Contents

Introduction

by

A. Churchill Ettinger

Why They Enlisted

It must be difficult for today's generation to understand why one and a half million American boys would enlist to fight in an overseas war having little perceptible threat to their country's national security. Yet, even before the United States formally entered World War I on April 6, 1917, hundreds of young men, mostly college boys, had joined the French Army through the LaFayette Escadrille, the Foreign Legion, or as volunteer ambulance drivers with the American Field Service.

After the United States declared war, the stream of volunteers became a veritable flood. Bill Ettinger, my father's older brother, joined the Fordham College Volunteer Ambulance Corps attached to the French Army because it was the quickest way to get into action. A younger brother, Churchill, was only fourteen years old, yet he and a school chum hitch-hiked to Montreal where they tried to enlist in the Canadian Army.[1]

The reasons for this flood of enlistments had roots in an acrimonious history involving the United States with Germany, Mexico, and Japan. An increase in anti-German sentiment had been developing in this country since 1880 with the "Samoa Incident," was intensified over events in China at the turn of the century, and was subsequently aggravated by diplomatic conflict with Germany in the Philippines, the Caribbean, and South America.[2]

These thirty-seven years involving hostile incidents with the Imperial German Government were reported in the press and periodicals of the day. However, while many of their readers had developed a critical attitude toward Germany, it was more than counterpoised by intense and cohesive anti-English sentiment embraced by our two largest European immigrant minorities, the Catholic Irish and Germans.

Between these contending bodies, the predominance of American opinion was decidedly neutral. That sentiment began to change when Germany invaded neutral Belgium, killed over three thousand civilians, and looted and burned several villages, as well as part of the city of Louvain and its precious university.[3] Then the Kaiser authorized an unprecedented policy of unrestricted submarine warfare, whereby any vessel approaching the British Isles or France was subject to torpedo attack without warning. While promising a victorious German counterpoise to a British naval blockade, that fateful policy resulted in the sinking of dozens of neutral ships, four of them American.

Most shocking to the American public was the U-boat sinking of the British passenger liner, *Lusitania,* with a loss of 1,195 persons including 124 Americans and 94 children. However, many citizens, particularly in the West and Midwest, would not have supported entry into a war over the *Lusitania,* or any number of American commercial vessels. The Midwest was heavily isolationist, and the West was more concerned about Mexico and the threat allegedly posed by Chinese and Japanese immigration.

Historian Barbara Tuchman persuasively argues that the critical change occurred on March 1, 1917, when President Wilson released an intercepted, secret telegram from the German Secretary of Foreign Affairs, Arthur Zimmermann, to the Mexican government. The message proposed an alliance with Germany and the involvement of Japan in a reconquest of Texas, New Mexico, and Arizona—should the United States enter the war. This was a normal act of diplomatic contigency planning on Germany's part. It was also incredibly foolish. War drums reverberated throughout the American West as the image of invading Mexican and Japanese hordes, led by Prussian Junkers, triggered longstanding and deeply ingrained concern and hostility. Thus did Western hysteria marshal forces with Eastern moral outrage to demand retribution.[4]

Woodrow Wilson did not "carry the United States into war." He had repeatedly importuned to convene a peace conference to negotiate differences between the belligerent nations and, for a few months, secured a cessation of Germany's submarine policy. But with the resumption of that policy and interception of the Zimmermann cable, he could no more have remained neutral in April of 1917 than Franklin Roosevelt in December of 1941. Had Wilson not called upon Congress for a declaration of war, which was overwhelmingly approved, he might have been impeached.

The Army

America's participation in the war was brief but brutal. In less than seven and a half months of active Army combat, our total armed forces lost 116,708 men, with an additional 204,002 wounded. This works out to 35,626 casualties a month, as compared with 24,504 casualties a month (over 44 mos) for American World War II servicemen, 4,146 a month (over 38 mos) for Korea, and 2,250 per month (over 94 mos) for Vietnam.[5]

While American losses were very high for the limited period of active combat, they were minimal compared with the casualties suffered by other nations, which had been fighting for three years before we became involved. Russian casualties totaled 6,650,000; German-6,000,000; French-5,600,000; Austrian/Hungarian-4,800,000; British-3,000,000; and Italian-1,600,000. These data aid in understanding the decisive impact that American fighting men had on the outcome of that conflict. In the spring of 1917, the United States could offer significant financial backing, an excellent navy, and potential manpower—healthy, eager bodies to replace Allied losses.

The German High Command understandably erred in believing its forces could prevail before American troops would arrive in sufficient force to turn the tide. When the United States entered the war on April 6, 1917, its Regular Army consisted of 133,000 officers and men, whose units could scarcely have filled a gap on the Western Front. Behind these regulars, however, were 382,000 National Guardsmen, soon to be organized into seventeen Guard divisions, and a respectable number of Guard officers had gained experience during the 1898 Spanish-American War and the 1916 Mexican border fracas.

The immediate need was reorganization, expansion, and intensive training in the kind of warfare that could be anticipated in Europe. Secretary of War, Newton D. Baker, had developed plans for an army of 3.5 million, and by the end of the war, one and a half years later, had raised four million men under arms, half of whom had been transported to France. This was accomplished through a flood of volunteers, the Selective Service Act of May 1917, and a remarkable performance by the United States Navy, which lost not a single troop transport under convoy to enemy attack, and reduced merchant sinking from a peak of 900,000 tons in April 1917, to 288,000 tons during November.

Three months after Congress declared war, a token force of thirteen thousand American troops arrived to march down the Champs Elysées. These were so-called regulars from the 1st Division, but two-thirds of them were raw recruits. Most of the real regulars of the "Big Red One" were home training the volunteer army of National Guardsmen that had begun to mobilize.

In early September of 1917, the 26th Yankee Division of New England National Guard arrived in France, shortly followed by a miscellaneous 2nd Division, so understrength in its Regular Army regiments that it included a Marine brigade. Then, in late October, the 42nd Rainbow Division landed, consisting of National Guard units from 26 states and the District of Columbia.

These four divisions became the shock troops of the American Army, and few other divisions served as long in the trenches or suffered comparable casualties—notably the 3rd and 4th Regular Army divisions, the 28th Pennsylvania National Guard, and the 32nd Guard division with units from Michigan and Wisconsin, these arriving during the spring of 1918.

The state of readiness of America's first troops abroad is well illustrated by a passage from Stallings' *The Doughboys:*

> Half of Europe was represented in Bailey's company [of the 2nd Division of "Regulars"]. . . . Three of the platoon leaders were . . . college boys with little more knowledge than Bailey, who confessed he knew nothing at all. Only the fourth platoon leader, who had been a Regular Army sergeant, knew something about

soldiering. . . . He recalled that his company of "Regulars" contained not a single man who had ever fired a
Springfield rifle, and few who had ever discharged a
firearm of any kind.[6]

Nevertheless, imbued with a determination to "make the
world safe for democracy," 287,500 doughboys had arrived
in France by April 1918, when the 1st Division counterattacked west of Montdidier and captured Cantigny. In late
May, our 2nd and 3rd (Rock of the Marne) Divisions
blocked the enemy at Chateau-Thierry and then attacked in
June. On July 15, the 42nd Rainbow Division and two black
regiments of the 93rd Division reinforced the French Fourth
Army and helped stop the German "Peace Offensive" cold
at the Battle of Champagne. Within a week, the Rainbow
deployed at Chateau-Thierry and joined the 1st, 2nd, 3rd,
26th, and 32nd Divisions, as well as four French armies, in
the Aisne-Marne offensive.

Two months later, five of the now veteran American
divisions, plus four green ones, with five additional in
reserve, were poised before the St. Mihiel ready to undertake the first operation of the war under the independent
command of its newly created First Army. By then, there
were over 1,200,000 American soldiers in France, and some
230,000 of them charged through the St. Mihiel salient in
three days against 90,000 Germans taking 15,000 prisoners.
The enemy, to straighten its lines, was in the process of
withdrawing from the salient, and the French had contributed 110,000 troops, most of the artillery, and all the tanks
and aircraft; nevertheless, the victory provided a great
morale boost for the fledgling American Army and its allies.[7]

With little time to rest, those blooded divisions effected a
logistic miracle by moving sixty miles over three muddy
roads, with all their equipment, to the forests and craggy
ravines of the Argonne. There, after 41 days and 117,000
American casualties, they had overthrown an elaborate
defense system and elements of the most proficient, albeit
outnumbered, army in the world. Simultaneously, more
numerous British and French troops attacked at Arras,
Flanders, and the Somme. The Hindenburg Line collapsed,
and a few weeks later the Armistice was signed as American

troops stood poised on the heights of the Meuse River across from Sedan.[8]

The Division

The fundamental, multi-function, autonomous unit of any modern army is its combat division. The division consists of everything necessary to wage land warfare—infantry and artillery regiments, as well as supply, sanitation, communication, engineer, transportation, and field hospital units.

When Congress declared war on April 6, 1917, the Regular Army had not a single division in combat-ready status, and the War Department had already concluded that its old table of organization would be inadequate to provide units that could tilt the balance of forces then in stalemate on Europe's Western Front. Thus, to develop a punch sufficient to pentrate the static trench defense system of the Central Powers, each American combat division was increased to 27,000 men, twice the size of its British and European counterparts.[9]

The existing National Guard divisions that formed the basis for this expansion were organized along state and regional lines, and the first of these that might have been prepared to embark for France were the 26th Yankee Division from New England, the 27th New York State Division, and the 28th Pennsylvania. Secretary of War Baker, however, was concerned about the state repercussions were one of these divisions to be selected over another. When he presented the problem to his aide, then Major Douglas MacArthur, the latter suggested the possibility of organizing a multi-state division from existing surplus Guard units.

After the details were approved, MacArthur, who was also the War Department's press representative, convened a news conference to announce the, as yet, unnamed and unnumbered first National Guard division to be designated for service in France. He stated that its organization included crack units from twenty-six states, which would represent the spirit of America as a whole, and that "in the make up and promise of the future of this division, it resembles a rainbow." At this, some perceptive correspondent declared: "Rainbow—there's the name for the division—I shall call it the Rainbow in my dispatch." Thus, the only composite National Guard division of the American Army got its name from a newspaper reporter even before it had been assigned a number. The "42nd" came later, after all the proposed Regular Army and conventional National Guard divisions had been designated.[10]

Major General William A. Mann was placed in command of the Rainbow, and MacArthur was promoted to colonel as its chief of staff. Together they selected a sample of the most experienced and combat-ready Guard units from 26 states and the District of Columbia to fill its ranks.

The division included two infantry brigades: The 83rd Brigade, commanded by Brigadier General Michael Lenihan, was formed from the 69th Regiment of New York City and the 4th Ohio, plus a machine gun battalion from Wisconsin. The 84th Infantry Brigade, first commanded by Brigadier General Robert Brown, later by MacArthur, consisted of the 4th Alabama and the 3rd Iowa, with a machine gun battalion from Georgia.

Heavy fire power for the division was provided by a field artillery brigade, which included artillery regiments from Illinois, Indiana, and Minnesota. Then there were a trench mortar battery from Maryland, engineer battalions from South Carolina and California, two companies of military police from Virginia, a Texas supply train, an ammunition train from Kansas, ambulance companies from New Jersey, Tennessee, Oklahoma, and Michigan; field hospital companies from the District of Columbia, Nebraska, Oregon, and Colorado; a signal corps battalion from Missouri, and a calvary troop from Louisiana.

Total armament for the Rainbow consisted of:

16,200	rifles (American Springfields)
260	machine guns (French-made Hotchkiss)
48	37mm guns (French one-pound cannon)
48	Stokes mortars (English)
48	75mm cannon (French)
24	155mm howitzers (French)
12	6" trench mortars

42nd RAINBOW DIVISION

(27,000 men)

Major General William Mann, commanding
Major General Charles Menoher, succeeded to command
Colonel Douglas MacArthur, chief of staff, later brigadier general

83rd Inf. Brig.	84th Inf. Brig.	67th F.A. Brig.	Support Units
Gen. M. Lenihan	Gen. Rbt. Brown	Gen. C. Summerall	
Col. H. Reilly	Gen. MacArthur	Gen. McKinstry	
165th New York	167th Alabama	149th Ill. F.A.	117th Engin.
(Colonels)	Wm. P. Screws	Henry J. Reilly	Wm. Kelly
John Barker		A.P. Smith	
Frank McCoy			117th Md. Trench
Harry Mitchell		150th Ind. F.A.	Mortars
Charles Dravo		Rbt. H. Tyndall	
William Donovan			117th Mo. Field
			Signal Batt.
166th Ohio	168th Iowa	151st Minn. F.A.	
Benson Hough	E.R. Bennett	Geo. E. Leach	117th Sanitary
	Matthew Tinley		Train
150th Wisconsin	151st Georgia		117th Tx. Supply
M.G. Battalion	M.G. Battalion		Train
Maj. Wm. Hall	Maj. Cooper Winn		
			117th Va. M.P.s

Note: Each brigade = 8,450 men, optimum
  Each infantry regiment = 3,600 men, optimum
  F.A. = Field Artillery M.G. = Machine Gun

A simplified schematic for the division, with its reorganized nomenclature, appears on the adjacent page.

The esprit de corps of the Rainbow was extraordinary. The men took great pride in their diverse origins, and each infantry regiment vied for honor on the battlefield. Of course, there was the spirit of the volunteer at its roots, but that was true of every National Guard division. What made the Rainbow unique was an awareness by the men that they had been selected to represent, not only their particular state, but the country as a whole. Nevertheless, it required more than federalization and new regimental designations to create the elan that developed. That very special intense comradeship was forged on several battlefields of shared experience, sacrifice, and life dependency.

The Regiment

The 69th New York National Guard had its origin early in 1851, when, to prepare for rebellion in Ireland, Irish citizens of New York City organized a militia known locally as the Second Regiment of Irish Volunteers. On October 12, 1851, this group was officially accepted as part of the New York State Militia and designated the Sixty-Ninth Regiment. The regiment fought with great distinction in all the major battles of the Army of the Potomac during the Civil War as part of Meagher's Irish Brigade. Reportedly, it was General Robert E. Lee, who accorded an accolade, quickly adopted by the regiment, when he respectfully referred to "that fighting Sixty-Ninth."[11]

Although left waiting to embark from the Tampa docks as the Spanish-American War concluded, in 1916 the 69th served on the Border as part of Pershing's operation against Pancho Villa.

In March 1917, just back from Mexico, the regiment strode up Fifth Avenue to the Gaelic beat of its regimental march "Garry-Owen" for muster out of the Federal Service.

One month later, when war was declared against Germany, the 69th had only 500 effective fighting men, so immediate effort was made to recruit up to the 2,000 then required for an infantry regiment. This was accomplished within a month, with hand-picked volunteers coming mainly from the Irish county societies and Catholic athletic clubs of New York City. At this time, only about five percent of the men were non-Irish, but even these, according to Father Duffy, the regimental chaplain, "were Irish by adoption, Irish by association, or Irish by conviction."

On August 25, it was announced that this grand group of "boyos" had been selected, along with experienced Guard units from other states, to form the Rainbow Division, which would be in the vanguard of the American Expeditionary Force.[12]

Steps were quickly taken to raise the regiment's strength to 3,600 men, as required by the new table of organization. The officers would have preferred to enlist their own, their own way, but the Army decreed a transfer of men from other New York City Guard regiments. As it turned out, most of these were Irish, and the regiment easily assimilated the non "Fish Eaters" who clamored to transfer. As for the misfits, Father Duffy reported that "the Company Commanders and Surgeons know 'thirty-five distinct damnations' by which an undesirable can be returned to civilian life."

The schematic on the following page depicts the regiment's organization and most of its officer personnel through the war. At least two-thirds of the company captains were wounded and four were killed.

The Doughboy

Albert Leonard Mark Ettinger was born in Haworth, New Jersey, on April 3, 1900, to Dr. William Louis Ettinger and Emma McCarthy. In spite of the German name, Dr. Ettinger was half Irish by descent, and Emma's parents had been born in Ireland. Thus, the narrator of these stories was three-fourths Irish; so much for ethnic identification by surname in the United States.

Although both of Albert's parents were Catholic, they taught in the New York City public schools, where the good doctor, a licensed physician as well as educator, established an enviable reputation. He initiated the city's first teachers' union, principals' association and complex of vocational schools and, according to his son, secured appointment of

165th U.S. INFANTRY (69th N.Y.)
(3,600 men)

Colonels Commanding

Charles Hine	Harry Mitchell
John Barker	Charles Dravo
Frank McCoy	William Donovan

Headquarters Company

Captains Commanding:	Walter Powers, Alex Anderson, Michael Walsh
Captains Adjutant:	Wm. Doyle, A. Anderson, Wm. McKenna, M. Meany
Reg. Sergeant Major:	Ambrose Steinert
Regimental Chaplain:	Major/Father Francis Duffy
Medical Department:	Major/Doctor George Lawrence

37mm Cannon Platoon	Signal Platoon
Stokes Mortar Platoon	Intelligence Section
Pioneer Platoon	Band Kitchens

Supply Company:	Captain John Mangan
Machine Gun Company:	Captain R.B. DeLacour

Infantry Battalions—1000 men each

1st Battalion: Majors William Donovan, Michael Kelly, Merle-Smith

Company (250 men ea)	Captains
A	George McAdie, *William Baldwin, William Hutchinson
B	Thomas Reilley, John Clifford
C	William Kennelly, Herman Bootz
D	*James McKenna, Edmond Connelly, Oscar Buck

2nd Battalion:	Majors William Stacom, Alex Anderson, Herman Bootz
E	Alex Anderson, *Charles Baker, John Conners
F	Michael Kelley, Frank Marsh
G	James Archer, John Prout, Louis Stout
H	James Finn, Kenneth Ogle

3rd Battalion:	Majors Timothy Moynahan, *Jas. McKenna, Tom Reilley
I	Richard Ryan, *Michael Walsh
K	John Hurley, Emil Guignon
L	Merle-Smith, William Given
M	Martin Meany, John Rowley

Note: A company consisted of 4 platoons of 58 men each.
        A platoon consisted of 6 squads of 8 men each.
        * Killed in action.

the first Jewish principal in a system then predominantly Irish Catholic.

In 1917, with the support of childhood friends, Governor Alfred E. Smith and Associate Justice Thomas Churchill (who was also president of the city's Board of Education), Dr. Ettinger became Superintendent of Schools.

As a youth, Dr. Ettinger had been the amateur welterweight boxing champion of New York City, representing the Pioneer Athletic Club. That combativeness was reflected during his tenure as Superintendent when he effectively prevented New York City's mayor, John F. Hylan, from saddling the school system with "sweetheart" building contracts and hack appointees. Gruff and forceful in demeanor, Dr. Ettinger stood in marked contrast to his beautiful, gentle, and warmhearted Emma. But Emma, too, had spirit, and on those rare occasions when disagreement was serious, she usually prevailed.

As boys, Albert and his brothers, Churchill and William, lived in two different worlds. In Manhattan, where Dr. Ettinger was employed, they played and fought in the streets, while in Haworth, New Jersey, to which the family had moved in 1898, they attended school, prowled the neighborhood woods, peddled newspapers, and caddied on the new village golf course.

Apparently through association with friends and relations, young Albert acquired a pervasive distrust of the English—in spite of the fact that Wordsworth, Pope, and Kipling were among his favored poets. In those days, Americans of Irish descent generally had a strong aversion to any and all things English, and the closest friends of the Ettinger family were second generation Irish. Two virtues emerged from that otherwise parochial attitude: a disdain for pretense of any kind, and a reflexive identification with whomever might be the underdog of the moment.

By age 17, Albert was a handsome, slender young man who, through some remarkable alchemy, managed to synthesize in his behavior the warm generosity and sensitivity of his mother and the tough courage of his father. That courage was refined by paternal boxing lessons so that, at 135 pounds dripping wet, young "Red" would take on anyone at the first hint of insult to himself or his brothers. In sum, Albert "Red" Ettinger was an empathetic, adventurous youth, quick to take offense, and inclined to cherish both friendship and enmities.

Cautionary Note

Among the dozens of characters described by my father in this book, he took serious umbrage with only five. For two reasons, I have adopted pseudonyms for most of these persons and have so indicated at appropriate places in the text. First, out of respect for memories their descendants might hold of these soldiers. Second, my father may have been in error in some of his judgments or stories pertaining to them.

RECONNAISSANCE NO. 1

"Mr. President and gentlemen of the Rainbow Division . . . It was with you I lived my greatest moments. It is of you I have my greatest memories.

". . . those days of old have vanished tone and tint; they have gone glimmering through the dreams of things that were. Their memory is a land where flowers of wondrous beauty and varied colors spring, watered by tears and coaxed and caressed into fuller bloom by the smiles of yesterday. Refrains no longer rise and fall from that land of used to be. We listen vainly, but with thirsty ear, for the witching melodies of days that are gone. Ghosts in olive drab and sky blue and German grey pass before our eyes; voices that have stolen away in the echoes from the battle-fields no more ring out. The faint, far whisper of forgotten songs no longer floats through the air. Youth, strength, aspirations, struggles, triumphs, despairs, wide winds sweeping, beacons flashing across uncharted depths, movements, vividness, radiance, shadows, faint bugles sounding reveille, far drums beating the long roll, the crash of guns, the rattle of musketry—the still white crosses!

". . . my thoughts go back to those men who went with us to their last charge. In memory's eye I can see them now—forming grimly for the attack, blue-lipped, covered with sludge and mud, chilled by the wind and rain . . . driving home to their objective and to the judgment seat of God. . . .

"And tonight we are met to remember."

—Douglas MacArthur. Address before Rainbow Division Veterans, Washington, D.C., July 14, 1935.

"The name Rainbow was a happy choice. There was something about it that appealed. The men felt that the eyes of the nation were fixed on this Rainbow, it was going as a rainbow of hope to a tired nation at war. Its men were hand picked. Old traditions must be upheld. Each must aid the other; each must see that his end was held up; none must falter; the Rainbow must be kept in its high place. Thus was born the spirit of the Rainbow—a spirit never excelled by any division in the Army. Because many said it couldn't be done, the men from the North, East, South, and West quietly—did it."

> —R.M. Cheseldine, *Ohio in the Rainbow* (Colombus: F.J. Heer, 1924), pp. 56–57.

"It is to be remembered that every man in the organization was a volunteer, and of all the foundations upon which a soldier's training may be based there is none so promising of success as the spirit of the volunteer. In an army of conscripted men or professional soldiers, some may start with this spirit, and some may acquire it, but in the Rainbow Division every man had it when the Division was first organized. It was not only that every man was a volunteer, but that he knew that every other man was a volunteer."

> —John H. Taber, *The Story of the 168th* [Iowa] Infantry (Iowa City: Iowa Historical Society, Vol. 1, 1925), p. 64.

"In barricks or out of it, as you say, Sorr, an Oirish rig'mint is the divil an' more. 'Tis only fit for a young man wid eddicated fisteses. Oh the crame av disruption is an Oirish rig'mint, an' rippin', tearin', ragin' scatterers in the field av war! Me first rig'mint was Oirish—Faynians an' rebils to the heart av their marrow was they, an' *so* they fought for the Widdy betther than most, bein' contrairy—Oirish. They was the Black Tyrone."

> —Private Mulvaney in "With the Main Guard," from Kipling's *Soldier Tales.*

1

Son of the 69th

★　★　★

*The Allies were losing very definitely from
March to July, 1918. We have their word for it
that their backs were to the wall and that they
must have help, quickly and in force, or the best
they could hope for—and that highly unlikely—
was a draw.*

—Major General Hunter Liggett, A.E.F.

In June 1916, when I was sixteen years old in high school,
the National Guard of the United States was called into the
federal service to punish Pancho Villa for his invasion of
American towns along the Mexican border, so I and a school
chum, Angelo Salerno, decided to fight with General Pershing in Mexico.

One day we played hooky and went across Manhattan to
the 69th Regiment armory determined to enlist, but another
kid who knew about our plan snitched to the principal, Mr.
Lowie. Lowie immediately telephoned my father, and they
both arrived at the armory as Salerno and I were waiting to
be interviewed by the recruiting sergeant. Dad yanked us
out right then and there, but he assured me that if we really
had to go to war, I could serve my country. First, however, I
had to finish high school, and that was that.

After that hurdle, I planned to attend the University of
Cincinnati, where my brother Bill was studying chemical
engineering, because, at that time, I wanted to be a civil
engineer. I applied but was turned down for lack of a few

courses, so I went to Hackensack High School and took those courses, intending to reapply. Then April came along, war was declared on the 6th, and on the 8th, I enlisted.

Enlistment in the "Kid Glove 7th"

I wanted to join the "Fighting 69th", because that regiment had a glorious reputation among my friends. My father, on the other hand, preferred that I enlist in the 7th New York National Guard, mainly because a good friend of his, Claude Leland, who was chief librarian of the Board of Education, was also the first sergeant of Company L in that regiment. So, dutifully, I reported there, and Claude greeted me warmly and enlisted me in that Company.

Now, the 7th Regiment was a pretty classy outfit. It had recruited sons from the most wealthy families in New York, sported West Point grays for its dress uniforms, and held some of the finest social affairs in the city. There I met Nick Harris, with whom I spent weekends at his family's beautiful estate outside Newburgh; this became a life-long friendship. Nick's cousin, Fancher Nicholl, was the captain of Company L, and everything was fine.

Soon after uniforms were issued, the family celebrated my enlistment with a party, and there were all kinds of "Oh's" and "Ah's" when I walked into the room—except for my older cousin Frank Lambert. Frank was then 37 years old and had been a Marine Corps corporal during the Philippine Insurrection, where his nose was smashed in by a Moro spear. He just took one look at this skinny seventeen-year-old kid and dubiously shook his head. The next day, Frank reenlisted in the Marine Corps as a sergeant major. I guess he thought if the war was to be fought by the likes of me, we didn't have a chance.

Training in the 7th Regiment was a picnic. Central Park was our drill field, and we took every opportunity to wave at the pretty girls sitting on the park benches—we had regular cheering sections—and during the lunch hour, we'd make dates for the evening. We had the choice either of staying overnight in the armory or, if we lived in the city, going home in the evening, as long as we reported back by seven

4

o'clock the next morning. I can't imagine a more utopian army duty.

Then, in July, the War Department decided to build up the 69th to full war strength, because it had been assigned to the newly formed 42nd Rainbow Division by Douglas MacArthur. MacArthur, then a major, was military assistant to Secretary of War Newton Baker. The 42nd Rainbow Division, which was to consist of crack National Guard regiments from across the country, was his idea.

The effectiveness of National Guard troops had been questioned during the Civil War, but those that had served on the Mexican border in 1916, and the 69th was there, were generally topnotch, and since time was critical, MacArthur believed that the best of these regiments could be beefed up, combined into a single division, and quickly shipped overseas. Moreover, MacArthur was intrigued by the idea of reflecting the nation as a whole in a division of volunteers from units that would span the country from coast to coast; hence, he named it the "Rainbow Division."[1]

The 69th Calls

The Army's table of organization had been changed, and the 69th, which formerly comprised about 1200 men, was to be expanded to 3600 men. The regiment put on a great recruiting campaign and could easily have filled its ranks from the streets and the Irish clubs of New York, but the War Department decided to speed up the process by having a complement of men sent to them by the other Guard regiments in the city. These were the 7th, 12th, 14th, 23rd, and the 71st. There was also the 15th New York Guard, which was a black outfit; but in those days, they didn't have integration in the Army, and I guess the 15th wasn't invited—a damn shame because they were a good outfit.

When word came to the 7th that men were needed in the 69th, because it was to be sent overseas before any other regiment in New York, virtually everyone in the 7th wanted to transfer. I immediately jumped at the chance and asked Captain Nicholl to be included among those going, but he wouldn't make the reassignment. It was not to be a voluntary procedure. Instead, every seventh person on the roster was designated for transfer to the 69th. I wasn't the right number on the roster, but there were two sets of brothers in Company L who would be separated by the count, so Nick Harris and I volunteered to take the place of one each of the pairs. Well, my request was granted, but Captain Nicholl refused to let Nick join me, and Nick was brokenhearted. Then, another fellow from L Company, Tom FitzSimmons, succeeded in replacing the other brother. Tom became the first sergeant of HQ mortar platoon in the 69th, and, later, a very dear friend.

It was a wonderful day when the entire 7th Regiment, with those who were to be transferred taking up the rear, marched down Park Avenue over to the 69th Regiment armory at 26th Street and Lexington. Upon arriving, the main body of the regiment opened ranks, and our contingent of transfers marched between them into the armory.

The ceremony was unforgettable. As we entered, those Irishers of the 69th gave us a rousing roar of welcome. Men were up in the balcony and hanging from the rafters, and they cheered and cheered, because we were the first troops from the other regiments in New York to make the transfer.[2]

Headquarters Company

The old Headquarters Company of the 69th included a clerical staff, headed by a sergeant major, a regimental sergeant major and his staff, a small medical section, a band, and several foot and horse orderlies. According to the new table of organization, HQ[3] Company would be expanded to 360 men, to include new weapons platoons and special sections. There would be a pioneer platoon of combat engineers, an intelligence section, a Stokes mortar platoon, a 37mm gun platoon, a signal section, and a beefed-up medical section. Eventually, we would have the largest company in the regiment; the average company had 250 men.

One day, Captain Walter Powers, our regimental adjutant, assembled the men and explained our new organization, especially that of HQ Company. He described the duties of each section, and when he came to the pioneer platoon, he gave a glorious account of how they would cut the barbed wire in front of every infantry advance and be the heroes of the whole regiment.

After Captain Powers completed this great story, I immediately volunteered to join the pioneer platoon, believing it would be a good way to combine glory with preliminary training as a civil engineer. Unfortunately, Powers had neglected to mention the thousands of sandbags that would have to be filled, the miles of trenches to be dug or repaired, the latrines to be handcrafted, and the dead to be buried. Oh, well, it turned out to be a great platoon anyway because of the men we had.

The Pioneers at Camp Mills

Within a few weeks, the newly formed pioneer platoon of HQ Company was ordered to old Camp Mills in Hempstead, Long Island, to lay out company streets and erect squad tents for our company.

We found an area of farmland inhabited only by rabbits and skunks. Regular Army engineers had already staked out the grounds, and we lost no time in pitching our pup tents. Next, we erected a field kitchen and then set up model squad tents at the head of each company street for the regiment. Finally, we pitched the squad tents for our own company. It was laborious work, but we went at it with zeal, feeling rather proud to erect the first squad tents at Camp Mills. We laughed as we worked, supervised by Dick Heins, our first sergeant at the time and a great guy.

Our only problem was the food, which was terrible. Inexperienced cooks served up boiled beans with gobs of pork fat one day and canned corned beef stew the next. Men soon sickened from the greasy pork, and we were assaulted with an epidemic of boils. However, we persisted, and it was a happy day when the last squad tent was in place.

In early July, ours was the first regiment in the division to arrive at the camp, and other units followed from all over the United States. Eventually, Camp Mills housed nearly 30,000 men of the Rainbow, plus other units. It was truly spectacular to see that many troops under canvas.

7

The 4th Alabama and New York's "Men of Bronze"

As the other units arrived, our regiment always sent a HQ detachment to the railroad station with our band to greet them, and I thoroughly enjoyed these details.

One of the infantry regiments of the Rainbow was the famous 4th Alabama, later to become the 167th U.S. Infantry, as the 69th became the 165th U.S. Infantry. When we welcomed them at the station, the comradeship was great, but it didn't last very long, because they soon received hometown newspapers deploring the fact that the 4th Alabama and the 69th New York were to be brigaded together in the division.

These newspapers carried stories reminding their readers that, during the Civil War, the 4th Alabama and the 69th had clashed in several important engagements in which the two regiments almost wiped each other out. Only the history buffs of either outfit knew about this, but after reading those articles, the boys from Alabama became unfriendly, and fist fights erupted at the taverns in Hempstead, where the fellows hung out.

That condition worsened when the 15th New York arrived in camp. The 15th New York Guard was comprised of Negro troops, and it was a hell of a good outfit.[4] They had superb officers, black and white, and some of their noncommissioned officers came from the black 10th Cavalry, so they were pretty well trained. As a matter of fact, they had rifle practice at Camp Whitman near Peekskill, which we never got until arriving in France. They also had the best band of any regiment in the United States Army.

There was a great Negro musician in those days, James Reece Europe, who had a terrific dance band that played at the Cotton Club in New York. When war broke out, Europe was commissioned a lieutenant in the 15th Regiment, and he persuaded almost his entire group to enlist in the same outfit, at least those who could pass the physical. Then, with financial support from his colonel, who dunned wealthy friends, he recruited additional talent from Chicago and Puerto Rico.

When the 15th New York arrived at Camp Mills from

Spartanburg, South Carolina, a detail with the 69th band was turned out to welcome them, but our band was nothing compared with theirs. As soon as they got off the train, they formed up behind forty professional musicians led by Lieutenant Europe, and when they marched into camp, it was a sight to behold, and their music was simply out of this world! Europe had injected syncopated rhythm in his march selections, and we laughed and cheered like crazy. Europe's drum major was Noble Sissle. In peacetime, Sissle was a famous black singer and composer. Now a 2nd lieutenant and a high-stomping drum major, with a twirling baton and a fancy headdress, he was something else!

Our boys from the 69th received those of the 15th New York as buddies. Not so the Alabamians. They resented Blacks coming into camp. Hell, they resented us! The first thing you know fights erupted all over the place, and the 69th guys usually stood up for the 15th men and fought alongside them against the Alabamians.

It got so bad that the men of the 15th were required to turn in their ammunition. Not so the 4th Alabamians. We thought that was unfair, so a number of us slipped ammunition to our fellow New Yorkers. They never forgot that, and once, when I visited with a unit of the 15th in France, some of the fellows thanked me for it.

A riot nearly started when over a hundred fellows from Alabama attempted to invade the 69th camp intending to tear it down. (I'm sure they believed they had sufficient provocation. Our language alone was not the most elegant.) The Rainbow's military police unit from Virginia drove them back with fixed bayonets, and one of the Alabamians was killed. It was hell to pay, but finally the officers of both regiments, and Father Duffy in particular, calmed down the situation.[5]

As we left Camp Mills for France, men of the 69th and 4th Alabama were not very good buddies. However, as we got into combat, we came to appreciate each other and became good comrades, even though we were in different brigades. They usually fought on our right flank, or we would relieve one another, and we could always count on them. They were terrific fighters! After the war, at our Rainbow reunions, the

Alabamians would usually seek out our fellows to drink with, and we had some good times together.

Joe Hennessy

Many of us in the pioneer platoon had transferred from the 3rd Battalion of the old 7th Regiment. A few of the men had higher education, and most were Irish-Americans. We settled down with 12 men to a tent, and I found myself with eleven unique characters.

The only one in my group from the old 69th was Joe Hennessy, the Colonel's horse orderly. Joe was the biggest con artist and wiseacre in the platoon. "Fuck you. If you got any sisters, fuck them too." That was Hennessy. It's a wonder he survived. But he was such a likeable guy, and he looked so innocent, he could get away with murder.

Hennessy had been born and raised in the circus. His parents were circus performers, and he had become a typical "carny" in his attitude, language, and skulduggery in every respect. He was one of the nicest-looking fellows you ever saw, with big blue eyes, light brown hair, and smooth skin. Hennessy had the face of an angel with the soul of a devil.

Joe started out as a stunt man in the circus; then decided there was more money in the newly emerging movie business, so he became a movie stunt man. His greatest claim to fame was a double for Pearl White in a silent movie series, "The Perils of Pauline." Joe could do this because of his baby face.

One evening, Hennessy burst into the tent and proudly announced: "While you guys are ploughing through mud up to your ass, I'll be riding a motorcycle." Colonel Hine had told him that when we got to France, Joe could ferry him around in a sidecar.

There was a profound silence. Then Unc Shannon, recently a star fullback at Fordham College, decided to string Joe along:

"Listen Hennessy, we've been listening to your lies and assorted crap until it comes out of our ears. What the hell do you know about motorcycles?"

Joe replied that he had driven them in the movies. "Didn't you see the movie where Pearl White is speeding along, and a draw bridge opens, and she goes right through the air over the bridge? Well, that was me."

Unc, with great authority: "Well, you better know what you're talking about Hennessy, because in this tent is one of the greatest motorcycle riders in the world."

"Go on," scoffed Hennessy. "Who's that?"

"Why, Red Ettinger, of course. Haven't you heard of Ettinger out at the Velodrome? Don't you ever read the newspapers?"

The other guys picked up on it right away. "Come on, Hennessy, what's the matter with you. Ettinger is famous." Etc., etc. As smart and worldly wise as he was, Hennessy swallowed Unc's story hook, line, and sinker. (I had been on a motorcycle but once in my life, then had wrecked it, and my mother made me get rid of it.) The biggest con artist of the platoon had been conned, and from then on Hennessy treated me with great respect. As the Colonel's horse orderly, he let me ride his horse, which I thoroughly enjoyed. Joe liked me because I didn't tease him like the other fellows. I'd listen and pretend to believe his every word. He became a bosom friend until we arrived overseas; then we separated for a while as he became a motorcycle dispatch rider—and he often did drive the Colonel around in a sidecar.

Hennessy was a great story teller, and he constantly regaled us with tales of his dare-devil performances in the circus, most of which were wholly unbelievable. The only person in the tent who really believed his bunkum was Charlie Holt, scion of the Holt Publishing Company, who believed and trusted everyone.

Charlie Holt

Charlie Holt was a perfect gentleman who came to the 69th from the old 7th Regiment. He was a college graduate, and his parents were quite wealthy. I don't think that Charlie had ever lifted anything heavier than a set of golf clubs. He was about six feet tall, with bright red hair and light complexion, and he wore horn-rimmed glasses that framed big blue eyes. When he peered out at you from behind those glasses, he looked for all the world like an owl.

Every Sunday, a chauffeur-driven limousine would pull up with his mother. The chauffeur would get out with a large lunch hamper in one hand and a pair of sheets over his arm. Mrs. Holt was horrified that her Charles might have to sleep between rough blankets, so every Sunday she brought him fresh sheets. Well, to please her, Charlie used them. He had to put up with a lot of ribbing from the other fellows, but he was good-natured and took everything in stride.

Now this hamper was loaded with goodies—salad, roast beef, chicken, caviar and crackers, a bottle of bourbon, and sometimes a couple bottles of wine—all of which Charlie generously shared with his tentmates.

We had another character in our tent, Jimmy McKic, a former Marine. He was pretty much of a wise guy and he knew all the angles from his experience in the Corps. He kind of rubbed us the wrong way because of his superior attitude. He'd sneak out of camp almost every night, go into town, get a load on, and wake everyone up when he came back about four o'clock in the morning. After he came in, McKic would help himself to the whiskey that Charlie kept under his cot.

One night, we decided to lay a trap for McKic, so while he was in town, we found an empty whiskey bottle, took turns urinating in it, then put it under Charlie's cot. When McKic came in that morning, he immediately reached down, grabbed this bottle, and took a swig. We were all waiting for it and we howled. He was furious and challenged everybody to a fight. We just laughed.

Another night, while on guard duty, my post included the company latrine. There was a pea-soup fog, and you couldn't see more than a dozen paces. Suddenly, I heard a moaning sound, and a white apparition flitted from the direction of our squad tent. I thought it was one of the boys intending to give me a scare, so I circled around, and as this character approached the latrine, I jumped out from behind him and flourished my bayonet with a yell. He shouted and turned around . . . and it was Charlie Holt.

"Red, oh Red, you gave me a scare. God! . . . oh Red, it's too late." Poor Charlie had soiled his undershorts and the sheet. He'd had a touch of dysentery and was wearing one of his sheets for warmth as he stumbled, moaning, to the latrine.

Charlie Holt, the pampered "momma's boy," ended up with the Stokes mortar platoon and became the best Number One gunner we had. Tom FitzSimmons, top sergeant of our mortars, admired him a great deal because of his accuracy. Tom used him for the first shell to get the range, and Charlie was almost always on target. Everyone thought the world of Charlie Holt; he was such a gentle man and a good soldier.

Major Timothy J. Moynahan

The first few weeks at Camp Mills were fine. We enjoyed every bit of it, and I remember some funny incidents.

The 3rd Battalion of the regiment was commanded by Major Timothy J. Moynahan, a strict but good-natured officer, who was quite the dandy, with a black, waxed moustache turned up at the ends. Moynahan spoke with a loud, distinctive brogue that could be heard a block away. As often as possible, Major Moynahan rode his horse, "Fanny."

Every Saturday evening we had Retreat, an elaborate ceremonial affair in which officers of the various regimental units reported up the chain of command: "All present and accounted for, Sir!"

This particular Saturday, having accepted the report of his company commanders, Major Moynahan was trying to turn Fanny, so he could ride down the line to report to Colonel Hine, but Fanny was skittish and wouldn't turn in the right direction.

"Now Fanny; now Fanny; be a good girl, Fanny," the major said. No cooperation from Fanny. Finally, in exasperation: "Come on, Fanny! T'is no damn buck private talkin'. T'is your Major!"

At this pronouncement, out from the ranks someone shouted: "FUCK FANNY!"

"WHO SAID THAT!" bellowed Moynahan, his face beet red as he frantically tried to get Fanny under control.

The ranks roared with laughter.

That was our regiment.

A few months later, I was on sentry duty in the trenches outside the Rouge Bouquet. It was a dark night, and all was quiet. Then I heard a small group approach along the duckboards, and I could identify Major Moynahan by his loud and unique brogue. Apparently, he'd been imbibing generously with a group of French officers and had been inspired to escort them on a midnight tour of our sector. As he emerged from behind a turn in the trench, I stepped out and shouted: "WHO GOES THERE!" Major Moynahan must have jumped two feet in the air. Then he exclaimed: "My God, man. Don't you recognize the footsteps of your own major?"

Training Under Bill Cavanaugh and Mike Walsh

Our company commander was Captain Walter Powers, a fine officer, who was also the regimental adjutant. He had already served 15 years in the 7th Cavalry and was General Pershing's sergeant major when Pershing went into Mexico after Pancho Villa. In France he became a major and the division adjutant to Colonel MacArthur.

Responsibility for training HQ Company was initially assigned to First Lieutenant William Cavanaugh, a sweetheart of a guy from a wealthy New York family. Cavanaugh was familiar with the intricacies of high society and was a perfect gentleman. He didn't have a very strong voice, so during drill he'd have to shout through a megaphone.

One day, after assembly on the parade ground, he introduced us to Michael J. Walsh, a husky, rough looking second lieutenant, and we were advised that, from then on, Lieutenant Walsh would be in charge of our training.

Well, Mike Walsh was a soldier's soldier. Formerly a first sergeant with the 5th Cavalry, Walsh was as tough, brave, and fair a man as ever lived. Although we didn't have a firing range at Camp Mills, Walsh got us in shape for the more strenuous training we were about to experience in France— and he never needed a megaphone. All Mike Walsh had to do was whisper, and he could be heard halfway across the parade ground. When he shouted, it was like the roar of a cannon.

Soiree at the Vanderbilts

Some time later, Lieutenant Cavanaugh approached me with an invitation to attend a Red Cross benefit on Long Island at the home of Mrs. Albert Vanderbilt. Of course, I accepted. Mrs. Vanderbilt had requested a military escort for a super pageant to be held on her large estate in Huntington, and she had asked Lieutenant Cavanaugh to recruit a dozen men for that purpose.

Needless to say, I was quite proud to be one of the chosen.[6]

Well, you never saw such a sight in your life—the beautiful grounds, and this enormous mansion. The Vanderbilts had an open-air theater on the grounds, with seats terraced into the lawn, and the stage was a grassy island, surrounded by a fairly deep stream. It was a truly magnificent setting.

Marjorie Rambeau, a famous singer, was dressed to resemble Columbia. She wore a long, white, translucent gown, with a wreath around her head, and she sang the "Star Spangled Banner" and "Columbia, the Gem of the Ocean." She was so beautiful and had such an inspiring voice that, had the opportunity presented itself, I could have wiped out a whole platoon of Germans single-handed.

We stood in a semi-circle on this island stage while she performed. Then Caruso sang, and Irene Fenwick and half a dozen other famous actors and actresses performed. But the climax was an aquatic demonstration by Annette Kellerman and twelve swimmers costumed to resemble mermaids, tails and all. Led by Miss Kellerman, they swam round and around this island to a musical accompaniment.

After this extravaganza, we had a ball. There were tents all over the lawn, the largest containing all the food and liquor one could possibly consume. Lieutenant Cavanaugh had asked us not to drink anything until after the performance, and we didn't. But then we made haste to the refreshment tent and started to pour it in.

In the meantime, Lieutenant Cavanaugh fell in love with Margie Rambeau. I know, because I caught a glimpse of him hugging her in the corner of a tent. By the time we got on the bus to return to camp, we were all loaded and singing our heads off. That's the neatest detail I had at Camp Mills.

Donald Adair and the Footrace

Another of the lieutenants, Dillon his name, had been a famous runner at Boston College, having set a couple of track records up there. Toward the end of our training, he decided to see how good our endurance was, so he scheduled a two-mile race, with all of us carrying a rifle and bayonet and 150 rounds of ammunition around our waist. There were about 300 men running, and by golly, I came in ninth. I was proud of my finish, because I'd never run two miles before. At the same time, I was furious with one of the other runners, who had given me an elbow toward the end of the race, throwing me off stride.

This guy's name was Ed Hussey, and he was a bully of a sergeant who had come to us from the 71st New York. He used to run for the regiment in competition and thought he was pretty hot stuff. After the race, I was determined to tie into him, even though he was quite a bit bigger than me. As soon as I got my wind, I told Frankie McGuire, "I'm going to clobber that son of a bitch."

Standing next to Frankie was a slender, intelligent looking young man I hadn't met before. His name was Donald Adair, and he, too, had come from the 71st New York, knew Hussey, and justified his use of the elbow. Adair concluded his technical critique by declaring: "You're a silly shit. Hussey will take you apart." "Maybe so," I replied, "but you can't."

There followed additional unkind dialogue before we were separated. Don Adair later became one of my closest buddies, and Ed Hussey was killed in action at the Ourcq River.

Enter the Villain

Among the new officers assigned to our regiment from their training school in Plattsburg, New York, some proved to be excellent, but the pioneer platoon drew the worst of the lot, Cedric Quirt, a second lieutenant, who thought

16

himself a combination of Ceasar, Napoleon, and Hannibal.
He was meaner than hell and disliked by most of the men.
["Cedric Quirt" is a pseudonym.]

About a month after enlisting in the 7th Regiment, I had
been promoted to private first class. In the 7th, an examination was required for every promotion, even private first
class. There was a written and an oral examination; then
you had to go through the manual of arms, so I was rather
proud that I had become a PFC before many of my other
comrades. When we went to Camp Mills, I did all I could to
conform to the rules and regulations and considered myself
a good soldier.

Everything changed when Quirt came along. His arro-
gance was unbelievable. Furthermore, we soon discovered
that he distrusted anyone with a German name. That
included Dick Heins, a sergeant, Herb Schwartz, and me. I
found this to be particularly ironic, because I was three-
fourths Irish by descent, but I never gave him the satisfaction of telling him.

Dick Heins had worked for the Edison Company and was
an expert in underground tunneling. Anyone who could
tunnel under the sidewalks of New York knew his job. He
was also well-grounded in other kinds of construction.
Schwartz had been a superintendent for the Smith Foundation Company, which had laid the foundations of some of
the biggest skyscrapers in the city, and Herb had a wealth of
experience in construction. Here we were a construction
outfit, and Quirt refused to listen to either of the two men
most qualified to give advice. After a few attempts to
straighten Quirt out on some of our problems, they gave up
in disgust and never offered their suggestions again.

I managed to get along with him for several weeks, until
one evening at formation, Quirt asked if anyone in the
platoon had experience in draftsmanship. Foolishly, I raised
my hand, because I had studied drafting in high school, and
he ordered me to report to his quarters after evening chow.
There he had a table laid out with drafting instruments and
a French Army textbook on engineering problems that
illustrated the construction of trenches and dugouts, the
disposition of barbed wire, building roads and drainage
ditches, camouflage techniques, etc. This book was in

French, and the diagrams were so small, I had to use a magnifying glass to bring out the dimensions. He intended to translate it into English so that "his" book would become the standard text on pioneer work for the United States Army.

The only French I knew was "Oui, Monsieur/Madame." (I had not yet learned to say "Voulez-vous coucher avec moi ce soir?") And Quirt, all he knew was high school French, yet he was going to do the translation, and I was to transpose those little plans and change all the metric measurements into standard American measurements.

We fussed around and fussed around, and he got angry because it took me so long to transpose from the metric system, and I didn't get out of his tent until after one in the morning.

I had drilled eight hours that day and was dead tired. Stumbling into my tent, I didn't even undress but flopped on my cot and didn't hear the bugle blow the next morning. Sergeant Blaustein, who commanded our tent, knowing that I had been on special duty with Quirt, and seeing me come in so late, took it for granted that I would be excused for morning formation, so he didn't wake me up.

The first thing I knew, someone was shouting and kicking me, actually kicking me! I sat up, and there was Quirt, livid with anger, demanding to know why I was not out to answer reveille. So I grabbed my rifle and got out on the line, and he proceeded to place me in front of the whole platoon, saying that I was a disgrace, not only to the pioneer platoon, but to the old 7th Regiment as well. I had never before felt so humiliated, and from that time on, I had no use for Lieutenant Cedric Quirt.[7]

AWOL and William J. Donovan

As the days passed, I did my regular turn on guard duty. Then Joe Hennessy reported from HQ that we were going to board ship for France within two weeks. I had been home only once since our arrival at Camp Mills, so I put in for a 48-hour pass, but Quirt turned it down. Finally, I decided, to hell with the pass; I was going home anyway to say farewell to my mother and father before going overseas.

Every day we were supposed to check a bulletin board for special assignments, and I saw my name was on for guard duty. Having stood guard only two days before, I was angry because, ordinarily, we pulled sentry duty less than once a week, so I left camp and went home. Of course, I didn't mention that I was AWOL to my parents, and we had a wonderful weekend. My mother prepared a sumptuous dinner, and I visited all my old friends in Haworth.

I arrived back at camp early Monday morning in time for reveille, but as soon as Quirt spotted me, he placed me under arrest, and it was off to the guard tent.

The next day, I went before Major William Donovan, who commanded the First Battalion, for summary court-martial. That was my first meeting with Major Donovan, and it was inauspicious, to say the least. God, he was impressive. He had eyes like blue ice that drilled straight through you.

As I stood before him, scared to death, he studied the charges that Quirt had prepared against me and wanted to know if I had anything to say in my defense. I told him what had happened. Then he said:

"Well, Ettinger, you had an excellent record, and it's a shame that you've blemished it. You must understand that the most important thing in the Army is to obey orders, regardless of personal problems, regardless of what you may think. Charges have been brought to me by your platoon commander, and it's up to me to find you guilty or not. It is evident that you were absent without leave, so I must sentence you to one month at hard labor and fine you two-thirds of one month's pay. I hope this will be a lesson to you. You are dismissed."[8]

So they took me to the guard house, which was actually a tent at the end of our company street. There were half a dozen other fellows there, all for the same reason, AWOL. Two of them had been born in Ireland and had been brought before Major Moynahan, himself born in Ireland, and even though they had been AWOL for two whole weeks, he let them off with the same sentence as mine.

Boy! I was angry. It was my first exposure to military justice. Well, the hard labor wasn't very hard. Those of us in the guard tent spent a few hours every day policing the camp area by picking up paper, and the rest of the time we played

19

cards or shot craps. It was almost a vacation; no drill or inspection, and no Quirt around to worry about.

Anyway, come Sunday morning, we were shooting craps on a blanket laid over the tent floor when someone shouted: "ATTENTION!" I looked up, and there at the entrance of the tent was my father, Uncle Tom Churchill, and Father Duffy, our regimental chaplain. Oh, I was embarrassed— first of all, having them see me in the guard house, but also seeing me shooting craps—on a Sunday morning no less.

Father Duffy took me outside and gave me a good talking to; so did Pop, and I felt terribly ashamed. The next day, I was released from the guard house, and a week later we were on our way to France.

RECONNAISSANCE NO. 2

The Sixty-Ninth is on its way—
France heard it long ago,
And the Germans know we're coming,
to give them blow for blow.
We've taken on the contract,
and when the job is through
We'll let them hear a Yankee cheer
and an Irish ballad too.

The Harp that once through Tara's Halls
shall fill the air with song,
And the Shamrock be cheered as the port is
neared by our triumphant throng.
With the Potsdam Palace on a truck
and the Kaiser in a sack,
New York will be seen one Irish green
when the Sixty-Ninth comes back.

We brought back from the Border our Flag—
'twas never lost;
We left behind the land we love,
the stormy sea we crossed.
We heard the cry of Belgium,
and France the free and fair,
For where there's work for fighting-men,
the Sixty-Ninth is there.

The Harp that once through Tara's Halls . . .

The men who fought at Marye's Heights
will aid us from the sky,
They showed the world at Fredericksburg
how Irish soldiers die.
At Blackburn Ford they think of us,
Atlanta and Bull Run;
There are many silver rings on the old flagstaff
but there's room for another one.

The Harp that once through Tara's Halls . . .

A DOUGHBOY WITH THE FIGHTING 69TH

God rest our valiant leaders dead,
  whom we cannot forget;
They'll see the Fighting Irish
  are the Fighting Irish yet.
While Ryan, Roe, and Corcoran
  on History's pages shine,
A wreath of laurel and shamrock waits
  the head of Colonel Hine.

The Harp that once through Tara's Halls . . .

—Joyce Kilmer, "When the Sixty-Ninth Comes Back," *Joyce Kilmer, Vol. 1, Memoir and Poems* (New York: George H. Doran Co., 1918), pp. 110–112.

2

Over There

★   ★   ★

As [men of the regiment] thronged the deck-
space available and looked . . . at the lights
along the fast receding shore, they showed a
contentment, a mirth that amazed the crew, long
accustomed to transporting troops. . . . [One
sailor] had helped carry over all sort of soldiers,
he said, Marines, Regulars, and Guardsmen, but
he had never before seen passengers so seemingly
indifferent to the grief of leavetaking and the
perils of the wartime sea. He couldn't understand
it.

—Joyce Kilmer, Appendix in
Father Duffy's Story, p. 338.

In Transit

When the Rainbow left Camp Mills in late October 1917,
it was by no means a mass embarkation. Remember, there
were 27,000 men in that division, equivalent to the population of a small city. Each unit had its own schedule
and, without warning, would simply disappear overnight.
Of course, this was done for security reasons. For all we
knew, there were a dozen U-boats waiting for us off the
Battery.

Even our own regiment split up. Donovan, with the 1st
Battalion, took off on the night of October 25, and we didn't
see them again until arriving at our training area in France

23

several weeks later. Then we discovered they had taken a train from Camp Mills to Montreal, where they joined an English convoy bound for Liverpool. There they entrained to Southampton, then steamed across the English Channel in another ship to Le Havre.

The bulk of the regiment left Camp Mills during the night of October 29, boarded a train for New York Harbor, and embarked on the SS *America*. The *America* had been a German passenger vessel of the Hamburg-American Line and was one of the largest ships afloat. It had been impounded upon our entry into the war and converted for troop transport use. There were about ten other ships in our convoy carrying other units of the Rainbow, and most of the way across we were escorted by a U.S. Navy cruiser.

No sooner were we underway than Quirt generously offered our platoon to Captain Powers for submarine watch. Then he asked for volunteers from among the men. Like most of the fellows, I raised my hand, only to become the butt of an insult. "Ettinger," said Quirt, "I wouldn't allow you to be a lookout. I'm suspicious of you as it is. For all I know, you might be a German spy."

At the time, I thought he was serious, although, in retrospect, he was probably being sarcastic. When he left our quarters, the whole platoon roared with laughter.

As it turned out, the fellows who stood submarine watch soon tired of it, while Willie McBean and I hid behind a lifeboat so we wouldn't get stuck with any kind of extra duty. Then we taunted our buddies on lookout—until we reached a zone where we were solemnly informed, submarines might really be on the prowl.

Father Duffy tells the story of one of our lookouts being challenged by a ship's officer:

"What are you staring at, soldier?"

"Lookin' fer somethin Oi don' wan ter foind," our lad replied.

The fellows not on lookout were either singing, playing cards, or shooting craps when the officers weren't around. You'd have thought we were on a grand picnic. Our holiday spirit was enhanced by the weather, which was perfect throughout the voyage.

There was a bit of confusion on the chow lines during the

first few days, but that was soon straightened out. The order was remarkable, considering the fact that ours was the first full division to sail across the ocean under American naval command.

All the way over, our ships took a zig-zag course to avoid possible submarine attack. One night, about two days from the coast of France, we heard a terrible sound and thought a German submarine had attacked one of the transports. In case of submarine attack, the convoy was supposed to scatter in every direction and reassemble when the order came through that all was clear. Our transport heeled on its side in a 45-degree turn, and I never realized a ship that size could go so fast. The entire vessel almost shook apart as the engine was put to full speed.

We were ordered out on deck, put on our life jackets and stood by the lifeboats, thinking that at any second we might be hit by a torpedo. But it was a false alarm. What actually had happened was that the SS *Baron Von Steuben* had collided with a ship called the *Agamemnon.* One of them zigged instead of zagged that night and hit the other just below the bow. One man from the *Agamemnon* was thrown to the deck of the *Von Steuben,* but the luck of the Irish prevailed, and he landed, uninjured, among a group of Army nurses. When he looked up, he thought he had died and gone to heaven.

Although the *Von Steuben* suffered a terrible gash in its bow, it was able to continue, and the convoy reassembled at daybreak.[1]

A few hundred miles from France, a flotilla of American destroyers came out to escort us the rest of the way through the most dangerous waters, as far as German submarines were concerned. They were a beautiful sight as they came across the horizon at full speed. Those coal-burning destroyers could really travel!

We arrived in the harbor of Brest at dawn on November 12, 1917. The sun was just rising on the most eventful time of my life, a year and a half of intense excitement, adventure, and heartbreak.

Standing on the deck of the *America,* we welcomed the dawn with great relief at having arrived safely and marveled at the beauty. The hills around the city were covered with green trees, and the green fields were spotted with white buildings that had red-tiled roofs. As the sun's first rays fell on those red roofs, white buildings, and the fields and trees, it was a magnificent sight, and we were most joyous.[2]

40 Hommes—8 Chevaux

For a week, we were bound in the harbor waiting for transport. Finally, we disembarked, and all the men looked forward to leave in Brest. We could see other soldiers fraternizing with the local ladies, and we definitely wanted to demonstrate Irish-American goodwill toward our French allies. Unfortunately, it was not to be. With his usual efficiency, Sergeant Blaustein quickly identified the railroad cars that were to transport us to the hinterlands, and we were hustled aboard.

Now these railroad boxcars were something else! Large lettering on their sides, *40 Hommes—8 Chevaux,* identified their purpose. They were to carry either forty men or eight horses, and there was straw on the floor suitable for both. The straw partially covered huge cracks and, every once in a while, it would blow around as the cold wind whistled in from below. Each man had two blankets, and to sleep, we would spread one blanket over the straw and use the other to cover ourselves.

There were no windows or toilet facilities in these cars, just sliding doors on each side, and we would relieve ourselves by hanging out the doors, or wait for the next stop where we could stretch our legs and line up to use the station toilet, such as it was.

When we first crawled aboard this boxcar, our hearts were filled with adventure, and each man looked for a place on the floor to bed down. I remembered the friendly advice of a hobo: "If you ever hit the road, my lad, sit in the front of the boxcar and in the center, as it makes easier riding." I, therefore, made a dash to the front and center of the car and proceeded to spread my blankets, looking forward to a comfortable ride.

While still on my knees, I noticed someone standing alongside, and a voice echoed through the car: "Pardon me, sir, may I sit next to you?"

26

I looked up, and there was a handsome young man, pale of face, in an ill-fitting uniform, sans overcoat.

"Hell, yes," I said. "Make yourself at home."

"Can I help you, sir?" he continued.

"Where do you get that 'sir' stuff?"

"Well, sir, I can see a stripe on your arm and thought you might be an officer."

I stood up in amazement, wondering if I should know this bird and whether he was kidding me. However, to my knowledge, I had never seen him before.

"My name is Al Ettinger," I said, offering my hand, "and I'm only a private first class, which in this outfit means that I'm only one rank higher than a yardbird. Who are you?"

"I'm Jack Perry," he replied. "I enlisted at Camp Mills the day before we sailed and was told to report to Sergeant Blaustein."

"Where's your pack and rifle?"

"They didn't have time to issue me any. All I have is what I've got on."

That was my introduction to Jack Perry, one of the finest men I ever knew and a brave soldier to boot.

It was freezing in that boxcar when we got moving. The wind whistled up through cracks in the floor, and the rain came through the open doors. When we closed the doors, we almost suffocated, so some men tried to rig a curtain of raincoats to keep the rain out, but it was a lost cause. As night came on, it got colder, and we huddled in our blankets. I shared mine with Jack to keep him from freezing to death.

Our troop train crawled along for four miserable rainy days and nights. Eventually, about 10 a.m., it stopped, and we were ordered to fall out. We tumbled into the pouring rain, and there was not a building of any kind to be seen. I gave Jack one of my blankets to help shield him from the rain and cold. It later took me two weeks to get it dry, because it was that long before we got any sunshine, and we were prohibited from having any kind of fire in our billets.

The regiment then hiked several miles to the little village of Naives-en-Blois where, soaked to the skin, we were billeted in various haylofts. Poor Jack was more dead than alive when we arrived.[3]

I spoke to Sergeant Blaustein about Jack, and he took him

to the medics, who, in turn, sent him to a hospital. A few weeks later, he returned to duty and looked me up to tell me that he had been assigned to our billeting officer as an interpreter. Before the war, Jack had traveled extensively in France with his parents and was fluent in the language. From then on, we were close buddies, visiting one another whenever we had the chance.

Naives-en-Blois and Mme Dumanois

The regiment trained outside Naives from just before Thanksgiving to the second week in December, and it rained constantly the first two weeks we were there. Then the rain turned to snow, and we were out in that rain or snow at least eight hours every damn day.

All the platoons slept in haylofts, and the men were wet and cold most of the time. We had no fire of our own. The only fire permitted was in the company kitchen, and only friends of the mess sergeant were allowed to warm themselves by "his" fire. My buddies and I had insulted him so often, we weren't welcome there at all.

The woman who owned the barn in which we were billeted lived in the adjoining house. (Most of the houses over there were connected to their barns through a passageway.) Her name was Madame Dumanois, and she was one of the most gracious ladies I had ever met. Her husband was in the army, and she ran their farm all by herself. She had three girls, from six to about twelve years of age—cute little rascals. She was so kind and sympathetic, and every evening she insisted that a group of us come to her kitchen to dry ourselves before an open-hearth fire, which not only provided heat for her house, but also was where she prepared her meals.

Twelve or fifteen of us would gather there. We would scrape the mud off our boots ever so carefully, but invariably, we would leave tracks on her spotless kitchen floor. She didn't mind at all, and she gave us fresh milk from her cow, and cheese and apples that we roasted over the open fire. Of course, we would try to reciprocate her kindness with goodies when we could get them—candy for the children, and cans of corned beef and salmon that we swiped from our mess, things like that.

Madame Dumanois was radiant with the happiness of her little children, and it was truly wonderful to have her company during those long winter evenings. We would sit around the fire and sing American songs, and she and the children would sing French songs. Of course, we made a big fuss over the kids; they were adorable. And they were so surprised that most of us were Catholic and that we could join in when they sang hymns in Latin. That seemed a miracle to them. It was quite an experience. Oh, she was a lovely woman.[4]

Jack Perry's Birthday Party

It was pretty tough training during that fall and winter, but there were a few diversions.

In a few weeks, Jack Perry recovered his strength from the exposure he had endured en route to Naives. He once complained to me that his interpreter duties were too soft, and he was afraid that when we went into combat he'd be kept in the rear.

"I'm trying to get back into good physical condition," he told me. "I was on the track and baseball team at Lawrenceville Academy, so I run every day to restore my wind, and my lieutenant has a set of bar bells that I exercise with."

While determined to be fully engaged in the struggle, Jack had a distinct premonition that he would not survive.

One day, as I was talking to a mutual friend, Spencer Sully, Jack came to me and said, "Red, today is my birthday, and by golly, we've got to go out and celebrate. I've never had a birthday without a party of some kind."

Spencer and I reluctantly replied that we were broke.

"Oh, the hell with that," said Jack, "I've got a five-dollar gold piece that my girlfriend gave to me for good luck. Hell, I'm not going to have any luck in this war. I know the Krauts have my name written on one of their shells, so come on; let's forget about the war and have a good time."

After evening chow, the three of us went to this old French

cafe. Jack took out his five-dollar gold piece and tried to explain its value in francs to the old Frenchman behind the bar. Jack spoke fluent French and, after considerable persuasion, the old fellow reluctantly agreed to exchange the gold piece into francs.

Well, he had francs we had never seen before. Some French provinces printed their own paper currency, and Jack had his campaign hat full of this crazy money before he was through.

As the evening wore on, we kept guzzling beer amid loud singing and laughter, much to the consternation of the elderly proprietor. By two in the morning, we had downed eleven liters of beer each and were flying high when the owner of the bistro threatened to call the MPs if we didn't leave. We had decided to drink a dozen liters apiece, so we departed for our billet singing and swigging from our last bottles, cajoled from the owner as a condition of leaving.

Somehow we managed to climb the ladder leading to the hayloft and announced our arrival with shouts of joy and words of pity for the men we had left behind. A shower of boots, accompanied by threats of instant death, quieted us somewhat, and with much giggling, we finally went to sleep.

My God, when the bugle blew a few hours later at six o'clock, we were still drunk. We grabbed our rifles and helmets and started down the ladder from the hayloft to the barn floor. Exhilarated, I decided to descend fireman style, sliding down the rails, which was fine, except that my heel caught on the second rung and I fell nearly a dozen feet, landed face down on the barn floor, breaking my nose, and had to have it taped by the medics.

Army Food and Civilian Rationing

Our HQ Company, the largest company in the regiment, had the worst mess of any company through lack of experienced cooks. Our mess sergeant had been appointed because he was an inspector of markets in New York; the first cook had been a veterinarian; the second cook, a Wall Street runner; and the third cook, a hobo.

The beef issue in the American Army was very good, but when our kitchen received a side of beef, instead of cutting it into small steaks and using other parts to prepare pot roasts and such, they just made stew out of the whole side of beef. We were stewed to death! That's why, wherever we were billeted, we were on the alert to find some family or cafe to cook for us.

As we were among the first American troops to arrive in France, the logistics were far from ideal. Much of the food issued to our mess sergeants was spoiled before they received it. Our bread and potatoes were often moldy. We probably had the best grade of bacon of any troops over there, except the German Army, but it was often rancid, and combined with the fact that our cooks were so inept, that chow was terrible.

During the regiment's first two months in France, our main meals consisted of canned corned beef hash and canned corned beef stew. We'd have rice for breakfast that was half cooked, like chewing gum for the most part, topped off by a large spoon of Karo syrup, which I detested. On a cold day, when you swallowed that rice and Karo syrup, it would form a ball that never seemed to reach your stomach and you had heartburn all day long.

Our only vegetable, besides the moldy potatoes, was canned tomatoes. The French Army would forage for vegetables, but we were not allowed to do so. Highly valued were those few enterprising mess sergeants who had been cooks or chefs in civilian life and who knew how to forage for fresh fruit and vegetables.

French civilians were rationed very strictly. It was difficult for them to get beef, but because of their culinary art, they could prepare horse meat, usually in the form of pot roast, that couldn't be distinguished from beef. They also seemed to be able to find rabbit and veal, but those were the only kinds of meat I saw in French households.

Wood for French families was also rationed. Even if a farmer had a large wood lot, it could be cut only under supervision of the French Forestry Service. Every bit of wood in France was under the control of that agency, although people in the country were free to gather twigs and small branches, and it was amazing to see them cook a meal with only a small bundle of twigs.

In the American Army, we used a great deal of wood in

our kitchen stoves, and we had a contract with the French government for all the wood that we needed. Men would often be detailed to cut and carry in wood for the kitchens, but they were strictly supervised.

From Naives-en-Blois to Grand

When the regiment was ready to leave Naives-en-Blois, we had not cut our entire wood allotment. Father Duffy decided not to leave any wood behind that the Army had contracted for, so on the Sunday prior to departure, he had the whole regiment go to this wood lot, bring in all the wood that we were entitled to and pile it in the courtyard of the local church, with agreement of the pastor that it be divided among the people of the village. We got such a charge out of doing that, we didn't mind the work at all. And the poor French pastor was in tears over the generosity of the great Father Duffy.

However, the beneficence of the church or army is one thing; taking care of your own is another.

Most of us carried only one log on our shoulders, the smallest one we could grab; but on my first trip, I took a log on each shoulder, and as we passed the home of Madame Dumanois, our benefactress, I threw one of them in her front yard. One of the few obnoxious guys in our platoon shouted: "Look what Red Ettinger is doing!" I told him to keep his mouth shut. He made a few wisecracks, and I wound up smacking him a couple.

Several men of the platoon who were billeted with me then followed suit with the logs, and Madame Dumanois rushed out to gather them into her house. She had enough wood to last the winter, I can tell you that.

The regiment marched out Naives-en-Blois about the middle of December 1917. Within a day, we were into hill country, and after two days' strenuous hiking in ankle-deep snow, we arrived on a plateau, and there was the beautiful city of Grand. There are a hundred Grands in France, but this one was an ancient city that had been occupied by the Romans centuries ago. It had a beautiful cathedral built on the ruins of a pagan temple, historically very interesting.

There we were billeted in an ancient stone barracks that looked like a fortress.[5]

Inspection by General Pershing

The next morning, although exhausted, we were ordered to clear the snow off the main street of Grand, which seemed to stretch for a mile. After shoveling, we had to use brooms right down to the cobblestones. The reason for all this nonsense was a planned inspection by General Pershing the following day.

Before dawn of the great event, we were rousted to police our sleeping quarters and had full inspection to ensure that everything was in perfect order for review by the famous General John J. Pershing. Then, at the break of day, we were marched out of town about a half mile or so, and our whole regiment lined up on either side of the road leading to Grand.

It was snowing and bitter cold. We stood there stamping our feet trying to keep warm. Eventually, about eleven o'clock, the bugle blew and an order came roaring down the line:

"ATTENTION!" So we stood at attention.

Then: *"PRESENT ARMS!"* And we presented arms.

In the distance, I could see a cloud of snow coming down the road, and here came General Pershing in a great big limousine with half a dozen staff cars trailing behind. They were doing about sixty miles an hour when they passed, covered us with flurries of snow, and went through the city of Grand like an express train. They didn't even slow down!

We were madder than hell! For four damn hours we had stood there, and God! it was cold. Well, I never particularly cared for General Pershing after that.[6]

During the two-day march from Naives-en-Blois to Grand, many of the fellows had developed frost-bitten feet and blisters so bad they couldn't walk. These men had been treated in the medical dispensary in Grand, located in an old building we called "The Castle." We kidded them by calling them "Castle Feet." Little did we realize that soon we'd be in the same or worse predicament.

Christmas Dinner with Mme Bouvier

It was Christmas Eve. Tony Catrona, Fred Young, and I went exploring, entered an old deserted church, and there were the most unusual stations of the cross I had ever seen. They were carved from wood and painted, and the paint had peeled quite a bit. But it was really the age of this little church that impressed us so much.

We went back to the village looking for something to eat and came across a butcher shop. The proprietor was a Madame Bouvier whose husband was in the French Army. Of the three of us, Tony Catrona spoke the best French, so he did most of the talking. Well, she made us a lovely lunch of summer sausage, crackers, and cheese; then she invited the three of us to share Christmas dinner that evening with her family and other guests. Naturally, we accepted.[7]

Among the guests were two young French soldiers with their girlfriends, Madame Bouvier's sister, and two aunts. The soldiers were home on leave and were nephews of our hostess. They were most hospitable to us, and we had a great time. And the dinner was a feast! our best meal since arriving in France. She had rabbit, veal pot roast, turnips and potatoes, and all the wine we could drink.

Father Duffy was to say midnight mass in the large cathedral, so all of us went to the service. It was a beautiful, moonlit night, a light snow was falling, and we felt particularly good after all that delicious food and wine. We strolled down the street singing Christmas carols, and all of us attended mass. It was so lovely.

During mass, Father Duffy told us that the collection was for the local parish, so he urged us to be generous and said with a smile, ". . . and I would hope not to hear any metal in the collection box." Well, when that box ended its passage, it contained about two thousand dollars. As we left, the parish priest was in tears. He had never before seen so much money.

The next day was Christmas, and Madame Bouvier had invited us to her home for afternoon refreshment. So Tony, Fred, and I enjoyed a delightful spread with wine and cognac, while the two French soldiers told us about their war experiences.

The hospitality of the French people was beyond belief during our entire stay in that venerable country.

Parlez-Vous Francais?

Most of our time was spent in small rural villages like Grand. These truly constituted the backbone of the French Republic. Small farms were located on the outskirts of these villages, and the people could easily walk to work on them.

By the time we got to France, the only males we would see in these villages were old men, young boys, and disabled French soldiers. The whole rural area was run by women. Women ran the farms, operated the stores and cafes, and for the most part, they were a wonderful, strong-willed group of people. They received the Rainbow with open arms, because we were among the first American troops to arrive. They had so little themselves, yet they generously offered us a portion of their bounty.

The difference in language didn't mean a thing. Those of us from New York City were more sympathetic, I believe, than troops from other parts of the United States except, perhaps, those from other large cities where there were large numbers of foreign-born. Practically every New York kid knew a few words of German, Italian, or Yiddish, and it didn't take him very long to learn a little French. Of course, Italian-Americans caught on very easily.

On the ship across, we had been issued a little pocket dictionary of French phrases. Well, it wasn't much of a dictionary, but it did help, and we were able to pick up enough of the language to get by. We had such fun trying to talk to the French people, because they so enjoyed the mistakes that we made. It just tickled them to death, and we joined in their amusement.

RECONNAISSANCE NO. 3

"Promptly with the advent of Christmas week, the division received a warning order for a movement further south past Chaumont to begin on December 26th. By Christmas Day, a great deal of snow had fallen. The hilly roads were heavily glazed; the wind was high, and under these circumstances, the thermometer could do nothing but keep on dropping—which it did, below zero. The march was a long one. The bulk of the division's animals had not reached it as yet. There were but a handful of trucks, scarcely twenty, and a few small ambulances. On Christmas Day the mules were received—for the most part unbroken and unshod. With the equipment available and the distance to be traversed, the march had to be made in as short a time as possible in order to feed the columns on the road.

". . . In a blinding snow storm it commenced. The roads were deep with snow, with a treacherous glassy base and full of long grades and sharp turns. The thermometer kept on dropping and the men proceeded through these conditions in the same uniform in which they passed in review before the Secretary of War on that balmy Sunday afternoon in Indian summer . . . except for the inroads of four months' hard wear. At the very last moment . . . a few thousand shoes were rushed to the division.

"The march the troops had previously passed through had so broadened and swollen their feet that it was extremely difficult to make use of what had been so obtained. There were many men without overcoats; and gloves were the exception. Over an average of three full march days and 75 kilometers distance, the division bucked the adversity of a blizzard and pushed steadily ahead on the slippery roads. . . . Many a foot left a red trail on the snow. . . . In the history of this division there is no page more full of courage and determination than that on which this journey is recorded. The columns, with gallantry and grit, drove ahead at least 25 kilometers a day and came in well closed and accounted for. . . .

36

Reconnaissance No. 3

"From this march, the spirit of the division was born. The experience settled each man who took part—he became a veteran, at least so far as contending with the elements was concerned, and he had shown a tenacity and nerve which, when the Rainbow took the field, was never more surely demonstrated. It was a great march; such was the judgment of those who observed it, whether at Chaumont . . . or on the white and drifted roads on which the column passed." [But it was not a "great march" to the ill-clad doughboy who endured it.]

—Major Walter Wolf, *The Story of the Rainbow Division* (New York: Rand McNally & Co., 1919).

3

Final Maneuvers
at Longeau

★ ★ ★

> *I am absolutely in love with France, its people,
> its villages, its mountains; everything about
> it. . . . It has suffered tremendous hardships with
> dignity and humor, and kept its sanity and faith.
> America, to judge by the papers, grows hysterical
> over a little self-denial . . .*

> —Letter from Joyce Kilmer to his mother,
> May 1918, *Memoirs and Poems,*
> Vol. 2, p. 158.

Dysentery for Christmas

According to American newspapers, that past November
we Doughboys had been treated to a traditional Thanksgiving dinner—"roast turkey with all the trimmings." What
the 69th dined on for Thanksgiving was beef stew. The
turkeys didn't arrive until Christmas! So we patiently waited
in line for this well-advertised, glorious dinner and filled our
mess kits with turkey, mashed potatoes, squash, and giblet
gravy.

Well, the turkey was awful. Taking so long to reach us, it
had spoiled. I needed but one taste, having previously
feasted at Mme Bouviers', but many of the men were so
hungry they devoured a large portion of this turkey. Consequently, most of the regiment came down with dysentery

overnight. As if that were not enough, the bugles blew at four the next morning, and we were ordered to pack up to continue our march across the hills of the Haute Marne.

After the regiment left Grand, the slopes were much steeper than before. It was bitter cold and snowing, and a fierce wind lashed at our gloveless hands and faces. Going up those slopes, the lead company had to break through snow up to their knees, while the rear company slipped on packed-down icy snow.

It was a terrible ordeal. We would march for fifty minutes and rest ten, and all that day during the ten-minute breaks, we would hurriedly discard our packs and overcoats and rush into the woods on either side of the road because of the dysentery.

We carried a 55-lb. pack, a rifle that weighed over eight pounds, plus bayonet, and 150 rounds of ammunition around our waist. The accoutrement dragged and dragged on you. The straps of the pack dug into your shoulders, and after the first mile, you felt you couldn't go another step, but you did. Oh, it was a grueling march.

The supply wagons and field kitchens were started one hour before the troops every morning. Still, on the very first hill, there would be the supply train in utter confusion, the mules unable to pull the wagons up the icy slopes. A team of mules from one wagon would be hitched to another to make a four-mule team, but these mules weren't used to being harnessed in that manner, and they balked. Finally, you'd see forty men of the supply company on a long rope attached to the wagon tongue, struggling . . . and . . . foot . . . by . . . foot . . . getting it up those steep grades.

Consequently, we'd arrive at our night's bivouac long ahead of the supply wagons. They wouldn't come in until midnight. Then they had to set up the kitchens to prepare food, and it would be two o'clock in the morning before we had anything to eat. Most of the men were so exhausted they wouldn't bother to eat.

Breakfast was at 4:00 a.m., only a couple of hours after dinner, because the kitchens had to be broken down and sent on their way before the troops started. It usually consisted of rice with Karo syrup, a couple of slices of moldy bread, and black coffee. For lunch, there would be two bacon sandwiches for each man. That sounds good, but the damn bacon was rancid.

During the march, we would plunge our little finger in and out of the mouth of our canteen to keep the water from freezing. The men started to eat snow, and the officers tried to stop it, but you had to, that's all there was to it; you got so thirsty you just did it anyway.

The second day was worse than the first. It had stopped snowing, but it was colder. When we reached the summit of those hills, the wind cut right into us, and without winter clothing, I don't know how we survived. The men struggled on with noncoms constantly shouting: "Don't fall behind!"

At the time, the 1st sergeant of HQ Company was "Red" Murchison, a great big son of a bitch and a bully, who would repeatedly threaten those men who had difficulty in keeping up. Yet, hell, he only carried a little knapsack and no rifle. ["Red Murchison" is a pseudonym.]

Introduction to James Collintine

Murchison's measure was soon taken by "Big Jim" Collintine, a powerful Irishman in my platoon, who had shoveled coal on transatlantic liners for years. He was older than most of us, probably in his 40's, and a giant of a man in every way.

Collintine trudged along with his own pack, in addition to two buddies' packs, one over each shoulder. Many of our stronger men would carry the pack of a buddy who could no longer manage the burden. When Murchison ordered Jim to return the extra packs to his exhausted buddies, Jim grabbed him by the front of his tunic with powerful hands and hissed:

"Red Murchison, wan more word out av e an' O'il break yir neck! Go back t' th' rear whir ye belong an' stop shoutin' at moi lads!"

Murchison didn't say a word. He just dropped to the rear of the column and stayed there from that time on.

All the fellows in the pioneer platoon were Jim Collintine's "lads," as he called them. Oh, he was a lovely person, God rest his soul.

No one from our platoon fell out during this march. Several staggered to the rear, but they managed to keep going, usually arriving at our night's bivouac an hour or two after the others.

John Mahon

The man who had the greatest difficulty in our company was John Mahon. A lovable person, and our only avowed atheist, John was several years older than most of us and had given up a law practice to enlist. Over six feet in stature, with a gaunt bearing and striking resemblance to Abraham Lincoln, John, nevertheless, was not very strong, and our every hike was an agonizing effort for him. Never once, however, did he complain and his courage shamed those of us who felt sorry for ourselves. Although unable to keep up, John never dropped out, even on the most punishing hikes.

On this particular march, John would come in hours after most of us had bedded down in some hayloft. His feet bleeding, he would suffer the agony of the damned.

In other companies, some men just fell on their faces and stayed there. They couldn't move. During the four days of that march, five men in our regiment died of exhaustion. They were placed alongside the road to wait for an ambulance, but the muledrawn ambulances also had trouble on the grades and by the time they arrived, it was too late.[1]

The Feet . . . The Feet . . . The Feet

Thank God, in my company we didn't have that kind of casualty. But the feet . . . the feet . . . the feet. Blood on the snow from bleeding feet. At day's end, our socks would oft-times be caked with blood from broken blisters. We'd gingerly peel the socks off and wash our feet in the snow, rub them to regain circulation, and then apply iodine from our first-aid equipment to the broken blisters. We'd also rub our feet with vaseline, then change socks. We all had several pair of fresh socks, thank God.

When we took our boots off, they'd be soaking wet, and by morning they'd be frozen stiff and you couldn't get them on. The men would stuff them with hay and then fire it off. The

41

fire would thaw out the boots all right but it also burned the thread around the soles, and within a day, the soles would fall off.[2]

I had a problem with frostbite of my left foot. Then a huge blister developed, turned black and split open. All the medics could do was apply iodine to prevent infection, and every evening I rubbed it with vaseline to keep it soft.

Shortly after this hike, we were issued new boots that had been made in England. I had to get two sizes larger than normal to fit my sore foot. Consequently, for several weeks, I had to shuffle around until the foot healed. Frankie McGuire started to call me "Blue Jay" because, back in the States, billboards advertised Blue Jay corn plaster, with the picture of a tramp shuffling down the road, a bindlestick over his shoulder, and the advertisement read: "Blue Jay corn plasters make hard roads easy."

Diversion and Inspiration

One incident during that march caused us to forget our troubles, at least momentarily. During one of the rest stops, Lieutenant Quirt insisted that Mike Walsh spar with him to keep warm. Mike demurred. Quirt kept at him, kept at him. Finally, Quirt squared off and, right out of the blue, threw a haymaker. Fortunately, Mike ducked, then put over a lightning left cross and knocked Quirt on his fatty. Boy! it was a wicked punch, and the guys howled. Oh, it was so good to see Quirt go down. Mike said to him: "I thought you wanted to spar, but if you want to fight, get on your feet." Quirt didn't want any more of it.

One of the most thrilling sights I witnessed in France was on that miserable march. Our column was a couple of miles long, and at the head of the regiment were the color bearers with the Stars and Stripes and the regimental flag. This particular day, it had been snowing. Momentarily, the snow stopped and the sun emerged. Looking ahead, I could see the vanguard of the regiment climbing a high ridge with the Stars and Stripes at the fore. It was quite a distance off but an incredible sight. Both the flag and our regimental banner, with its silver battle furls reflecting in the sunlight, inspired me to keep going. Exhausted as I was, it gave me new life and spirit that day. I will never forget it.

By the end of the fourth day, New Year's Day of 1918, the regiment staggered into the village of Longeau, while the band played "In the Good Old Summertime." At least HQ Company did; the line companies were billeted in four neighboring villages.[3]

American engineers had constructed barracks for us, our first regular barracks in France. Until then, we had been living in haylofts, for the most part. First off, we were issued ticks, which we filled with straw. These were placed on the floor of the barracks to sleep on. At each end of the barracks was a potbellied stove in which the engineers had laid a fire, and they were cherry red. When we entered those barracks, it felt like heaven! Those engineers were a great bunch.

The Feather Bed

After we got squared away, Don Adair, Willie McBean, and I decided to check out the village. As we walked along the main street, we came to a store with a large plate glass window, covered with frost, with light flickering from behind. At first, we thought the place was on fire. Then, rubbing a patch of frost from the window, we saw a half-dozen American soldiers lounging around a big fireplace. One of them saw us and motioned us in.

These men were from the same group of army engineers who had built our barracks. They were all noncommissioned officers and the last to leave the area. They invited us to share their cheese and wine and French bread. We warmed up by the fire, and they had us take off our boots and dry our socks. It was so comfortable there, we stayed with them for a couple of hours. They told us they were leaving first thing in the morning.

One of the sergeants turned to me with a grin and said, "Red, how'd you like to have this mattress?" He showed me a huge feather mattress about two feet thick.

"Oh, my God," I replied. "Great!"

"If you can be here by six tomorrow morning, that mattress is yours," he promised.

Don Adair and I decided that we were going to be there, no mistake about it. We were, and the sergeant gave us his mattress. We brought it back to the barracks, put it on top of our straw ticks, and had a feather bed during our entire stay in Longeau.

The three of us slept together, Adair, McBean and myself, with McBean in the middle. With six blankets between us, we were as cozy as bugs in a rug. It was a great ending to that horrible march.

Collintine and Quirt's Boots

Big Jim Collintine had served seven years with the British Army fighting in India and Mesopotamia. When teased about being an Irishman in the British Army, he'd reply with great indignation:

"Oi niver served fer no England. Oi was a mimber av th' Queens Own Regiment an' was servin' fer me King an' me Queen; an' dey wasn't English, moind you, dey was Germans." [Apparently, someone had told Jim that George the Fifth's grandfather was of the German nobility, as was the father of Queen Mary.]

So, Jim never did fight for England; if anything, he fought for Germany.[4]

Collintine was every inch a soldier, and he frequently gave us fatherly advice. While everyone else in the platoon would be cussing Lieutenant Quirt, Jim would admonish us that no soldier should make derogatory remarks about his commanding officer. Lieutenant Quirt was our superior officer and should be obeyed at all times.

One day at Longeau, Quirt ordered Collintine to report to his billet, and when Jim arrived, handed him two pair of muddy boots to be cleaned. Jim never said a word. He went out, threw the boots in the snow, then walked over to the guard house and turned himself in. Lieutenant Walsh was on duty, and when Collintine told him the story, he said: "You go back to your barracks; I'll take care of this."

When Jim came into the barracks—it was early evening

and we were getting ready for chow—he was red as a beet. We could tell he was angry, and no one said anything, because when Jim Collintine was riled up, you had better keep your mouth shut.

"Oh me God," he said, "what iver did happin? Oh, God, t'was a bad pap dat man sucked."

He never defended Quirt from that day on.

Jim transferred out of the pioneer platoon after our first tour in the trenches and was assigned to drive a combat wagon that carried ammunition for the Stokes mortars and the 37mm cannon. In so doing, he became a regimental institution.

Collintine was something else! He loved his mules and would talk to them like a father to delinquent sons. The men would tease him terribly, telling him that he had long ears and thick skin like the mules, and so forth. They drove him out of his mind with their teasing; but when they wanted advice or protection, guess who they went to.

Everyone knew that Jim was the bravest mule skinner in the regiment. He carried that ammunition as close to the lines as possible, way ahead of the other supply wagons, always ahead, right on the heels of the advancing troops. One of his mules was killed at Chateau-Thierry, and that broke Jim's heart, but he continued to defy enemy artillery to the end of the war.

Jim Collintine and horseshoer McEnroy were great pals, although you'd never know it the way they used to cuss each other while McEnroy was attempting to shoe Jim's mules. The air would turn blue with insults, recriminations, and giant oaths. Gradually it would clear when, the job accomplished, the two men would mellow to the swig of a bottle and reminisce about the "Auld Sod."

Shortly after arriving in Longeau, the entire regiment began a period of intensive training. Every day, we were in the field going through maneuvers, rifle and hand grenade practice, and bayonet drill—eight hours a day, in snow, sleet, no matter what. Our feet eventually got better; I don't know how, because we were on them so much. It was incredible to see several hundred men limping around during those first few weeks in Longeau.

Rusky

In preparation for combat maneuvers, the pioneer platoon was ordered to build a defensive position on the top of a ridge four miles from the barracks.[5] Immediately after breakfast, we would load up with full pack and rifles, and some men would carry picks and shovels, while others had to shoulder stakes with rolls of barbed wire. We then trudged up a mountain road to this ridge where we proceeded to dig a trench system. It was tedious work because every swing of the pick made contact with a rock anywhere from the size of your fist to an enormous boulder. When we hit a really big one, we would call for Rusky.

Rusky was a giant of a man, so powerful, yet so good-natured. Born in Russia, he had emigrated to the United States only a few years before the war and immediately enlisted when we became involved. His first name, as I recall, was Vladimir, but we could never pronounce his last name. It was one of those long Russian names full of consonants, so when the sergeant called the roll, he settled for "Rusky," and the other fellows just picked it up. He didn't mind a bit and always responded with a big grin.

Now some of the stones we uncovered on that ridge were regular boulders, and it was impossible for the average man to lift them; but Rusky was so proud of his strength and so accommodating, he was always willing to help. He could hoist the biggest boulders and heave them over the side of the trench. Well, a few of the men began to take advantage of his generosity. Every time they uncovered a stone larger than a man's head, they'd call to Rusky for help, and he would charge down the line and lift the stones for them. It seems to be a cruel streak that some men have to take advantage of other men's simplicity, but Rusky never got angry with them.

Poor Rusky never came home. He was killed at Chateau-Thierry, but I shall never forget him, never.

From "Die Wacht am Rhein" to KP

As the men worked on this trench, Lieutenant Quirt stationed himself a hundred feet away, peering out over the valley with his binoculars "so the Germans won't surprise us." As a matter of fact, the nearest Germans were miles away; but Quirt insisted that we work under combat conditions at all times, and "Quiet there!" was his most frequent comment, although you could hear the picks on those rocks a thousand yards off. It was unbelievable!

One day, Frankie McGuire started to whistle "Die Wacht am Rhein," a popular German marching song. Other fellows joined in, and up and down the whole line, they were humming and whistling "The Watch on the Rhine." Then Quirt thought he recognized the tune, and he rushed toward the trench.

"WHO ARE THOSE TRAITORS!" he shouted. "WHO ARE THOSE TRAITORS!"

Of course, everybody clammed up.

"I want to know who the traitors are that were singing the enemy's national anthem!"

Nobody said a word, even those who knew the difference between "Deutschland uber Alles" and "Die Wacht am Rhein."[6]

"Well," he declared, "you're all traitors and you will all be punished." He put the entire platoon on KP for the following day, which was a Sunday.

It was some sight as 42 men reported to the kitchen for KP duty, since it could accommodate only half a dozen men. Sergeant Goldstein, the mess sergeant, was so astonished he didn't know what to do with us. We couldn't even fit in the kitchen.

A few minutes later Lieutenant Walsh came along on an inspection tour. He saw us hanging around and wanted to know what the hell we were doing there. Sergeant Goldstein explained. Walsh said: "You men go back to your barracks, and if Quirt says anything, you let me know." (Walsh, by this time a 1st lieutenant, outranked Quirt, who was still a 2nd lieutenant.)

It was almost noon before Quirt discovered that we were loafing around the barracks instead of working on KP. He was fit to be tied, but we explained that we were there on Lieutenant Walsh's orders, and that was that.

Michael J. Walsh and the Mother Superior

Michael J. Walsh was one of the most admired officers in our regiment. He had been the first sergeant of C Troop in the 5th Cavalry, and he was a great buddy of Herman Bootz. As soon as we entered the war, Bootz and Walsh had been sent to Plattsburg Officers Training School, and both were assigned to the 69th after graduating as second lieutenants. Fortunately, Walsh was attached to HQ Company and put in command of the Stokes mortar platoon.

The Stokes mortar was a British weapon and entirely new to the American Army. Mike Walsh studied every detail of it, and he trained the fifty men of that platoon to perfection in the use of this extremely effective weapon. (He was the one who trained Tom FitzSimmons as first sergeant of the mortar platoon. Of course, Tom adored him, and Mike was very fond of Tom.)

Here was one tough gazebo! Mike Walsh was not very tall, but he had a powerful physique, even if his legs were slightly bowed from years in the saddle. He was a great officer, admired by every man in the company. He was just something else—rough, tough, and so profane—you never heard anyone who could rip out oaths as he did, one after another. To be called a "Son of a Bitch" by Mike Walsh was almost a privilege, because then he knew you. I know, because he called me that one time.

I was on sentry duty in Longeau one cold winter night, and my post was to guard a store house in the courtyard of a convent.[7] There was a gate leading into the yard, with a fence all around, and all I had to do was watch that gate to ensure that no one entered without proper authority.

Oh God! it was cold. I went on the post about midnight and was walking up and down when I heard someone call in a low voice. It was the Mother Superior, standing on the convent stoop with a big bowl of hot chocolate for me. I accepted with great pleasure, and in English, she said, "You poor boy, you must be very cold."

With infinite self-pity I agreed, "It is cold, Ma'am." By golly, a few minutes later out she came again . . . with a chair and a charcoal foot warmer, insisting that I sit down and warm my feet! Like a damn fool, I did.

It was quiet, no traffic at all, and I sat there in the chair a few minutes . . . put my feet on the charcoal foot warmer . . . and pretty soon they were nice and warm . . . and I felt so cozy. Then I jerked up, pulled the lapels of my overcoat up around my ears, and started walking again. But the temptation was too great, so I went back to the chair and the foot warmer. This time I lay back. . . . Suddenly, the sound of hobnail boots cracked the stone sidewalk. Damn! I probably was half asleep.

Lurching up with a start, I reached for my rifle, which was propped up against the building, and accidentally knocked it over. The rifle fell with a hell of a clatter down the stone steps. By the time I had retrieved it, I saw a figure coming toward me. Oh my God, it was Mike Walsh. He was Officer of the Day, inspecting the different posts. Jesus! I challenged him properly, but he must have heard the rifle clatter, and he probably saw me trying to rescue it. As soon as he saw the chair and foot warmer, he knew what had happened.

"What the hell are you doing there! What's that chair doing there! And (indicating the foot warmer) what the hell is that . . . that . . . that thing? By God, I'll bet you've been SLEEPING!"

(I could see Quirt lining up the firing squad.)

As I began to sputter a reply, the convent door opened and the Mother Superior emerged like a guardian angel.

"Now, now, Lieutenant, you should be ashamed of yourself, using such language in front of this fine young man. The poor boy was freezing to death out here, and I told him to sit for a while and warm up. You should not scold him so."

Poor Mike blushed and mumbled something about military discipline, but she cut him off: "Would you have him disobey a Mother Superior?"

For the first time in his life, I suspect, Mike Walsh was at a loss for words; but after my savior went back into the house, he whispered fiercely: "You red-headed son of a bitch, I ought to have you shot for this! I'll see you later."

With great concern, I reported back to the guard house at the end of my tour. Mike Walsh was there by himself, but he didn't even put me on report; he just said: "Get the hell out of here, and never let me catch you like that again!"

That's the kind of a guy he was. He'd call you every name

in the book, but he seldom, if ever, put a man on report. Unfortunately, HQ Company lost him because he was promoted to captain in command of I Company right after Chateau-Thierry. Mike Walsh made a wonderful record for himself and was one of our most inspirational leaders.

Rubin Bernstein

One day in Longeau, a sleet and snowstorm raged through the countryside. We were ordered to remain in our barracks, clean our equipment, and rest after we had finished. Quirt wasn't satisfied with that. He hated to see us relax, so he acquired a blackboard from the local school, set it up in the barracks, and proceeded to give a lecture.

He started off by making a circle of twelve crosses with a check mark in the center. Then he said:

"Now, men, this is the problem we have before us. One of you is this check mark, and no one is more appropriate for this example than Private Bernstein."

(Rubin Bernstein was about 6'2", skinny, and a lovable kid. Everybody liked Bernstein; everybody except Quirt.)

Quirt continued:

"Bernstein, you've been out on a wire detail in No Man's Land and got lost from your detail because you're so stupid. You're wandering through No Man's Land, and suddenly you find yourself surrounded by a patrol of German soldiers. Now, these twelve crosses represent the German soldiers. This check mark in the center of the circle represents you, Bernstein. Now, I ask you Bernstein, under the circumstances, what would you do?"

Without hesitation, Bernstein said, "I'd surrender."

The whole platoon roared with laughter, and Quirt was furious.

"BERNSTEIN!" he shouted: "YOU STAND AT ATTENTION!"

Then he called upon Willie McBean to tie Bernie's hands behind his back with a tent rope, made a dunce cap out of a piece of cardboard, put it on Bernie's head, then had him stand in the corner with his back toward the platoon.

"Bernstein, you stay there for the rest of the day!" ordered Quirt, and he continued with some other lecture.

Nobody listened to a word he said. Every once in a while, someone would snicker; then the whole group would break out laughing. Quirt was so angry, if he could, I think he'd have shot us all.

Somewhat later, Lieutenant Walsh came into the barracks, took in the situation at a glance, and asked Quirt what he was doing.

"Well, I'm giving my men a lecture."

"Don't you know that the men are supposed to have the day off so they can clean their equipment and rest? What's the matter with you, Quirt? Men, you are dismissed."

Oh, Walsh detested Quirt, and he insulted him in front of the men on several occasions. But poor Bernstein. We laughed many a time through the years over that incident.

Gilman, Gilroy, and Tarrytown Murph

Life in the Pioneers was made tolerable by our resident comic, Frankie McGuire, and a good quartet consisting of the tallest men in the platoon—George Gilman, Ben Gilroy, Jack Murray, and Herb Schwartz. Our quartet would break into song at the least inspiration, and they made up several songs about Quirt, all very profane. Moreover, they would preface every song with the following insult:

> *You must admit——Boom, Boom*
> *You must admit——Boom, Boom*
> *That Quirt is full of shit.*

One day, Quirt came in unexpectedly, just as they were expositing what he was full of. He hit the ceiling and assigned the whole quartet to KP duty for a week.

We had a character in the Pioneers whose name was Murphy. He was one of five Murphys in HQ Company, so we called him Tarrytown Murph because he came from Tarrytown, New York. Murph had been a streetcar conductor in civilian life, and he was a tightwad. Oh, what a tightwad he was! He would go to the local cafe on payday and sponge drinks off the other fellows; never would he buy his own or treat anyone else.

Murphy had an old-fashioned soft leather purse that he kept his money in, and it was just bulging with francs. He would secure this purse to his undershirt with a large blanket pin when he slept. We accused him of having amassed a fortune by stealing nickels from his streetcar.

Gilman and Gilroy decided to do something about Murphy's fat purse; so, one night, while he was snoring away, they snuck up, unpinned the purse from his undershirt, and beat it back to their bunks. The next morning, when Murphy discovered his loss, oh, he carried on terribly! He grabbed his rifle and threatened to shoot everyone in the platoon, until Big Jim Collintine took his rifle away. He cried out: "It ain't th' money; it ain't th' money dat I loose. But thim damn thieves stole th' rosary dat me blessed mither giv t' me."

The rosary, imagine that.

A couple of nights later, while he was snoring away, Gilman and Gilroy snuck up again and pinned the purse back to his shirt with the rosary in it. When he awoke the next morning and saw there was nothing inside but the rosary, he started all over again. The guys said: "What are you bitching about? You don't care for the money; all you're interested in is the rosary; you got it back; what are you crying for?"

Gilman and Gilroy were very generous about sharing their loot with the rest of the platoon at the local cafe, and they themselves remained drunk for almost a week. After the war, they both joined the New York City police force.

The O'Day Incident

William O'Day was tall and thin and very awkward, with big feet that he stumbled over all the time. During drill, the squad would go one way, and he would go the other. The poor kid really wasn't all there; he really wasn't. Consequently, the fellows called him "Dizzy" O'Day. That was a cruel nickname, but he didn't seem to mind, and he was as good-natured as they come.

I used to recite poetry to the fellows once in a while. They liked to hear Kipling and Joyce Kilmer, and I knew many of their poems by heart. One evening, as I was holding forth, O'Day stood there listening with his mouth wide open. When I finished, he marveled: "Gee, Red, you must have gone to college."

"No, I haven't, Diz," I replied. "I only have a high school education."

"By golly, you sound like an educated man. I didn't have a chance to get educated, because I had to leave school to help support my mother."

"Willie," I suggested, "I'll tell you what to do. You just read as much as you can and you'll make up for it in no time at all. Read everything you can get your hands on."

"Oh," he said, hopefully, "that's a good idea. You know, I read my prayer book, but the Bible—I can't understand those big words in the Bible. I remember my prayers but I can't get those big words."

Well, I almost cried, but I slapped O'Day on the back and urged: "Go on now, Diz. You read all that you can and pretty soon you'll begin to catch on to those big words."

O'Day was always in trouble with Quirt, who found fault with everything the kid did. Quirt thought O'Day was intentionally resisting his orders, when, in fact, the kid just couldn't cope half the time. After a while, however, O'Day began to resent Quirt's constant hectoring and became very sullen when Quirt was around.

One morning, about a month after arriving in Longeau, the platoon was getting ready to move out, and O'Day fell in beside me with his rifle slung over his left shoulder and a roll of barbed wire on a stake over the other shoulder. A fellow came in from the kitchen with large bags of bread for lunch. Quirt grabbed one of the bags and thrust it into O'Day's chest for him to carry. The kid reached out with his left hand to grab the bag of bread, which had started to fall. In reaching for it, he sprawled head first onto the floor of the barracks. Quirt kicked him and shouted: "GET ON YOUR FEET, YOU CLUMSY OAF!"

O'Day started to cry and struggled to get up, but the roll of wire got loose from the end of the post and caught him behind the ear, and the back of his head began to bleed.

Oh, it was a terrible thing! Enraged, O'Day groped for his

rifle and cried: "If I can get this thing unslung, I'll kill you, you son of a bitch!"

That was it. We jumped in, grabbed the kid, and tried to quiet him down. But that wasn't the end of it. Quirt had him brought up on general court-martial charges: Insubordination and threatening to kill an officer.

Almost every man in the platoon was furious. Unfortunately, we weren't notified of the date of the court-martial, and only two men of the platoon were called as witnesses, Sergeant Blaustein and a Corporal Taggart from New Jersey, and the story was they supported Quirt.[8]

If only we had had a chance to testify, or if Father Duffy had not been on leave, O'Day would never have been convicted; but the court-martial was over before we even knew about it, and O'Day had been sentenced to 15 years at hard labor! We were told he had died of pneumonia on Governor's Island, en route to Leavenworth.

That was one of the most awful things I saw during the war, because you expect to be killed or wounded by the enemy, but brutality from your own is unforgivable.

Abraham Blaustein

Sergeant Abraham Blaustein was an unusual man in a difficult position. An Austrian Jew, whose every action bespoke that of a trained soldier, he was about 5 feet, 10 inches tall, powerfully built, and he frequently exercised to keep himself in excellent physical condition. During those frigid months of 1918, the coldest on record, Blaustein often went out into the fields and washed himself in snow, which we looked upon with amazement. As a matter of fact, he had been a member of the Polar Bear Club of Coney Island, which, during the winter, finds pleasure in breaking the ice and swimming among the floes.

Although an excellent soldier, Blaustein was aloof and lacked camaraderie with the men. The men resented that, but they resented even more his "ass wagging," as far as Quirt was concerned. He never questioned crazy Quirt's orders and did his best to please him, and we all held him partially responsible for O'Day's conviction. Blaustein was peculiar in that, while a few of the men insulted him, one even calling him a "Jew bastard," he wouldn't turn them in. It was like water off a duck's back. Sometimes I felt sorry for the guy, because I don't like that kind of thing.

The only thing that made Blaustein's authority possible was a recognition of his competence and his demonstrated courage after we entered the lines. At the Rouge Bouquet, he was heroic in the attempted rescue of 26 men entombed in a dugout. He not only directed the operation, but got down as far as he could to excavate the dirt and timbers that had fallen in, when, with the shellfire going on, he himself could have been buried alive at any second. For that action, he received the *Croix de Guerre,* one of the first men in our regiment to be so honored; and we all felt good about that because, after all, he was our sergeant.[9]

Fire at Longeau

One night, soon after midnight, the bugles blasted out assembly, and we were told to leave our arms behind and assemble on the Company street. We discovered that there was a fire in the warehouse where we stored our clothing, which was adjacent to our ammunition storage room. This warehouse was on the church property in Longeau, where I had previously stood guard.

In the center of the church complex was a great courtyard, at one end of which was a convent. Behind the convent was a church. At the other end of the courtyard was a row of attached buildings, each separated by a stone wall. The first building was a stable where the sisters kept a herd of twenty-two milk cows. Adjoining the stable was a milk house and cheese storage room, in the center of which was a spring, where large cans of milk were cooled for processing cheese. Shelves around this room held all kinds of cheeses. Next to the milk house was a room where the regiment kept its clothing stores. Finally, divided only by a stone wall, was the room with our ammunition. The fire had started in the clothing supply room, and as it was immediately adjacent to the ammunition storage room, the situation was quite perilous.

We rushed to the scene and formed bucket brigades from a big wash house in the center of the street, not far from the convent, and the spring house. These were the only sources of water we knew about at the time. Four lines were formed, two to carry water to try to quench the flames in the clothing supply room, and two lines to haul out cases of ammunition from the room next to it.

Lieutenant Walsh took charge of putting out the fire in the clothing supply room, while Captain John Mangan, commander of our supply company, took over evacuation of the ammunition. I was on the ammunition detail.

We noticed sisters hauling cheese from the milk house to the convent, and Captain Mangan ordered several of the men to help them. It was amazing to see those frail sisters carrying such large rounds of cheese. Several of the nuns also went into the stable to release the cattle into an adjacent street.

In the midst of it all stood Lieutenant Quirt, shouting contradictory orders at the top of his lungs. None of us paid much attention to him, but the Mother Superior rushed up to tell him that there was a large supply of water in a cistern at the end of the courtyard, adjacent to the convent. Quirt was so excited, he rudely pushed her aside. Captain Mangan, who saw this, strode over to Quirt, grabbed him by the tunic, and exploded:

"Lieutenant, how dare you lay your hands on a daughter of Christ! Go to your quarters, Sir! Go to your quarters immediately!"

Quirt slumped away. We didn't see him for two days and don't know what happened to him. Captain Mangan was a very gentle person. That was the only time his men saw him aroused to such anger.[10]

No sooner had this happened than we heard a bugle call from down the cobblestone street, and John Robertson, who had served in the American Field Service before we entered the war, told me it was the French Army call for "Charge!"

Well, you never saw such a sight in all your life. Down the street and into the courtyard came this old man in an outlandish uniform, blowing the bugle, followed by another old fellow with a wooden leg—he was actually running with that wooden leg—and behind him came an ancient fire wagon, pulled and pushed by old men and young boys. Basically, it was a wheeled platform with a pump and a coil of water hose. The pump was operated by two men on either side, up and down, like an old railroad work car.

The old Chief, he of the wooden leg, ran directly to the cistern at the corner of the courtyard and pried up that heavy lid—I don't know where the old man got his strength —but he got it loose; then others helped him to remove it. One end of the hose was dumped into the cistern, and the other, leading from the pumper, was rushed to the fire. All of this was accomplished with great speed and precision, which was a godsend, because our water supply was getting low. The local firemen saved the day, no question about it.[11]

In the meantime, Lieutenant Walsh, stripped to the waist and black with smoke and soot, led the bucket brigade and a squad of men with pitch forks, heaving out bales of burning clothing, while the company under Captain Mangan cleared the ammunition room. That was quite a job. We started by passing cases of ammunition from one to another, but it soon became evident that it was faster to just grab a case and run out to the street with it. It was an exciting night, and thank God, no one was seriously injured.

Although there had been a sentry on duty at the gate of the courtyard, the fire was discovered by horseshoer McEnroy, who occupied the last of the storage rooms. That was his blacksmith shop, and he lived in the rear. It was a miracle that he discovered it, because old McEnroy was never too sober at any one time.

What a character he was! Although short in height, he had a powerful body. Born in Ireland, with a brogue you could cut with a knife, one of McEnroy's duties was to wake the bugler every morning. I don't know how the devil he woke up himself. He must have had a ferocious alarm clock. Remember Irving Berlin's song?

A DOUGHBOY WITH THE FIGHTING 69TH

Someday I'm going to murder the bu—gler,
Someday they're going to find him dead,
And then I'll get that other pup,
The guy that wakes the bugler up,
And then, I'll spend, the rest of my life in bed.

The Button Rebellion

After about a month of training around Longeau, our uniforms were so worn they couldn't take another wash, and our boots had nearly disintegrated. We were told to report to the supply depot to draw down a complete new issue, and this time, thank God, we got winter underwear and woolen gloves. There was only one hitch. Both the uniforms and the boots were British issue, and the crown of England was displayed on the buttons of the uniforms.

Now the men born in Ireland were really steamed. They didn't like the idea of wearing anything made in England, and they refused to wear the new uniforms. For them, those buttons were a hated symbol of their former oppressors. Some hotheads in the regiment built a fire in the main street of the village and started to burn the British issue, and there was great excitement as one after another joined in.

Our officers were in a real bind. Most were sympathetic with the men's indignation; at the same time, there was great concern about lack of discipline and how to restore order. You must remember that this was a regiment of volunteers, and our best officers were very close to the men. We would follow them into hell, but that was a personal, not a professional, relationship.

Finally, Father Duffy was notified, and he rushed out and put a stop to it. The affair had almost come to mutiny, but it never went any further because Father Duffy realized how those Irishmen felt about anything English. He calmed the rebels with a great speech on how their indiscipline would shame the regiment, and how we had yet to prove in this war that Irish volunteers were the best fighters in the Army—and that couldn't be demonstrated around a bonfire in Longeau. Later, he and Colonel Baker assured the men that they would have access to American issue as soon as it arrived. He also conceived an obvious solution to the button problem. With a detail of men, the quartermaster replaced the English buttons with regular U.S. Army buttons.[12]

Most of our 69th men who had been born in Ireland had emigrated as soon as the war broke out because they didn't want to have to fight for England. But when we entered the conflict, that was a different story. They readily volunteered to fight for the United States. That was the feeling. You cannot imagine the bitter feeling of the native-born Irish Catholic toward the English in those days; very bitter.

John J. McMorrow

John J. McMorrow was one of several native Irishers in the pioneer platoon. In the States, he worked as a laborer, as a fireman on transatlantic steamers, and on the railroad as a section hand. He also professed to be a barber. If so, he was the worst barber I ever knew. His scissors were never sharp, neither was his razor; but he had conned himself into an assignment as company barber, which enabled him to make a few extra francs.

To discourage body lice (we called them cooties), our heads had been clipped right down to our skulls as soon as we arrived in France, and they remained that way until the Armistice. When a fellow's hair began to sprout, John only had to use the clippers. Even so, he managed to cut your skull—and his razor was terrible! I know, because he once cut my face and neck in a dozen places.

At Longeau, John found a French woman to do the laundry for him and other doughboys, and he acted as her agent. He brought the laundry to her and collected for it upon delivery. He also moved into her house and lived with her while we were in Longeau, despite the fact that the only French he knew was "Bonjour, Madame."

John was a rummy. Sometimes he was a lovable rummy, but he could also be dangerous.

About two o'clock one morning, he stumbled into the barracks drunk as a coot. The barracks was dimly lit with two kerosene lanterns turned down low, and I was later told that John was having a problem trying to find his bunk. The story was that he had been in a fight and was in a rage, cursing at somebody. The guys were shouting at him to shut up and this and that.

On his way down the aisle, John tripped over my feet, which must have been hanging over my bunk. I was asleep at the time but awoke quickly when he almost broke my ankle. John pitched forward on his face, sprawled out on the floor, then turned around and accused me of tripping him.

Concerned, I tried to deny it. "John, I didn't trip you, you stumbled over my feet. I never tripped you; I'd never do a thing like that, John."

"By God, ye did, an' yil rue th' day dat ye thript John J. McMorrow."

I didn't realize how crazy he was, just crazy drunk.

Our rifles and cartridge belts hung on wooden pegs along one side of the barracks wall, and on each cartridge belt, we carried our bayonet in a scabbard. John ran over and tried to get a bayonet out of one of the scabbards. There was a little latch that had to be pressed to withdraw the bayonet, and he was fumbling with the latch.

Don Adair saw what was happening and, in great alarm, warned me: "Red, get out of here; get out of here quick!"

I jumped up, and in long underwear and wool socks, ran to the exit while John was still messing with that bayonet. He finally got it out, and as I gave a quick look behind, I could see him charging after me, weapon in hand.

I went out that door a mile a minute, out into the snow, and ran several hundred yards, when I heard a lot of shouting.

As it happened, Big Jim Collintine, who slept near the exit door, stuck his foot out and tripped McMorrow as he charged by. McMorrow tumbled to the floor, and was out cold for twenty minutes. They had to rub snow on his face to bring him around.

In the meantime, I looked behind, and no one was following me, so I slowly returned to the barracks and heard the men laughing. One of them yelled: "Come on back, Red! The coast is clear!" As I reentered the barracks, almost frozen, there was John still unconscious on the floor. When he came to, he didn't remember a thing that had happened. The next morning, when I told him what he had done, he wouldn't believe me.

"It couldn'a happin, Red. It couldn'a happin."

"By God, it did, you big donkey," I replied.

John was sincerely remorseful, and the following night he invited me to his billet where he had shacked up with his woman. She was older than he and crazy about John, and they were very hospitable to me that evening. Their communication never ceased to puzzle and amuse me, because John's French was so terrible. It was even worse than his English, and that was hard to understand sometimes.

McMorrow Guards the Still

Farmers from the area grew a large quantity of plums. They would dry and store these plums; then, during the winter, a portable distillery moved from village to village to process them. The product of the distillation was commonly called "prune," but the name used in the cafes was "Eau-de-Vie," the water of life. It was strong stuff, very strong.

One night, two elderly Frenchmen hauled such a still into Longeau, set it up in the courtyard, and asked the military to keep an eye on it for them. It was made one of our guard posts, and from eight o'clock to midnight, I was on guard duty, and my post was to protect this still.

I was very quiet and very cold—golly, it was cold—and I started fooling around with the still to find out if I could extract some "prune." I found out. There was a certain valve which, when opened, released the "water of life." So, I filled my mess cup to get on a healthy glow over the four hours of my guard duty, just a nice glow, because I spread it out only to keep warm.

Lo and behold! Who relieved me at midnight but John McMorrow, and like a darn fool, I told him how to extract the "Eau-de-Vie." Little realizing the consequences, I went on to the guard house and hit the sack there.

About three o'clock in the morning, there was a lot of shouting and commotion, and the guard was called out. What had happened? John McMorrow had liberally imbibed of the "prune" and started singing at his post. This awoke the distillers, who were sleeping in an adjacent house. When they realized the source of John's merriment and came down to protest, John calmly smacked both of them with the butt of his rifle and knocked them out cold. A woman who had seen this from her window screamed for the gendarme who, arriving on the scene, met the same fate.

By this time, the whole neighborhood was awake, and our man at the next post heard the commotion. When the corporal of the guard arrived, there was McMorrow, drunk as a log, singing away at the top of his lungs, with three unconscious men lying in the snow. John was hauled to the guard house but was released two weeks later to participate in our final maneuvers, in which he played a noteworthy part.

Final Maneuvers

We were in Longeau from New Year's until mid-February. Several days before the regiment was to depart for the front, we had final maneuvers, using the trenches that our pioneer platoon had spent over a month building on this ridge. Small defending forces in the trenches were attacked by a battalion advancing through the valley and up the hill. Live ammunition was used, and the battalions rotated morning and afternoon.

This first day of the maneuvers, our pioneer platoon was in the defending position. It was crazy as hell, because the attacking forces used live hand grenades, and while they were thrown short of our trenches, they would occasionally roll a short distance back down the hill, with guys yelling and jumping like crazy to get out of their way.

At noon, the maneuvers were stopped to have lunch. We had been issued newly designed rolling kitchens to replace the old-fashioned army breakdown kitchen. This kitchen on wheels was fine on level country, but beef stew had been prepared for lunch, and bouncing over this mountain road on the way up to our ridge, the stew went sour. Lieutenant Walsh, who always sampled the food before it was served, took one sip, spat it out, and raised hell with the mess sergeant; then he sent a detail four miles back to Longeau for emergency rations. That gave us some time off, so we stacked arms on the ridge and sat around in the woods, chewing the fat.

Earlier that morning, while on our way up the mountain

grade, I had noticed the roofs of a little village in the valley
to our left and had called it to Frankie McGuire's attention.
We'd been going up that damn road for over a month and
never noticed the village because of dead leaves on the trees,
now totally gone. [Either Verseilles-le-Haut or Verseilles-le-
Bas.]

With time on our hands, I became inspired.

"Hey Frankie, maybe we can find that village we passed
and get us some cognac or something, wha'd you say?"

"Sure, let's go," agreed McGuire, always game for adventure.

We beat it back to the woods, making believe we were
going to the latrine, and kept on going. We cut across fields
and found a road that led to this village. There we discovered a neat cafe where we ordered an omelette, potatoes,
and a bottle of wine.

While waiting for the food, we drank two bottles of wine.
Then, noticing a bottle of cognac behind the bar, I asked the
proprietor: "Avez-vous du cognac?" "Oui, monsieur."
"Combien?" It was fifteen centimes—ten cents—for a little
glass, so we ordered a whole bottle.

By the time we had finished lunch and a fifth of cognac, we
had lost all track of time. Finally, looking at a watch, it was
four o'clock. What to do? Because our rifle and packs were
still back on the ridge, we decided to return and infiltrate the
maneuvers.

We bought another bottle of cognac and had found the
road leading to the ridge, when we heard band music. It was
the regiment returning from maneuvers, the band leading
them, playing their heads off. We jumped into a ditch
alongside the road and lay flat. All I could see after the band
passed was bayonets, row upon row of bayonets.

At last the troops moved on. We picked ourselves up and
started for the ridge, and by this time it was almost dark.
Approaching the summit, we left the road and went through
the woods so as not to be detected. Sure enough, someone
was pacing up and down with a rifle on his shoulder, and we
could see our rifles and packs stacked nearby.

As we got closer, we could hear the lone doughboy
muttering to himself, and we recognized this guard as one of
our own platoon, John McMorrow. So we sneaked through

the woods, and McGuire picked up a stick and threw it in John's direction. McMorrow swung around with his rifle and shouted:

"CUM OUT AV THIR, WHOER YE ARE, AR OI'L KILL YE! CUM OUT! CUM OUT! OI'L SHOOT! OI'L SHOOT!"

Frankie called out, "John, you wouldn't shoot us, would you?"

"By God, Oi will! Sure as hell Oi will, ye damn bastherds! Kape me up here wit th' cold, waitin' fer yer ter show op. Cum on now, wit yer hands op!"

So we took out our handkerchiefs and waved them in surrender. Oh, he cursed us; he called us everything. In the midst of this fusillade of profanity, McGuire held up the bottle of cognac.

McMorrow queried hopefully, "Hoy, what's dat?"

"It's cognac, John," replied McGuire, innocently. "Want a drink?"

"Oh, me God, yis! Oh, me God!"

So Frankie passed the bottle to McMorrow, and he drank about half of it.

"My God!" he exclaimed. "Whir did ye git dis? Whir did ye git dis? Whir th' hell have ye bin?"

We told him how we found this little village, and so forth.

"Oh, me God!" swore John for the tenth time. "We gotta git sumore av dat cognac. But remember, yer uner arres'; yer uner arres', now. An' don't thry anny funny business, cause ye thry ter escape. Oi'l shoot ye; sure as God, Oi'l shoot ye!"

McGuire made a proposition: "Suppose we take an oath not to escape, John, will that satisfy you?"

"Well, maybe-ut-twill," said John, trying to convince himself. "Maybe-ut-twill."

After Frankie and I took an oath that we wouldn't try to escape, the three of us went back to the village and got so drunk that by eleven o'clock they kicked us out of the cafe.

Soon after leaving, we took a short cut through the fields to get to the main road to Longeau, even though the snow was almost knee deep. We hadn't staggered very far when I declared:

"I think I see some movement over in that woods."

"Whut would be moovin?" said John.

"Maybe the Germans are coming," I suggested hopefully, since we were now ready to fight somebody.

So, he looked—it was a nice moonlit night—and looked; the more he looked, the more he imagined something there. Probably the tree branches were swaying in the breeze.

"Oh yis, Oi see ut," he agreed. "Now min, we'll sprid out in th' field here an' we'll git thim God damn Germans out av th' woods in a horry."

Stealthily, we approached the woods; then McMorrow ordered us to open fire. McGuire and I still had 250 rounds of ammunition from our morning's exercise, as well as three hand grenades each, so we started firing into the woods. We loaded as fast as we could, fired and reloaded, fired and reloaded; then we decided to throw some hand grenades. When we hurled our grenades, two of them hit a tree and bounced halfway back. Had it not been for the snow, we'd have been killed surer than hell.

Then McMorrow yelled: "CUM ON, BOYS! LET'S FIX BAYONETS AN' CHARGE!"

We charged the woods with fixed bayonets. I stuck mine into a tree and broke it trying to pull it out.

Finally, satisfied that we had driven all the Germans out of the area, we got back on the road.

Flushed with victory, we had progressed a few hundred yards when McGuire shouted: "I SMELL GAS!" (He had probably broken wind.) So we put on our gas masks. With our masks on, we couldn't see a damn thing. We were holding one another, staggering down the road.

In the meantime, the noise of all that shooting had alarmed the village of Longeau. The officers couldn't imagine what it was all about and sent an eight-man patrol to investigate. Before long, the three of us, arm-in-arm, staggered into the patrol. They grabbed us, took us back to Longeau, and slapped us in the guard house.

A summary court-martial was held the following day, and we were brought before Alexander Anderson, our company captain. Alex Anderson was a tough but a good and brave officer, who became a general in World War II. He got our service records, but he didn't have to read McMorrow's. John had already been in the guard house four times. He slapped McMorrow with his service record and then shook his stick at him. Each of us was sentenced to thirty days hard labor and fined two-thirds of two months' pay. Then it was off to the guard house, but we were there only two days when the regiment departed for the Luneville sector.

Evidently the penalties were dropped, because we heard no more about it, and the courts-martial didn't appear in our service records. We later heard that Colonel Hine, a grand old gentleman, had witnessed our return from the "Pioneer Platoon Maneuvers" and had been highly amused. He persuaded Anderson to expunge the court-martial proceedings from our service records.

Colonel Hine was too old for combat, so he was transferred to a desk job at AEF HQ. He was so frustrated there, and so desperately wanted to see action with the regiment, he went over the top with us at St. Mihiel in a private's uniform.

Frankie McGuire

Francis McGuire, my companion in this episode, came from the Redhook section of Brooklyn, a pretty rough neighborhood, where his father ran a waterfront saloon. Its customers were mostly seafaring men, and Frankie grew up in that environment. Even so, and although full of the devil, Frankie was a gentle young man.

Both Frankie and Jim Collintine had transferred to us from Brooklyn's 14th Regiment. Between sailings, Jim was both a patron and a tenant of the McGuire saloon (he rented a room above the bar), and that's why Jim and Frankie were such close friends. Indeed, Jim was like an uncle to us both.

McGuire was a pistol! He was the platoon comedian and an excellent one. He could mimic anyone's voice to perfection and had a great sense of timing. Several times he got me into trouble by imitating my voice while insulting other fellows. Once he even had Collintine fooled, and Jim was about to break my neck.

One Sunday in Longeau, some of the men were lounging around cleaning their weapons, while others spread a blanket on the floor and started a crap game, which was against regulations. Our captain at that time was Alexander Anderson, who was rougher than hell. McGuire slipped out of the barracks, then cracked open the door and, mimicking Anderson's voice, shouted: "WHAT ARE YOU MEN DO-ING THERE!"

The men panicked. They grabbed money off the blankets helter skelter and high-tailed it for their bunks. McGuire ran like hell and didn't return for several hours. The men would have killed anyone else who pulled a trick like that, but Frankie was such a good kid, and he so often gave our spirits a lift when we were feeling low, he could get away with even the most atrocious stunts.

RECONNAISSANCE NO. 4

"The Division at this time, along with the 1st, 2nd and 26th Divisions, made up the 1st U.S. Army Corps under the command of Major General Hunter Liggett. As it moved into the Luneville area, it remained under this corps for administration, supply, and discipline. For combat and training, however, it came under the 7th French Corps . . . and held the line in front of Luneville and Baccarat.

"The Rainbow headquarters and staff were put in Luneville alongside the 7th French Army Headquarters. . . . The 83rd Infantry Brigade Headquarters was placed in Benamenill with Headquarters of the 14th French Infantry Division. Headquarters of the 84th Infantry Brigade were put in Baccarat with the Headquarters of the 128th French Infantry Division. . . .

"Aside from learning the routine of life in the trenches and methods of making reliefs, the principal activities of the Rainbow were . . . nightly patrols, between different centers of resistance, where these occupied salients in the line, and throughout No Man's Land, or the territory between the French and American front lines and the German front line.

"In Addition, the Division had two classes of experiences: The first consisted of raids, on a large enough scale to be called minor attacks, on the German trenches; the second consisted of German retaliations in the shape of fairly large raids and of heavy artillery concentrations on different parts of the trenches held by the Rainbow."

—Reilly, *Americans All,* pp. 121–122.

"It is characteristic of the American soldier to scatter the moment he breaks ranks. Like Kipling's British soldier, he is out 'for to admire and for to see,' and his curiosity demands to know what the other side of any given hill looks like. In the old Army, long before the war, I have marched a company 30 miles on a hot day over dusty roads without a straggler, seen them stagger into camp, certain that they could not move another step, and then had every man jack except the cooks vanish the moment camp was made. Old soldiers or rookies, in a wilderness or a settled country, it always is the same. I remember it in Georgia, Texas and Minnesota in peace, and I saw it again in France in war."

—Major General Hunter Liggett, *A.E.F.* (New York: Dodd, Meade & Co., 1928) p. 208.

4

Luneville Sector

★　　★　　★

> —By the way, I'm a Sergeant now. I'll never
> be anything higher. To get a commission I'd have
> to go away for three months to a school, and
> then—whether or not I was made an officer—I'd
> be sent to some outfit other than this. And I don't
> want to leave this crowd. I'd rather be a Sergeant
> in the 69th than a Lieutenant in any other
> regiment in the world. . . .
>
> —Letter from Joyce Kilmer to Father James,
> April 1918, *Memoirs*, Vol. 2, p. 141.

The regiment departed Longeau in mid-February and hiked
about ten miles to a railroad. There we boarded a train
bound for the Province of Lorraine. All the cars were regular
French troop carriers, and in large letters their sides proclaimed:

"40 HOMMES/8 CHEVAUX."

Quite an experience riding in those cars. Cracks in the
floor, one to two inches wide . . . cold winds whirling up
. . . sliding doors on either side . . . only stopping to take on
fuel or water . . . hanging out the open door to relieve
oneself . . . sleeping on a thin layer of straw . . . eating
preserved rations.

En route, the train made a stop at some village, and
French Red Cross women on the platform served us hot
milk laced with cognac. The men were cold, and that drink
warmed us beautifully. After two days and nights, we
disembarked and hiked about 15 miles into the city of

Luneville. That was the largest city in France we had yet seen.

Luneville had been the capital of the silk industry in France, but the Germans, who had occupied the city for two years before the French recaptured it, had converted the silk mills into arms and ammunition factories.[1]

Our whole regiment was billeted in the "Stanislas," a huge chateau built by King Stanislas during his exile from Poland over two hundred years ago. It could house several thousand men and had stables for several hundred horses.

We rested there for three or four days and had time off in the evening to browse around the city. In Luneville, we encountered our first ladies of the night since landing in France, and some of us had an introduction to sex with a capital "S."

Hospitality at Luneville

Don Adair, Willie McBean, and I went exploring the first evening we arrived. As we sauntered down a beautiful, tree-lined street, we were greeted by an old Frenchman sitting in front of his house, so we stopped to chat. He was a veteran of the Franco-Prussian War, and he insisted that we enter his house to relax and discuss the war. After meeting his charming granddaughter and her two children, we sat before an open kitchen fire and were treated to coffee "au lait" and fresh, home-baked cookies.

On the kitchen wall was a huge map of Europe, which the old fellow used to follow the battle lines. It was quite a war map he had up there, with colored pins to show the various positions of the armies. Every day, he read the newspaper to update this map, and he got very excited trying to explain activities along the front. (The *Paris Herald* was distributed all over France, and the people were very well informed, even in the smaller villages.) We couldn't understand much of what he said, but it was interesting just to hear him talk, and he was so proud to be a veteran.

The old gentleman was very lame and had to walk with a cane. According to his granddaughter, when the Boche occupied Luneville at the beginning of the war, he was a stationary engineer in one of the silk factories. The Germans made him stay on, and he had to work ungodly hours. One night, as he was returning home, exhausted, he encountered two German officers walking abreast down the sidewalk. He failed to step aside fast enough and brushed one of the officers, who took umbrage and knocked him down. An aide to this officer rushed up and stuck a bayonet into the old man's leg.

That was a lovely family, and a most enjoyable evening.

The second night of our billet in Luneville, I joined Fred Young and John Robertson for another walk to see the sights. As we ambled along, suddenly we heard a strange "sss . . . sss . . ." Turning, we saw two women in the shadow of a building. One of them asked, "American soldat?" We walked over, and they turned out to be very good-looking women, I would say in their thirties. John Robertson could speak fluent French, because he'd been there for over a year with an American Field Service ambulance unit, so he was our interpreter. Well, after talking awhile, they invited us upstairs to their apartment.

Soon we were receptive to staying as long as possible under intimate circumstances; especially John, who was interpreting like crazy and becoming fond of the same woman I was partial to. Well, the upshot was the women wanted seven francs each, which was only about a dollar and a half. So, we flipped a coin to see which two of us would spend the evening. Poor Johnny, who had been doing all the work, was the third man out.

They were very nice—they really were—and it was one of the most memorable evenings of my life. It was my first experience with a lady of the evening, and I became very fond of her. Her husband had been killed while fighting with the French Army, and since pensions in those days were not very generous, her income was supplemented by those men whom she favored. After becoming a motorcycle dispatch rider, I managed to visit her several times.

Baptism of Fire

A few days after this delightful interlude, Dick Hennessy, formerly a dear friend from HQ Company, now a sergeant major at Division HQ, told me we were going to move out the next day. I passed the word around, and there was very little sleep that night, the men were so excited about going into the trenches.

To tell the truth, I think the French knew about our move before we did, because, as we marched out early in the morning, quite a few elderly French men and women were up and about the main street of Luneville. With many an "adieu" and "bonne chance," they thrust garlands of flowers upon us, giving us their blessing.

The regiment made a leisurely ten kilometers that day in an easterly direction and arrived at a cluster of barracks in a wooded area, which the men immediately dubbed Camp New York. We sacked there overnight, and the following morning headed for the trenches.[2]

We were marching up this road in two files, one on either side, our hearts beating in anticipation. Suddenly, German artillery opened up. They had the range almost perfect. Fortunately, however, their shells fell harmlessly into the woods several hundred yards to our left. The sound and sight of those first shells exploding was awesome . . . terrifying . . . very humbling.

Following our training instructions, we fell face-down on the road and crawled into the ditches on either side. We could hear shrapnel whining through the trees and the limbs cracking, but none of us was hurt. That was our baptism by fire, and we were all mighty frightened.

During a pause in the shelling, it became deathly still; then a voice piped up: "If those damned Krauts aren't careful, someone is going to get hurt around here." It was Frankie McGuire, our comic from Brooklyn. Everyone laughed, and that broke the tension. From then on, we were pretty much able to take shellfire in our stride.

Moving on through the Forest of Parroy, we entered the trenches in front of the Rouge Bouquet sector on George Washington's birthday, 1918, relieving a French regiment that had previously held that position.[3]

The pioneer platoon was assigned its own dugout, which accommodated 40 to 50 men, 40 feet underground. At the trench level entrance to the dugout, woolen blankets were kept saturated with water as protection against gas. Going down the stairs, we entered a large room with bunks, three tiers high around the sides. There was another set of blankets at the second entrance, which also had to be kept damp. It was an eerie feeling down in that dugout. No one knew what was going to happen next.

The next morning, out in No Man's Land, there was a big sign on white cloth reading: "Welcome, Rainbow Division." We hadn't surprised the Germans.

This area of the front was known as a quiet sector. For both sides, German and French, this was an area where men were sent to rest and recover from previous action. However, the Rainbow Division had no intention of using it as a peaceful exercise area. Even as we entered the trenches, our 149th Illinois Field Artillery set up a terrific barrage on the German lines. Of course, they returned the fire, and it was pretty hairy during our next month in those trenches.[4]

Artillery did the most damage. From the very beginning, our platoon was busy repairing sections of the parapet and trenches destroyed by German artillery fire. We also had to repair our barbed wire, which was continually blasted by German shells. This we would do in the dead of night.

We were only a few thousand yards from the German lines and had to work very quietly so as not to reveal ourselves. Every once in a while, the Germans would send up star shells to illuminate No Man's Land, but you could hear them going up before they exploded, so we'd drop to the ground and remain motionless while the area was illuminated. It was exciting work, to say the least.

Once we had to repair wire that had been blasted by our own artillery. After several hours of German shelling, one of our sentries, anticipating an attack, thought he saw forms moving in No Man's Land. Actually, the poor guy had been staring out there so long the shattered tree trunks appeared to be moving, so he reported enemy activity, whereupon an impetuous major, without further investigation, called up our artillery, which sent over a ferocious barrage. More important to us than needlessly costing thousands of dollars, that barrage blasted our own wire so effectively it took us almost a week to make the necessary repairs.

The major responsible for this marvel of destruction was transferred out of the regiment to Italy, where he found himself a cushy job as a provost marshal for the rest of the war. He was a handsome man with a great gift of gab, and after the war, he strutted around the city for several years in uniform and became president of the New York Athletic Club.

AWOL with Don Adair

Don Adair and I had begun our friendship by almost having a fist fight at Camp Mills. Then, on the voyage over, Don came down with the mumps, and Willie McBean and I visited him in the ship's sick bay. I guess we were the only ones in the platoon to do so, and I think Don appreciated that. In any case, we became dear friends.

My buddy was game for anything. We would scout around wherever we were billeted to find a village nearby without American troops, and we were very fortunate in finding these small villages. They all had at least one cafe where you could get a meal, wine, and so forth. One time we sneaked away for two days and didn't get caught. Boy, we were lucky.

Don was a Presbyterian of Scotch descent. His father was both a minister and the manager of the Railroad YMCA in New York, and I later discovered him to be a very fine, humane person. Don wasn't particularly religious, and he was a canny son of a gun with a tight rein on the buck, but many a time when I was broke he kept me in cigarettes and wine, and of course, when possible, I'd do the same for him. I vividly remember one of our escapades.

We pioneers had crawled and dug in the trenches and No Man's Land of the Rouge Bouquet for two weeks without relief. The three battalions of the regiment could rotate in the lines, one each week, but every night, we had to go out and repair barbed wire and the trenches. At the end of those two weeks, we were caked with mud and various kinds of filth, infested with lice, and our uniforms had been shredded by barbed wire. When we got out of there, we could call ourselves soldiers.

At the end of this first tour, we were given twenty-four hours off to rest in the dugout. Big deal. Filthy as we were, Don and I decided to sneak back to Luneville to visit the

French family we had met during our first evening in that city. In other words, we planned to go AWOL; not a very smart thing to do because we were in combat. Hell, we could have been court-martialed and shot! But we were too young and dumb to think about that.

I had become friendly with a French truck driver and his pal, who carried supplies from Luneville to the "Blue Devils," our French Army trainers. They'd come up early in the morning and make a return trip in the evening.

Before proceeding with my story, let me tell you about the Alpine Chasseurs. They were called "Blue Devils" because their uniforms were blue and they wore blue helmets and berets. They helped us with our training when we first entered the line, and they were great soldiers with considerable combat experience.

The original Alpine Chasseurs had come from the Alps area of France. I was told that these men were quite tall and expert skiers, but their ranks had been decimated during the early years of the war, and the Alpine Chasseurs, as we knew them, had been recruited from the slums of Paris. Most of them were short and wiry, but boy, they were tough! They lived up to the reputation of the original Blue Devils, and they were the pride of the French Army. We were very fortunate to have had them assigned to us as instructors.

Anyway, I contacted these truck drivers, and they agreed to drive Don and me the ten kilometers to Luneville that evening. So, about seven o'clock, we got into their *camion* [French for truck] and went right into Luneville through a huge gate guarded by a dozen French and American MPs. When we located those dear people we had previously met, they screamed with delight and insisted that we have dinner and stay overnight.

It was only then that Don and I realized how really sorry-looking we were. Our uniforms were torn and covered with mud, and we were filthy with body lice. Oh, we had a nerve calling on anyone like that! They had us strip off our clothing, which they boiled in a big iron kettle, gave us a bath, and put us in a feather bed. Of course, we immediately fell asleep. About eleven o'clock, we were awakened to find that our clothing had been dried by the fire, and we sat down to a wonderful dinner. We yakked away until four in the morning; then I decided it was time to get back to the platoon.

The problem was how to pass unobserved through those stone gates guarded by the MPs. I had planned to catch another *camion* and sneak through as we had entered, but no trucks were on the road that early. Then we heard singing, and down the main street of Luneville came a spirited regiment of French Chasseurs—"Blue Devils." They immediately guessed our predicament and motioned us to join their ranks. As we did so, two of them whipped off their capes and helmets to cover our uniforms. Here we were in platoon formation in the middle of their ranks, twelve men to a rank, and we went swinging by those MPs as bold as you please.

A few miles down the road, along came the same *camion* that had brought us to town, now on its way back to the trenches. Talk about dumb Irish luck! After thanking our French infantry comrades profusely, we jumped aboard the truck and arrived back at our dugout just before reveille. As we entered the darkened recess, someone asked, "Where you guys been?" "Latrine," we replied.

The War with Quirt Resumes

The Germans had leveled a twenty-foot span of trenches as flat as a pancake. It was extremely difficult to repair because they had that section zeroed-in with their machine guns, and it was worth your life to cross that level space. This night, a squad of us were on our way along the trenches when we came to this open area. Sergeant Blaustein at the lead. Quirt taking up the rear.

The Germans were very methodical in their machine gun fire. As we listened, we could tell that they were timing their bursts about twenty seconds apart, so just as soon as a burst would stop, Blaustein would have two men run across the open area. He continued to do this, and all was well. Then Quirt became impatient, and pushing up from behind, he wanted to know what the problem was. Blaustein explained, but Quirt insisted that the rest of the men—there were six who had not yet made it across—should go as one group.

The fellow next in line to go was Paul LeClair, a long-

77

shoreman from the Brooklyn waterfront. Brother, he was a tough customer! Quirt gave him a push without waiting to time the machine gun fire. After regaining his balance, Paul swung around, shoved the butt of his rifle into Quirt's stomach, and spit through his teeth: "Don't you push me, you son of a bitch!" Quirt didn't say a word, and the rest of us proceeded to cross that open space in good order, and no one was hurt.

Another night, we were repairing a section of trench, and Quirt was standing on a firing step overlooking the parapet into No Man's Land. I was right next to him. He was so afraid he was shaking—this at a time when there was no enemy fire at all. Every time anyone made a noise with his pick or shovel, Quirt would accuse him of revealing our position to the enemy, as if the enemy didn't know where we were. Naturally, the men got rather testy about it.

Jim Quinn had a stage whisper you could hear a half-mile away. He was working about twenty feet down the trench from me and, imitating Quirt, loudly whispered to the guy next to him: "Don't make so much noise!"

Quirt shouted: "WHO IS THAT! IS THAT ETTIN-GER?"

"No Sir," I protested, "it isn't Ettinger; Ettinger is right here alongside you."

Quirt swung around and put his .45 right up against my chest and scolded: "How dare you talk aloud! Where's your overcoat! You want to get pneumonia?"

Jesus, I was scared. That damn fool was so afraid of the Germans, he could have killed me!

Quirt was such a coward. He never went out on a wire detail. As a matter of fact, you could count on his never being around during shell fire.

We'd been up there about a week, and Sergeant Blaustein had twelve of us out on a night wire detail. Suddenly, we heard a noise like someone running, and Blaustein ordered us to lie low. We dropped into shell holes, wondering what that noise was until, before we could even see him, we heard Quirt call out:

"Sergeant Blaustein, get your men out of there! I have a premonition the Germans are going to send over a barrage!"

With that, he turned and ran back to our lines.

Well, at the sound of his voice, the Germans sent up flares and swept the area with machine gun fire. We had to hug the dirt for three hours and didn't get back to our lines until four o'clock that morning. Fortunately, no one was killed or wounded. Had we been able to find Quirt when we got back, one of us probably would have shot him; but he had gone to the medical dugout, claiming that he'd been gassed, when there wasn't any gas around at all. However, in his hasty retreat, he had been cut by the barbed wire, so they sent him to the hospital.

Rouge Bouquet

An unforgettable tragedy occurred during our second week in the lines. One night, when German artillery fire was particularly intense, a shell came over, went right down the entrance of a dugout, exploded at the bottom of the stairs, and killed or imprisoned twenty-four men below. Many of them were still alive, but the entrance of the dugout had been torn apart, and soil was constantly filling it in.

The Pioneers were called out to try to rescue these men. All night long we labored. I wasn't on that rescue detail because only a few men could work at a time, and only the largest and strongest were selected, but I was there. It was terrible as they tried to lift those shattered timbers, all the while hearing the survivors plead for help forty feet below.

Quirt wasn't there.[5] You never did see him in a real crisis. Two lieutenants (Tarr and Oscar Buck) gave general direction, but it was Abe Blaustein who really took charge and led by example. The men worked in relays, but Blaustein always took the most dangerous position.

Many of the Company E men, buddies of the entombed, insisted that they join the rescue effort. Plenty of help, but my God, only a few men could work in that narrow opening, and the Germans were shelling constantly during the rescue attempt. No sooner would we clear away a partial opening than the concussion from another shell explosion would fill it in.

A call went out to Regular Army engineers, who arrived at

daybreak. By that time we had managed to rescue two men alive and recover several bodies, but we couldn't reach the rest, and there was no further sound coming from the recess of the dugout. The engineers conducted several tests to determine if there was anyone still alive down there. They drove down pipes to signal and to provide air and water, but there was no response. Finally, the engineers said it was hopeless, and orders came to fill in the entrance with sandbags.[6]

This tragedy had a shocking effect on the men and was the episode so movingly described by Joyce Kilmer in his poem "The Rouge Bouquet."

Murderous Intent

The next night, Jim Collintine, Frankie McGuire, and I were assigned the job of filling the dugout entrance with sandbags. Forty men were detailed to bring up the bags. We'd take them, crawl down and pack them into the hole. We were working there about an hour, at the same time talking about Quirt—that dirty, lazy, lousy, yellow, son-of-a-bitch; why wasn't he here, and why wasn't he here last night?

McGuire exclaimed, "Oh, I could kill that bastard and wouldn't have a bit on my conscience." Collintine, one of the most gentle men I ever knew, who, when we talked about Quirt, would hush us up—"Now, yer jus a bunch av buys, ye don't know; ye don't unthersand discipline."—and all this and that, finally broke his peace:

"By God! if th' bastherd shows up, Oi'l hit 'im on th' head wit th' butt av me rifle; we'll trow 'im down dat damn hole, put th' bags on top, an' no wan 'ill know th' difference. How could dey?"

So, we made a pact right then and there. If Quirt turned up, Collintine would bust him with his rifle, and we'd throw him down the hole. In the meantime, we allowed the sandbags to pile up on the parapet in order to readily accomplish the execution. About three o'clock in the morning, who arrived on the scene but Captain Mike Walsh.

"What the hell are you guys doing?"

"Sir, we're just resting; this is hard work."

"What the hell have you done? Get those damn sandbags down that hole, and get them down right now!"

So, we had to work like crazy. Thinking back, I shudder, but that's how we felt about Quirt.

Soon after that, almost everyone in the Pioneers tried to transfer to some other platoon in the company. Adair and Fred Young got a transfer to intelligence, and both went from private first class to sergeant in a matter of weeks.

Several of us went to our first sergeant and asked him if something couldn't be done to get Quirt away from us, and he suggested that we see Father Duffy. So some of the men wrote up charges citing Quirt with twelve incidents of cowardice, and I was one of about twenty men to sign it. They took it to Father Duffy, who had already heard many complaints about Quirt, and he said: "That's the last straw. I'll take this to the Colonel."

Our colonel at that time was Frank McCoy, a great soldier, who later became a general. Rumor had it that Colonel McCoy didn't know what to do, because Quirt's uncle was a general with another New York division, but eventually he transferred Quirt to Company C of the 1st Battalion. Captain Herman Bootz was in command of C Company, a tough old guy of German descent—and this was particularly ironic, because Quirt so disliked anyone of German heritage.

Father Duffy

Our first service for the dead was held following the shelling at Rouge Bouquet. During those first ten days in the trenches, we had lost twenty-six men. Father Duffy located a little clearing in the woods near Croixmare, about four miles behind the lines, surrounded by pine trees. The clearing itself was like a beautiful prairie. There we buried those few men we had been able to excavate from the blasted dug-out, in addition to several others who had been killed by artillery.

After conducting the regular service, Father Duffy recited Joyce Kilmer's "Rouge Bouquet" to the accompaniment of taps on the bugle. Several hundred of the roughest, toughest men in New York stood by with tears rolling down their cheeks. I will never, never forget that beautiful service or that poem:[7]

In a wood they call the Rouge Bouquet
There is a new-made grave today,
Built by never a spade nor pick
Yet covered with earth ten meters thick.
There lie many fighting men,
    Dead in their youthful prime,
Never to laugh nor love again
    Nor taste the Summertime.
For Death came flying through the air
And stopped his flight at the dugout stair,
Touched his prey and left them there,
    Clay to clay.
He hid their bodies stealthily
In the soil of the land they fought to free
    And fled away.
Now over the grave abrupt and clear
    Three volleys ring;
And perhaps their brave young spirits hear
    The bugle sing:
"Go to sleep!
Go to sleep!
Slumber well where the shell screamed and fell.
Let your rifles rest on the muddy floor,
You will not need them any more.
    Danger's past;
Now at last,
Go to sleep!"
There is on earth no worthier grave
To hold the bodies of the brave
Than this place of pain and pride
Where they nobly fought and nobly died.
Never fear but in the skies
Saints and angels stand
Smiling with their holy eyes
    On this new-come band.
St. Michael's sword darts through the air
And touches the aureole on his hair
As he sees them stand saluting there,

82

> *His stalwart sons;*
> *And Patrick, Brigid, Columkill*
> *Rejoice that in veins of warriors still*
>   *The Gael's blood runs.*
> *And up to Heaven's doorway floats,*
>   *From the wood called Rouge Bouquet,*
> *A delicate cloud of buglenotes*
>   *That softly say:*
> *"Farewell!*
> *Farewell!*
> *Comrades true, born anew, peace to you!*
> *Your souls shall be where the heroes are*
> *And your memory shine like the morning-star.*
> *Brave and dear,*
> *Shield us here.*
> *Farewell!"*

Francis Patrick Duffy was a tall (6′3″), handsome man, arrow straight. He had the most beautiful speaking voice I have ever heard. When he preached a sermon from the pulpit, it was like the peal of an organ with a master at the keyboard.[8]

Father Duffy was appointed chaplain of the 69th several years before the war and there found great pleasure attending to the morale of the troops. Before we went overseas, he held the rank of captain in the Army, but soon after arriving in France, he was promoted to major. Eventually, he became a lieutenant-colonel in command of all the chaplains in the division. But rank meant nothing to Father Duffy. He was always with the men, on or off the battlefield. Everybody, every man in the regiment, loved Father Duffy.

His method of hearing confession was unusual, to say the least. When we were in the rear, he always made his headquarters in the parish house of the local church, and on Saturday mornings, he would stand like a giant monk in the middle of the street of whatever village we were in, and men would come to him for confession.

He never missed a trick! I shall never forget one time, while walking up the main street of Deneuvre, I saw Father Duffy listening to a man's confession. For some reason or other, I hadn't intended to make my confession at that time.

He had his back to me, and I thought it safe to walk by him, but as I started by, he reached out, grabbed me, and held me with an iron grip. Oh, he was powerful! He held me off to one side while he continued to listen to the confession of the man he had his other arm around. At its conclusion, he pulled me to him and said: "Albert, don't you think it's about time you came to confession?" Well, I didn't have much choice.

The man was also a public relations wizard. He would learn the history of whatever village or city we were billeted in, and at Sunday mass, he would fascinate us with that history. This brought us closer to the French people, which was his purpose.

During his sermon on the eve of departure, he would tell us about the poverty of that church and the villagers, and how it was our responsibility to help those people who had been so kind to us—and he didn't want to hear any silver in the collection box. Then he would caution us that we would soon be going into the lines, where we wouldn't need that money, because you couldn't use money in heaven or hell! At the conclusion of his sermon, that collection box would be piled high with francs, and when presented to the local cure, the poor man would weep with gratitude. And the little charity we dispensed made us feel pretty good also.

Unfortunately, Father Duffy was on leave when Willie O'Day was court-martialed. Otherwise, O'Day never would have received the sentence he did, because on several occasions, when men had committed far more serious offenses, Father Duffy managed to get their sentences commuted.[9]

Father Duffy had a remarkable memory. He knew the names of most of the men in the regiment, as well as their wives, and even their children. It was almost unbelievable to hear him hail a man and ask how Mary was, when had he last heard from her, and how Timmie and Mikie were.[10]

Every Sunday, Father Duffy conducted several masses. In addition to regular service in the local church, he held a field mass for the men of each battalion. When held for the 1st Battalion, Major Donovan served as his altar boy. A field mass was beautiful to witness—several hundred men under the open sky in reverent prayer to Almighty God.

When we were in the trenches prior to an attack, with shells falling like rain, he was right there, accompanied by medics, attending to the wounded, giving last rites to the dying and absolution to the dead. On the open battlefield, he was everywhere. He would appear like a gigantic apparition, emerging from a haze of smoke, undaunted by shell fire or machine gun bullets.

Coming upon a seriously wounded man, Father Duffy first established his religion. If a Jew, he would say the appropriate prayer in Hebrew; if Protestant, he'd say the Protestant prayer. Should a man be dead, he gave absolution, then took one of the two dog tags, and as soon as possible, after ensuring that the man got a proper burial, he'd write to the man's parents—always a very personal and lovely letter.[11]

Cooties and Rats

The dugouts and trenches were infested with body lice. These "cooties" sucked your blood like ticks. They'd bloat up, and if you could get them between two fingernails, you could pop them like firecrackers. When off-duty, we would inspect the seams of our underwear where they congregated. Some of the men would run a candle up and down the seams to hear them pop. Unfortunately, the thread would burn, and the underwear soon fell apart.

We engaged in a lot of good-natured kidding about being lousy. I'll never forget Big Jim Collintine lying on top of his bunk, smoking his pipe, while watching the rest of us search for cooties. He feigned disgust:

"Oi can't unersthan how ye min can be so filthy. Now just look at me, fer exsample. Oi keep meself clean like a good soldier should. Oi've got no cooties."

Frankie McGuire retorted: "Oh you big donkey, you've got such an elephant skin you can't feel them."

There was a roar of laughter. Collintine then admonished McGuire whom he dearly loved:

"Now, Frankie buy, ye shouldn't talk dat way; remember me buy, Oi'm yer real father." (Making reference to his apartment above the McGuire tavern in Brooklyn where he lived when between jobs as a ship's stoker.)

Jack Ryan and Jim Moore

Practical jokes were rough and rife in the 69th. One of the craziest was played out in the 37mm Platoon. They had a light field piece, called a one-pound cannon, that was mounted on wheels and could be pulled by two men. This platoon was under the command of Sergeant Willermin, a little guy of German descent, very proper, with no sense of humor. He was unable to maintain discipline among the men, but they were good soldiers who didn't require much discipline. They did their job, and they did it well.

In this platoon were two characters, both corporals. One, Jack Ryan, became the heavy-weight boxing champion of the Rainbow Division; the other, also a big fellow, was Jim Moore. Ryan and Moore were buddies and crazier than hell.

There were big fat rats in the trenches that often got into the dugouts. These rats were as large as cats. Ryan and Moore delighted in shooting them with their .45s, which sounded like cannons in the dugout, much to the dismay of Sergeant Willermin.

One night, while Willermin was snoring away, these two culprits encircled his bunk with barbed wire; then fired their .45s in the air, shouting: "THE GERMANS ARE COMING! THE GERMANS ARE COMING!" Willermin awoke, grabbed his rifle, and struggled to get out through the barbed wire, while the rest of the platoon howled at his predicament. Willermin was a good enough sport not to put them on report; just cussed them out.

Jack Ryan became the best first sergeant that HQ Company ever had. That company consisted of over 350 men, many of them college graduates or undergraduates, divided into a number of special sections and platoons, each highly independent. Each platoon sergeant thought that his platoon was the best in the regiment, and it was very difficult to get them to cooperate.

Headquarters Company went through five first sergeants between Camp Mills and Baccarat. None of them shaped up except Denis O'Shea at Camp Mills, but he was taken from us and sent to officer's school and, after receiving his commission, was assigned to the 1st Division.

At Baccarat, Jack Ryan was promoted to first sergeant and

put in charge of HQ Company, and he turned out to be a natural leader—but of course, he was a natural leader when raising hell as a corporal. Although an easygoing fellow, when Jack gave an order, you knew damn well he meant it, and his reputation as a boxer ensured that he could enforce it; but he rarely had to, because of his leadership qualities. Jack never said: "Do this, and that's an order!" No, indeed. Rather, he would pat you on the back and say, "Buddy, how about helping me with . . ." this or that; and you'd jump to do it because you liked him, and because whatever he asked you to do made sense.

I don't believe that Jack ever put a man on report. We had one bad apple in the company; a thief and a bully who would pick fights with smaller and weaker men. One day, he was caught redhanded stealing a comrade's blanket. Jack didn't bother to turn him in for punishment. He took him out behind the latrine and beat the hell out of him; then assigned him to permanent KP to the delight of us all.

In combat, Jack assisted Sergeant Willermin in the one-pound cannon platoon, and he handled this 37mm piece as if it were a toy, making every shell count. After the war, Jack became a New York policeman, and we remained the best of friends until he died back in the '40s.

Silent Night—Unholy Location

Up in the Rouge Bouquet sector, it came one night a full moon, and it was almost as bright as day. Therefore, it was foolish, actually suicidal, for any kind of patrol action. Seemingly, as a miracle, all firing stopped, and the silence was amazing! Then, as we stood at our positions along the trenches, we heard a chorus from the German lines, which was only a couple of thousand yards away, a beautiful chorus singing "Silent Night." We stood there, listening, and the strangest feeling came over us.

As it happened, a member of our regiment, Sergeant Tom O'Kelley, had been a tenor with the Chicago Opera before the war and had a beautiful voice. As soon as the Germans stopped singing, O'Kelley got up on top of the parapet in full view of everyone and also sang "Silent Night." When Tom finished, the Germans actually cheered. It was a wonderful occasion, but the silence was short-lived, because before dawn, the moon disappeared, and then sporadic firing resumed along the lines.

Raid with the Alpine Chasseurs

Elements of two other infantry regiments of the Rainbow had already conducted raids on the enemy trenches. Our first prisoners were captured by the Alabama regiment, and two details of the 168th Iowa had done themselves proud with Colonel MacArthur along as an observer. In each of these raids, French Alpine Chasseurs had participated in equal strength to show our boys the ropes.

The French seemed to be pleased with their aggressiveness; if anything, they were thought foolhardy. In any event, a lot of them were awarded the *Croix de Guerre.* Needless to say, we 69th boys were champing at the bit to get a few medals of our own.

In early March, a group of forty volunteers from the 1st Battalion of the 69th, plus forty Blue Devils, undertook the largest raid on the German lines that had yet been held in our sector. Lieutenant Herman Bootz was placed in command of the raiding party, and his advisor was a Blue Devil lieutenant. Fifteen miles behind our lines, they undertook a strenuous training exercise in preparation for the raid. Trenches and barbed wire were constructed by the engineers to simulate the enemy lines, and No Man's Land was duplicated in fine detail.

I had just become a regimental dispatch rider and was particularly thrilled to carry dispatches to Lieutenant Bootz and return with his progress reports. I was one excited kid over the prospect of what was to happen.

Late on the afternoon of March 20, I was given final orders, confirming the raid, to deliver to Major Donovan at the front, where the men had assembled. Major Donovan, who, after the Battle at the Ourcq River, was called "Wild Bill" Donovan, was in command of the 1st Battalion.

The trenches were crowded with these eighty men, and after they went over the top, I was determined to stay there until they returned. But Major Donovan took me by the arm, led me back into his command dugout, and said:

"Ettinger, there is no reason for you to stand out here. You must get all the rest you can. I want you to lie down on one of those bunks over there and rest until the raiding party returns. It's very important that a soldier rest whenever he has the opportunity. I don't expect you to sleep, but lie down and close your eyes."

Naturally, I followed his orders, but I couldn't sleep, and when word came down the line that the men were returning, I jumped up and went out to greet them.

The object of the raid was to capture prisoners for interrogation. Unfortunately, it wasn't very successful from that point of view. Our artillery preparation had been so intense and effective that the Germans, anticipating an attack, pulled out of their front line trenches. Then, when our men got there, they poured in their own artillery fire. Rather than risk an attack on their secondary lines, which we knew little about, Lieutenant Bootz wisely decided to retire. That was some task in itself, because the Germans made a living hell out of No Man's Land.

In returning from the raid, one of our men stepped on a land mine, which shattered his leg.[12] Bootz ordered the raiding party to continue back to our lines while he stayed behind to apply a tourniquet and, with his trench knife, amputate the man's lower leg. Then he slung the doughboy over his shoulder and returned to our lines.

Our casualties were surprisingly low but very sad. Jim Minogue, who was a member of the raiding party, had a brother in the same company, Tom Minogue. Tom went berserk when Jim failed to return from the raid, and despite a direct order to the contrary, he broke away over the parapet in search of his brother. Shortly thereafter, we heard a loud explosion, which could only have come from a land mine, then silence. That was Tom—killed. An hour later, his brother, Jim, returned unharmed. He had been lost but finally made it back to our lines.[13]

Herman Bootz

Herman Bootz was a fabulous character. Born in Germany, he immigrated, alone, to the United States when only eight years old and lived with an aunt and uncle in New York

City. He went to night school to learn English, but at age 15, he ran away and joined the Army. Within a month, Bootz was in the Philippines and, shortly thereafter, saw his first combat. He stayed in the Army, transferred from the infantry to the cavalry, and eventually became the first sergeant of Troop A of the 13th Cavalry. To be a first sergeant in any cavalry outfit, you had to be a tough cookie.

Bootz became an expert on mountain artillery, and when General Pershing went into Mexico after Villa in 1916, he placed Sergeant Bootz in command of the supply train, which in those days consisted of pack horses and mules. Bootz was highly commended by the General, sent to officers training school at Plattsburgh, New York, then assigned to the 69th as a second lieutenant.

At Camp Mills, Bootz was placed in command of Company D, which had a reputation of being undisciplined, to say the least. Almost all of D Company were longshoremen, and their first sergeant was a boss stevedore who had made himself proud by enlisting a host of his Irish confederates. They were so undisciplined their first officer couldn't do anything with them, so Bootz was given the job, and he whipped them into shape in no time.

A fellow who was there told me how Lieutenant Bootz first assembled the members of D Company. He got up and, in his heavy German accent, addressed them as follows:

Now, I am about to introduce myself. My name iss Lieutenant Herman Bootz, und I been in dis man's Army before some of you vas born. I vas da first sergeant of C Troop in da 13th Cavalry, da toughest troop in da toughest cavalry outfit in da vorld. Now, let me tell you someding. I iss da Papa und you iss da kids, und if da kids don't do vat da Papa says, da Papa knocks da hell out of dem! Remember dot! Und if any of you tink da Papa can't do dot, I vill take off my blouse anytime, und you can try me out.

That became a favorite story in the 69th, and this gang of Irishmen just loved that Dutchman! They roared their approval after he had finished his speech, and from that time on, he was their idol, their "Papa Bootz." Oh, he was stern! But he was always fair, and he knew what he was doing at all times. Upon arriving in France, Bootz was promoted to first lieutenant along with his buddy Mike Walsh, and after our first raid, he was promoted to captain in command of Company C of Donovan's 1st Battalion.

When I was detached to HQ for motorcycle dispatch, I was told by one of the sergeant majors that, shortly after we arrived in France, someone wrote to Pershing questioning whether Lieutenant Bootz could be trusted, because he had been born in Germany. General Pershing reportedly exploded (his paternal grandfather had emigrated from Alsace) and replied that he wished he had a thousand Herman Bootz in his command, and that was the end of that.[14]

Bootz won the Distinguished Service Cross and was decorated several times by the French, and the men adored him. He was so brave, and he always led his men; he was always ahead of them. By the end of the war, he had been promoted to major, but that was only a temporary commission, a wartime commission. Many officers from the Regular Army who had obtained high rank during the war lost that rank afterward and had to serve in their previous capacity. However, because of Papa Bootz's heroism, he was accorded the permanent rank of major in the Regular Army. There were very few men so honored. Eventually, Bootz served forty-two years in the United States Army, retiring as a full colonel.

Mustard Gas and Sergeant Pierre

About an hour before our March 20 raid led by Herman Bootz, the Germans, almost as if they knew the date of the raid, hit us with a massive attack of mustard gas. Their timing was perfect, but they hit the wrong sector of our lines. While I was comfortably ensconced in Colonel Donovan's dugout waiting for the raiding party to return, regimental HQ area was being plastered with gas, Company K suffering the most casualties. This was the worst gas barrage we experienced during the war.

Now, mustard gas could kill you, if you inhaled enough of it, although it was not as poisonous as the phosgene gas the Germans used. It was chiefly effective as a painful disabling agent. Wherever it touched moist skin it caused burns, particularly under the armpits, on the head, sweating under your helmet, and around the genitals.

The 3rd Battalion was in the lines at the time of this gas attack. Dense clouds of it came over and caught them by surprise. Many didn't have time to put on their masks and were severely affected. Still, they had the guts to stick it out in those burning trenches until relieved by men of the 2nd Battalion.

The following morning, when I went up to 3rd Battalion HQ on my motorcycle to get a report on the attack, several hundred men out of the twelve hundred in that battalion were lying alongside the road, most of them from Company K, moaning and groaning. They had wet rags over their eyes and were waiting for ambulances to take them back for medication. At that time, most of these men were blind. Had the Germans realized the extent of their damage, they could have walked right into our position. Perhaps one reason they didn't was because the wind changed and blew a lot of this gas back on their own lines. Maybe they were too busy taking care of themselves to think about attacking us.

The men were being evacuated as fast as possible, especially by our own service, the 165th Ambulance Company from Red Bank, New Jersey. They were the same boys who later saved my life in the Argonne. Other unit ambulances were also called out, and they all rushed to carry the men to a first aid station, then drove the most seriously burned to an evacuation hospital in the rear.

About 400 men were temporarily blinded by this attack, the most casualties the regiment ever suffered within such a short time. Fortunately, most of the men recovered fairly quickly with medication and returned to the lines within a few days. But some were not so fortunate, including Sergeant Tom O'Kelley, who inhaled so much of that gas that his singing career was ruined. I personally knew only one fatality—our beloved friend, Sergeant Pierre.

Sergeant Pierre had been assigned to us from the French infantry as our resident instructor on chemical warfare. He was one of the most unforgettable characters I met in France. I never knew his last name because we all just called him Sergeant Pierre. He taught us how to use our gas mask quickly and efficiently, how to distinguish different kinds of poison gas by their odor, and so forth.

Pierre had already served four years in the army, two of them at that hell-hole of Verdun (there was the ultimate horror), and he had the *Croix de Guerre* with two palms and the *Medaille Militaire,* the most treasured honor in the French Army, awarded only to those who had distinguished themselves in combat through display of exceptional courage.

Soon after his arrival, Pierre built his own dugout in the remnants of an old trench with logs from the forest. He had a cozy little nest in there, with a table and chair, and a bunk built into one of the log walls. He also kept a blanket over the door, which he wet down daily to prevent the entry of poison gas. But the most unique feature of Pierre's dugout was the wine cabinet that he had carefully crafted to the wall above his table. This he kept well-stocked with several bottles of different vintage wines, along with bread and cheese.

Pierre enjoyed company, and when we'd visit, he'd immediately offer some cheese with bread and a glass of wine. One day he said to me: "Give me my loaf of bread, a piece of cheese, and a good glass of wine, and I am content." Evidently he was, because he always had a nice glow on.

Pierre was such a happy, animated guy, always laughing. He would walk along the trench, see a doughboy, slap him on the back with a hearty "Bonjour, Camarade," chat awhile, and then walk on.

One day, Pierre was walking along and came across Lieutenant Quirt, whose back was turned to him, and he slapped Quirt on the back. Jesus! Quirt wheeled around, furious; and fellows who witnessed the event told me that Quirt cursed him for daring to touch an officer. Pierre just walked away.

We loved the old guy. He would tell us stories about the war, and although we could hardly understand a word he was saying, he would laugh, and we would laugh, and while we were with him, the world was a happier, better place.

On the morning after the gas attack of March 20, the French camion driver who supplied food and wine to Sergeant Pierre, looked into Pierre's dugout, and our comrade seemed to be sleeping. Then the driver noticed that the candle on his table had burned down, and Pierre didn't respond to efforts to revive him. Strangely, his gas mask, which usually hung on a nail at the dugout entrance, was also on the table, together with a couple of empty wine bottles. Evidently he had been drinking and didn't hear the gas alarm.

What a pity it was! A pall of sorrow fell over the whole platoon because of the loss of our very dear friend, Sergeant Pierre.

RECONNAISSANCE NO. 5

"The French and the Germans watched the reactions of American divisions doing their first service at the front with no more interest and anxiety than that felt by the High Command of the A.E.F.

"When an American division by its conduct in this test earned the notation 'a first class combat division' the dismay of the Germans and the delight of the French were not as great as the pride and gratification of the American High Command.

"This was the notation the Rainbow Division earned by its first month's service at the front. . . .

"The Germans had struck a furious blow against the Fifth British Army, had driven through its front, destroyed many of its units, and was rapidly driving the remnants to the rear. At the same time, they were widening their front of attack and spreading disaster. . . .

"The 128th French Infantry Division in the Baccarat Sector had an excellent reputation. It, therefore, was one of those wanted for the terrific battle then raging. Just back of it was the Rainbow, which had just proven itself fit for trench service and competent to hold a sector alone. Also it had double the strength of the French 128th Infantry Division.

"The answer was obvious. Put the Rainbow in line and send the experienced 128th French Infantry Division to what Marshal Foch always referred to as the 'Big Battle'."

—Henry J. Reilly, *Americans All,* p. 181.

5

Motorcycle Dispatch

★ ★ ★

> *Gallant hearts lay asleep*
> *'Neath the poppies that weep*
> *Hearts that thrilled at the*
> *Call of the Rainbow.*
> *'Twas a call to Crusaders*
> *From centuries past*
> *To champion Miss Liberty's*
> *Cause to the last.*
> *All the Rainbow Crusaders*
> *Who sleep 'neath the trail*
> *From the hills of Lorraine to Sedan*
> *Are the children of God*
> *For they hallowed French sod,*
> *With the blood of the Rainbow Clan.*

—Private Tom Donahue
Co. H, 165th U.S. Infantry
69th NY

New Assignment

It was an early Saturday afternoon, the second week in March, and we had just finished lunch. Then, after twenty-one days in the trenches, the pioneer platoon lined up to move back to Camp New York, where we had left our barracks bags with extra clothing. There you could shower, change, and rest awhile.

As we started down the road, Hennessy came up on his motorcycle with a sidecar. He was shouting something.

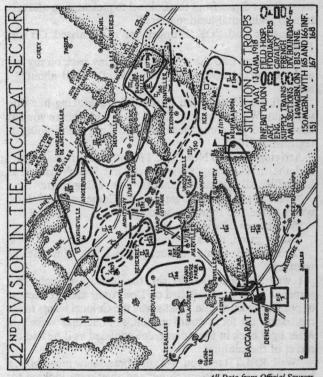

All Data from Official Sources.

Much to my surprise, he was calling out my name: "WHERE IS RED ETTINGER! WHERE IS RED ETTINGER!"

Sergeant Blaustein stopped the platoon and asked what he wanted. Hennessy replied imperiously: "I want Ettinger. I have orders direct from the Colonel to pick him up and take him to regimental headquarters."

Blaustein said, "OK, Ettinger, you're dismissed. Go with Hennessy."

I clambered into the sidecar, stowed my pack on my lap, and we started down the road. "What's it all about?" I asked.

"Well, I can't take you to the Colonel looking like this, you bum. We'll go back to Camp New York, where you can shower and get some clean clothes. Then we're going to regimental HQ."

Arriving at Camp New York, I found my barracks bag and had the first cleanup since leaving my French friends in Luneville. All that time Hennessy was yelling at me:

"For Christ's sake, let's get moving! Come on, the Colonel wants to see you right this second!"

"What does he want me for?"

"Never mind, that's a secret."

"Secret, hell! Come on, Joe, you're a pal. Why does he want me?"

I was apprehensive, to say the least. I thought that someone must have snitched on Don Adair and me because of our trip to Luneville. That's why the Colonel wants to see me, come up for a court-martial, . . . but that wasn't it. After I got back in the sidecar, Joe confided as if he had the secret of the century:

"Well, Red, I'll tell you. We got a brand-new motorbike, a beautiful Indian solo machine, and they were looking for someone who could handle it. I told the Colonel that I knew an expert motorcycle rider in the pioneer platoon who would certainly fill the bill, and I told him your name and what a famous racing driver you'd been back in the States. He said: 'You go and find Ettinger, and bring him back here right away'."

Oh my God! The con that the boys had put on Hennessy

back in Camp Mills had backfired. There, when Hennessy had bragged about his motorcycle stunts in the "Perils of Pauline," Unc Shannon and the rest of the fellows had told him that his feats were as nothing compared to the motorcycle exploits of Red Ettinger. They had concocted this wild story, and Hennessy, the consummate con artist, had himself been conned.

Well, I was damn scared. I had driven a motorcycle only once before in my life and had wrecked it. Desperately, I concentrated on every move that Hennessy made in driving that machine, particularly how he started and shifted gears.

Arriving at regimental HQ, we went down into the dugout, and here were Colonel Barker, Lieutenant Colonel Harry Mitchell, Captain Bill McKenna, the regimental adjutant, and Sergeant Major Ambrose Steinert. After saluting and presenting myself to the Colonel, this was the word:

"Ettinger, Hennessy has told me about your experience as a motorcycle racer. We have a new solo machine, and it's hard to find a man who can ride a solo machine. Hennessy recommends you highly, so I'm going to assign you as a dispatch rider and transfer you from the pioneer platoon to regimental HQ. It's now 2:30. Report to Captain McKenna at seven o'clock this evening to carry dispatches to division HQ in Luneville."

I was speechless and shaking from head to foot, but I couldn't do anything about it. Brother, I was in deep!

Colonel Barker then turned me over to Captain Bill McKenna, who sat me down and explained my new duties. I'd carry dispatches from regimental HQ to the various battalion HQ and also, from time to time, to brigade or division HQ. First he swore me to secrecy. I was not to tell anyone, except designated authorities, about the orders I would carry. Then he gave me a pouch that contained a map of the whole battle area in eastern France, a message pad, a military pass to any place occupied by the Allied armies, another pass that entitled me to eat at any Allied mess, and a pair of goggles. Finally, he talked to me very seriously about the importance of the job and how dedicated I should be. Then he excused me.

As I emerged from the dugout, Hennessy was waiting. He

led me to this new motorbike hidden in a grove of trees, pushed it onto the highway, started it for me, and said: "Now, Red, why don't you try it out. It's a beauty." With a show of confidence, I got on the motorcycle; then, turning my head, saw the Colonel emerge from the dugout with Captain McKenna. They were watching me, and that made it worse.

I put this monster in low gear, started down the road and kept going, too afraid to shift. Fortunately, about a hundred yards away, there was a sharp curve as the road entered a heavily wooded area. If I could get around that curve, I'd be out of sight of HQ. So I kept the motorcycle in low gear, and how I kept my balance I don't know, because you can only creep along in low gear, but I managed to get around the curve. Then I started to experiment with the gear shift, but in so doing, took my eyes off the road and landed head over heels in a ditch alongside the road.

Oh, God! it was a deep ditch. Very deep. And there I was, mortified and scared, imagining I'd spend the rest of my life in Leavenworth. Anyway, I crawled out of the ditch and got up on the highway. By the grace of God, along came a French camion. I hailed it down and indicated the crisis to the driver and his assistant. They got a chain out of the truck, and we put it around the front of the bike. As the driver slowly moved ahead, his assistant and I managed to haul that monster back onto the highway.

Well, that brand-new Indian motorcycle was covered with mud, and both the handlebar and the right footrest were bent. Nothing to do, my saviors got a can of gasoline out of the truck and washed the mud off; then they helped to straighten the handlebar and footrest. When we finished, that thing looked like the brand-new machine it had been an hour before.

Because both of these men were mechanics who had never seen an American motorcycle at close hand, the project was as exciting to them as it was desperate for me. (American bikes were much larger and more powerful than the French.) Well, God bless them. I gave them almost a full pack of cigarettes, all that I had, and they were pleased. After thanking them profusely, the motor roared at my first kick. It was now or never, so I started down the road again and this time succeeded in shifting gears. I did this repeatedly until satisfied that I could ride the damn thing.

It was after 4:00 p.m. when I got back to HQ, and Joe was fit to be tied. "Where the hell have you been?" he cried, "to Paris, for God's sake?"

"Naw, I was just trying it out, and she's a beaut."

At seven that evening, I reported to carry dispatches to division HQ, seven miles to the rear.

First Dispatch

I don't know how I ever lived through it all. In the first place, the machine had no lights—you had to drive at night without lights—then it started to rain, and the rain became a downpour.

About half a mile from regimental HQ, from out of the dark and the rain, charged an American four-wheel-drive truck. They were the damndest things you ever saw, because the rear end of these trucks would be on one side of the road and the front end on the other, and this son of a gun was taking the whole road. Trying to avoid him, I went ass-over-head in the mud.

Underway again, the next thing I encountered was a battalion of French troops headed for the lines, a file on each side of the road. God Almighty! They loomed out of the dark, and my reflexes were barely fast enough to avoid them. Fortunately, I didn't hit any, but I kept falling in the mud trying to dodge them, and the mud soon became ankle deep.

By the time I got to Luneville, it was midnight, and I had fallen exactly twelve times. The elbows were out of my blouse, my knees were exposed, I was bleeding from knees, hands, and arms, and caked with mud from head to foot.

In that condition, I walked into division HQ and reported to the adjutant, Major Walter Powers. Astonished, it took him a few seconds to recognize me. Powers had been the captain of HQ Company when I joined the 69th. Since then, he had been selected as division adjutant. (A twenty year man in the cavalry, Major Powers had been General Pershing's first sergeant when Pershing went into Mexico after Villa. He was a great soldier and organizer.)

When he recognized me, he let out a "Whoa hoo! My

God, Ettinger, what happened to you?" I told him the story and handed him the dispatches. He glanced at them, then exclaimed in anger:

"These aren't so damn important that you couldn't have waited until tomorrow morning. They shouldn't make you come down here in a storm at night for this kind of stuff."

Major Powers walked over to an adjoining office, knocked on the door, and a colonel emerged. It was Douglas MacArthur, then chief of staff of our division.

Introduction to Douglas MacArthur

Powers said, "Colonel, I would like you to meet one of my old boys from HQ Company of the 165th. His name is Al Ettinger, and he is their newly assigned regimental dispatch rider. This is his first trip at night, and I want you to see the dispatches that he delivered, because I think it's ridiculous that they sent him out at night in such weather for this kind of stuff."

After glancing at the dispatches, MacArthur came over to me (I was standing as stiff as a ramrod, scared to death) and shook my hand. At the same time, he put his left hand on my shoulder and said, "Ettinger, you are a good soldier."

I damn near died. Tears came to my eyes. No one, but no one, had ever called me a good soldier. Oh, my heart went out to him right then and there.

He turned and addressed one of the sergeant majors: "Go find my cook and see that Ettinger gets a shower and a hot meal; I mean a good meal. Then have the supply sergeant draw out a new clothing issue for him and find him a bunk to stay overnight. He'll not return to regimental HQ until after daylight, and then only if the weather has cleared."

After a dinner consisting of steak, potatoes, fried onions, and coffee with real cream and sugar (which I hadn't seen in six months), I was assigned to a bunk with a real mattress. I slept until after daylight; then had the most wonderful breakfast since leaving home: oatmeal with cream, fruit juice, four eggs with a rasher of bacon, toast, and again, coffee with cream and sugar. It was heavenly!

The storm had passed, the sun was out beautiful and

bright, and a strong, cool March wind helped dry the muddy roads. I started back to HQ shortly after eight o'clock.

Receipt for Damages

The main entrance to the city of Luneville was from the north. At one time it was a walled city, and the entrance was flanked by a remnant of this wall, with two huge stone gate pillars on either side of the road. Beside each pillar was a small sentry house for the MPs, one for the French, the other for Americans.

I was looking for that landmark as I drove down a beautiful boulevard. Knowing that the gateway was two blocks to the right from this boulevard, as I passed each intersecting street, I would quickly check to my right for the stone gate. Well, I traveled several blocks with a quick look to my right, and no gate, no gate. Finally, I saw the gate . . . but a little too late. Swinging over to make the turn, my machine mounted the sidewalk and immediately confronted a jewelry store display window. I yanked the handlebar, trying to avoid it, but the left end of the bar hit that plate-glass window, and . . . CRASH! . . . the entire window collapsed.

There were quite a few people in the street going to mass—it was a Sunday—and they were shouting with excitement. Then the owner of the jewelry shop, who lived in an apartment above it, emerged wringing his hands and crying. Oh! he carried on. His name was Monsieur Duvalier.

Finally, someone called the gendarme. He was a nice guy who, fortunately, spoke a little English. I asked him to tell the owner not to worry, that Uncle Sam would pay for the broken window, which the owner valued at 150 francs.

I took out my new dispatch pad and wrote: "THE UNITED STATES GOVERNMENT OWES MR. DUVALIER THE SUM OF 150 FRANCS." (With the seal of the United States Army emblazoned at the top, the paper was very impressive.) Then I scribbled my name at the bottom. The gendarme nodded his head in approval, and I continued out the gate and back to regimental HQ.

By the time I had returned to HQ, I was a dispatch rider;

not an expert dispatch rider, but I had learned the rudiments and had lost my fear of the machine. The most important thing I soon learned was that, in an emergency, my legs were long enough to stand up and let the motorcycle ride out from under. The bike would shoot ahead and topple over on its side with little damage except a bent handlebar. I discovered that trick through trial and terror.

Later, I learned from a HQ clerk, Dan Hennessy (no relation to Joe Hennessy), that among the return dispatches was a sarcastic note from Major Powers about dispatching a rider on a stormy night with messages that could easily be delayed. Captain McKenna, who was always very decent, told me I wouldn't have to do any more night riding until I had become more accustomed to the machine.

Comment on Cuisine

The best part of being a dispatch rider was the freedom. You were free as a bird. No officers breathing down your neck, except your own immediate command, and they were all great.

At night, we'd carry orders from regimental to battalion HQ—that was the prime job—then return with reports from the battalion. But we were also assigned to carry dispatches from regimental to brigade HQ; sometimes from regimental to division HQ. Occasionally, we'd take dispatches to some French regiment on our left or right flank. That was the most fun. I always enjoyed a visit with them.

I'd usually be on the road at meal time, and with a permit that entitled me to eat anywhere, I'd go twenty miles out of my way to eat where I knew there was a good mess.

Particularly enjoyable was the French mess, because they had better cooks. If you were a French chef as a civilian, you'd be a chef in the French Army. Hell, in our company, we had an undertaker as mess sergeant, a Wall Street runner as chief cook, and a couple of railroad section hands as assistant cooks.

The French soup was superb. We had stew, but never soup. It was bitter cold during the winter of 1917–18, and a good hot bowl of soup just hit the spot. Moreover, the French could do so much more with a side of beef than our kitchens. They'd carve steaks out of it, prepare the lesser cuts with delicious sauces, make ragout, then use the bones to concoct great vegetable soups. So I'd take full advantage of my prerogative to eat at the best messes.

Another neat part of the job was the way I was treated by our men, who thought I had inside information. They'd gather around when I was trying to eat. "Hey, Red, when are we going?" "How long are we going to be here?" "Where are we headed from here?" I usually knew no more than they did, and if I did, I couldn't tell them, but that's how I got to know a lot of fellows in the regiment.

From Luneville to Baccarat via the Bordello

After the regiment completed a month of on-the-job training in the Luneville sector, it was marched southeast into the lines outside the city of Baccarat. There, we were the first American division to occupy a sector entirely on our own, because our companion French division was needed to help block a German breakthrough on the northern front. Two days before the move, I was ordered to locate billets for HQ Company officers in the little village of Deneuvre on the outskirts of Baccarat.[1]

It was a brisk sunny day in late March, and approaching the city of Baccarat, I could see the Vosges Mountains off to the southeast. On the outskirts of Baccarat, I hailed down an Iowa dispatcher to get a briefing on the area because one of the Iowa battalions had previously been headquartered in Deneuvre. He said my best bet for information on billets for the officers could be obtained from the madame of the local bordello, and he gave me directions.

Well, it was a fine-looking house between Baccarat and Deneuvre, and as I tooled up on my machine, the madame came to the front door and graciously insisted that I enter and relax for a while. She was terrific and knew exactly where the officers could stay. She also introduced me to the other ladies and invited me to remain free of charge as long as I wished. Then she gave me a batch of business cards to distribute to my buddies.

At first, I was kind of embarrassed because I'd never before seen women dressed, or rather undressed, that way,

105

draped all over the room. But soon I became keen on a girl no older than I. She was absolutely lovely, and after a most pleasant sojourn, I took my leave. Before proceeding to Deneuvre, however, I checked in at the aid station in Baccarat for a prophylaxis. Then it was back to Deneuvre to confirm the billets recommended by the madame.

After returning to HQ, the first person I ran into was Hennessy. "Hey, Red, what's it like?" he inquired. I told him the story, embellishing here and there, and after I finished and gave him one of the cards, he was positively drooling. Nothing to do, he took off that very night for Deneuvre and joined the same girl I had been with. But he didn't bother with a prophylaxis, and several days later, he came down with a dose. He never forgave me—and he accused me of having infected that beautiful, sweet young girl!

Not long after the regiment arrived and settled in around the various suburbs of Baccarat, our MPs put that bordello off-limits—which was a damn dirty trick, because the officers were having a ball with these ladies in their billets assigned by the madame, but the poor enlisted men had no place to go.

Revenge on Quirt

Deneuvre was located on a hill, and the road from the front, when it got to the top of the hill, divided like a "Y"; one fork went over a block, and the other went straight ahead—those were the only two streets of the village—then they converged, and a single road continued out the other side of the village. To get to HQ from the front, you would normally take the right fork. The pioneer platoon was quartered on the street of the left fork.

About seven in the morning, I'd return from the trenches with a night report from battalion HQ. That was when the pioneer platoon would line up for morning formation. Arriving at the top of the hill, I'd swing to the left and gun down the street past the pioneer platoon, wide open. I'd power as close to the guys as possible, and they'd yell, pretend to be terrified, jump out of formation, and scatter all over. That would infuriate Quirt, who would shake his fist at me—which, of course, was the whole idea.

One day, Quirt went to Captain McKenna to put me on report and have me court-martialed. McKenna, who had no use for Quirt, told him to stop acting like a corporal and be an officer for a change. "You leave Ettinger alone. He's under my command. You have nothing to do with him anymore." Oh, it infuriated Quirt and tickled me to death.

Sex, Love, and the Orange

Two months and a few visits after first meeting my lady friend in Luneville, I had arranged another visit on a Sunday. Before leaving Deneuvre, I bought a couple of oranges from the Red Cross, one for each of us. These were beautiful oranges, the first I'd seen in France. A few miles down the road, I just couldn't wait any longer, so, driving without hands, I retrieved one of the oranges from my musette bag and began to peel it. Every once in a while, as the Indian hit a bump, I'd grab the handlebar with one hand to steady it. Well, just as I finished peeling this orange, the bike hit a large pothole, and to save it, I had to let the orange go. Up in the air it went . . . and down in the middle of the road, kerplop. After stopping, I got back to my precious orange and discovered it had landed right smack in the middle of a pile of half-dry horse dung. I spent several minutes pondering the dilemma, but so fond had I become of my lady friend that I saved the remaining orange for her and ever-so-carefully wiped off its slightly damaged companion. It was delicious.

That reminds me of another story.

There was a fine young man in our outfit who had come over to us from the 7th Regiment. He was very bashful about women and was always shocked when he heard the men describe their episodes with them. (Eventually, I learned that men who mouth off the most about women are often the least experienced.) Anyway, he was always lecturing us about the risks of intercourse, about remembering the girl back home, and how you should return clean, etc.

After the Armistice, when the regiment occupied

Remagen, he and another guy were billeted at the home of one of the leading burghers of the town. This distinguished gentleman had a beautiful daughter with whom our buddy fell madly in love. Well, one thing led to another, and he slept with her and got the clap. Now, it was impossible to keep that condition a secret from the other men, and you can imagine the ribbing that poor fellow had to take.

Jim Collintine Had Style

Big Jim Collintine never joined in our conversations about women. Once in a while he would "Humph" in disgust, so we thought he was too old to be interested. After all, he was in his forties. I later realized that our discussions of sex offended his sense of propriety and dignity.

Well, after Chateau-Thierry and the Battle of the Ourcq River, we were able to rest for a couple weeks while rebuilding our decimated regiment. The veterans received a complete new issue of clothing and were given a forty-eight hour leave to visit Paris, half at a time. I was absolutely broke, didn't have a dime, so I decided there was no use in my going. Jim Collintine offered to give me some money so I could buddy with him, but I wouldn't take it, thinking he would have difficulty paying his own way. "Jim," I said, "you'll need every franc you have to visit Paris." Besides, it was finally summer, the regiment was encamped at a delightful location along the Marne River, and I was perfectly content to rest an injured knee, soak in the sun, and swim from time to time.

When the boys returned from Paris, they had a great story. A couple of them saw Big Jim, sporting his new uniform, which he had had tailored his first day in Paris, strutting down the Champs Elysees with two beautiful young chicks, one on each arm. They followed him until the threesome entered a hotel so plush the boys daren't enter the lobby. They said that Jim looked like a million dollars, and that he walked along, proud as a peacock, as if he owned the city. When he returned, they started to tease him.

Frankie McGuire said, "What the hell could you do with two young chicks like that?" and Jim replied:

"God! Oi've had t' lisen t' ye young squirts talkin' about

ut fer months. If ye really wan' ter know, take down yer pants an Oi'll show yer how ter do ut."

Oh, how we laughed. And I regret to this day that I hadn't joined him, because I never did get to see Paris, and Big Jim knew how to do it in style.

Pat Carroll and the Motorcycle Race

Every day, I was on the move and kept improving in my ability to handle that Indian, and within a month I was pretty good at it. Moreover, I probably had the fastest machine in our division—I once had it up to 82 mph on a straightaway. Now, when I say 82 mph, remember, this thing didn't have a windshield. At 30 mph on dirt roads, it seemed you were going like the devil.

I soon became acquainted with dispatch riders from other divisions, other brigades, and the different regiments in the division. Then there were a number of officers who had motorcycle sidecars, and I got to know their drivers as well. One of these, Pat Carroll, became a good buddy.

Pat Carroll was from Ireland with a brogue you could cut with a knife. He was a fine looking man with black hair and blue eyes, and he drove a sidecar for Captain Mangan who was in command of our Supply Company. Back in New York, Pat had driven his own taxicab, and he was an excellent mechanic, who time and again helped me repair my machine.

One evening, four of us dispatchers were relaxing in a cafe—one from division, one from brigade, one from the Ohio regiment and myself. We decided to have a race to see who had the fastest bike. Pat Carroll was there, and he said he'd like to join us. We laughed at him because he had a sidecar. Naturally, a sidecar machine can't go as fast as a solo motorcycle. With offhand deference, he said, "I'll give you a chase anyway." So, hell, we agreed, and each of us put up twenty francs. That was about four bucks, a lot of money for us over there. We mapped out a route from Deneuvre that took us about twenty-five miles through the countryside. The race was to be held the following Sunday.

We started off about ten in the morning. Everything was going fine. My Indian was faster than the others, and I took a

109

short lead. They held on pretty well, but I could gain on them if really pushed. Then, much to my surprise, I noticed that Pat Carroll, with his sidecar, was keeping up with the rest of us.

Going up a hill, I turned, and there was Pat alongside, and the other guys were behind. We went over the brow of the hill and down into a beautiful valley, and—My God!—right in front of us was a farmer driving a herd of cows, and they were taking up the whole road! So we braked, but I slowed only momentarily because I could see a slight opening that I thought I could get through. Gunning the machine, I managed to zip through that opening, grazing cows on either side with my knuckles. Pat had to stop; he couldn't get through with his sidecar, so I won the race.

The other guys claimed a foul. It was a foul that the cattle were in the road; I was just lucky to get through and blah, blah, blah. But Pat said, "No one else did, but he had the nerve to try it, and he had the Lord breathing on his back."

Oh dear, it was great. But do you know? We discovered that son-of-a-gun Pat Carroll had obtained ether from one of the medics and had added it to his gas. That's what gave his machine the extra power—and, eventually, it burned out his engine.

Temporary Chauffeur for Colonel McCoy

When I was first assigned to regimental headquarters as a dispatch rider, Colonel John Barker was our commanding officer, but within a few weeks, he was promoted to brigadier general and transferred to another division, and Colonel Frank R. McCoy took his place.

Now, Colonel McCoy was something else. He was less formal and more outgoing than Colonel Barker. He had been Teddy Roosevelt's military aide when Roosevelt was President, and they were not only good friends, but they had the same kind of personality. Incidentally, Roosevelt presented Colonel McCoy with a beautiful horse and had it shipped overseas, and this horse was the Colonel's pride and joy.[2]

One Sunday morning, I had the day off and was sleeping in, when I was rousted out of bed by an orderly from HQ, who said that Colonel McCoy wanted to see me at once. So I rushed to dress and get over there, whereupon he asked:

"Ettinger, do you drive a car?"

"Yes, sir," I proudly replied, "and I have a New Jersey license."

"Fine. We can't locate my driver, and I have to make a trip to the lines because Colonel Post of the 77th Division's 308th Infantry would like to inspect the lines. They are going to relieve us in a couple of weeks, and I want to show him the territory."

"Yes, sir."

"All right, you go and get my car, and here's the key. I have an extra key because Mike Feeney, my driver, gets unreliable at times. You get the car and bring it up here." [Mike Feeney is a pseudonym.]

"Yes, sir."

So, I found his car and drove it to HQ; he and Colonel Post got in the back seat, and we started off. No problem driving, because we had a Buick at home, and I had had a license since I was fifteen years old. This was duck soup for me, and a treat in the bargain.

Going down the road, Colonel McCoy tapped me on the shoulder: "Ettinger, aren't you going a little fast? I wish you'd slow down a bit."

Gee! I looked at the speedometer, and we were doing over sixty, although it felt more like forty. So I slowed down; and every few miles, he'd tap me on the shoulder and caution: "Ettinger, please slow down some more." And I would.

Down the road, we saw a man on horseback going in the same direction. Braking down to a crawl, I also pulled way over to avoid contact; but the damn horse got skittish, pranced right in front of the car, backed against the front fender, reared, and threw its rider onto the highway. That unfortunate gentleman turned out to be Major Bill Doyle, adjutant of our 83rd Brigade, out for Sunday morning exercise. Of course, I stopped the car and went to Major Doyle's assistance, whereupon he exclaimed:

"You red-headed son of a bitch, I'll get you for this!"

"I'm sorry, Major, but I was almost stopped. Your horse . . ."

"God damn you, never mind any excuses!"

111

Just then, Colonel McCoy and Colonel Post got out of the car, and Colonel McCoy apologized profusely for the accident. Major Doyle was red-faced and embarrassed because his horsemanship had been impugned. The horse had run down the road a couple hundred feet and was browsing, so I went and brought it back, and we started off again.

McCoy cautioned: "Goddamit, Ettinger, for God's sake, be more careful, will you?" "Yes, sir."

Then he and Colonel Post started to laugh. They laughed like crazy, and that made me feel better.

Well, we visited two of our battalions, each holding a different sector of the trenches, and I was able to get a good meal at Company A's mess, which was a lot better than ours.

We started back that evening by a different road that wound through hilly country, heavily wooded on both sides, and much narrower than the road we had traveled earlier.

Suddenly, a motorcycle solo machine roared around a curve taking up the whole damn road. God! I pulled over to avoid hitting him head on, but I could hear his handlebar tick the rear fender. Looking in the rearview mirror, I saw the poor guy slide down the road, but he was getting up so I figured he was all right. Fortunately, Colonel McCoy didn't know of the accident. With some reassurance, he said:

"My God! that was a pretty close call, Ettinger, but it wasn't your fault."

"No, sir," I replied, and kept going.

Well, it turned out that this dispatch rider was from the Alabama Regiment. He was a big, tall kid and hardheaded as hell. And he thought that Mike Feeney, the Colonel's chauffeur, had been driving the car, because Mike also had red hair. So he came up to HQ in Deneuvre looking for Feeney that evening, found him in a cafe, and beat the hell out of him. Then he looked me up and told me what had happened. I sympathized. If he wanted to blame Mike Feeney, it was all right with me, and I'll tell you why. I had no use for Mike Feeney. He was a surly son of a gun, who had pulled a dirty trick on me that I wouldn't forget for the rest of my life.

One day while fixing the chain of my motorcycle, a fellow came along who turned out to be a war correspondent. He said he had heard that I was a demon on a motorcycle, and

112

that I had won a race among the dispatch riders. Then he asked me questions about dispatch riding, and wanted me to relate some of my experiences. So I gave him a lot of hokum and mentioned that the only tools I had to repair the motorcycle were a screwdriver and a pair of pliers. By golly, he wrote this up, and the article came to the attention of the Indian Motorcycle Company.

Soon afterward, George Kramer, our mail sergeant, hailed me:

"Hey, Al, a package came for you this morning from the Indian Motorcycle Company. It felt like there were tools in it. Mike Feeney was there, and he offered to deliver them to you. Did you get them?" "Hell no," I replied.

Well, George was upset, and he went looking for Feeney. Feeney told him that he'd delivered the package to my billet, which was a damn lie. Oh, I was mad! I collared Feeney and challenged him to a fight, and he wouldn't fight. He insisted that the Frenchwoman who cleaned our billet must have taken the package, but I had already spoken to her, and she denied having seen it. Moreover, I knew she was honest, and Feeney had a reputation as a liar. That's why I was not unhappy when the guy from Alabama cleaned his clock.

The Big Dive

One dark night, I was carrying dispatches to a French regiment on our right, and I'd never been over this road before. It was hard enough to see ahead when you were in open country, but suddenly the road entered a heavily wooded area, and it became black as pitch.

Along the right shoulder of this road was a narrow gauge railroad the French used for transporting ammunition, so I slowed down considerably and dragged my right foot along the rail. That's the only way I could follow the road. This went on for a couple of miles; then the woods disappeared, and I came out into a valley.

I knew from my map that a bridge crossed a river at the end of the valley. Approaching the river, I was still trailing the narrow gauge railway, unaware that the railroad and the highway crossed the river on separate trestles. I heard men shouting but couldn't understand what they were saying.

Pretty soon my tires were bumping along the railroad trestle; and the next thing I knew I had plunged into the river.[3] It was about 15 feet deep, and I was still sitting upright on the Indian when it hit the bottom.

After swimming ashore, a group of Army engineers gathered around me. They had been repairing the trestle and had tried to warn me about the break in the span. These engineers were great fellows. One of them dove into the river with a rope, got it around the motorcycle, and the rest of them hauled it out.

By this time, the moon had come out, and there was good visibility. The only damage to the bike was a broken chain. I started to fix it but discovered I didn't have enough spare links. The sergeant in charge then came up with a solution:

"Listen, our captain has a motorcycle and sidecar parked in a barn just down the road a piece. I'll send a man with you, and perhaps you can find some spare links to fix your chain."

In the meantime, I had removed the carburetor, drained the water and cleaned it, and the motor started, purring like a kitten. Then one of the engineers took me down the road to the barn. We looked around but couldn't find any spare links, so this guy said: "Well, I'll check out a workbench on the other side of the barn; maybe there's something over there."

As soon as his back was turned, I replaced the chain from the captain's motorcycle with my own. (I figured the captain didn't need his sidecar nearly as much as I had to get my dispatches through.)

"I found it," I hollered. "I got it fixed!"

I've often wondered what the captain's driver said when he found my broken chain around his sprockets the next morning.

Pursued by a German Pilot

When our regiment first entered the Baccarat sector, our HQ was still back in Deneuvre, about five miles to the rear; but soon it was moved up to the small, half-destroyed village of Reherrey. Amazingly, trenches ran right through the village, although the front was now a few miles to the northeast.[4]

After carrying dispatches to Reherrey for a couple of weeks, I discovered a shortcut, but getting there this particular day, the road was blocked by MPs, who announced that traffic was closed, because a German pilot had recently destroyed a French camion on that road, killing the driver. Nevertheless, I was determined to take that route to save a few miles, and they couldn't stop me.

The road was about five miles long, then came to an abrupt end, and you had to turn either right or left. The sun was shining, and I was halfway down the stretch when suddenly I saw a shadow, then heard the sound of an engine above that of the Indian. Looking over my shoulder, I saw an airplane swooping down. Instead of speeding up, I braked to a stop, and the plane overshot me. God! I could see his machine gun bullets kicking up the dust just ahead.

Brother, was I scared! There was no protection on either side of the road, only open fields; but ahead, just beyond the end of the road, was a forest. Before that pilot could turn to make another pass, I poured on the gas and went down that road as fast as he could fly.

At the end of the road was a six-foot ditch, and I was determined to jump it. Fortunately, there was enough slope from the road to the far side of the ditch, and horsing up on the handlebars, I jumped right across it into the woods. How I missed hitting a tree, God only knows. I skinned the knuckles of both hands doing so.

No sooner had I entered the woods, than that son of a Hun started shooting again. I could hear the branches breaking all around, but he didn't hit me. I just stayed there while he wheeled around and swooped around; but finally he flew away, and I continued back to HQ.[5]

Headache Hennessy and Billy James

The worst headache I had to contend with was that character Joe Hennessy. He was such a scheming rascal and so infuriating at times.

In Reherrey, there was a watering trough across the street

from the barn that was my billet. One day I had the motorcycle leaning on its stand on the ground floor of the barn, working on the clutch, and the damn thing fell on me. I was pinned to the floor and couldn't move; that machine weighed several hundred pounds, and I just could not get out from under it.

Joe Hennessy, who seldom cleaned his machine unless ordered to, had just got hell from the sergeant major for having such a dirty motorcycle. He was across the street washing it. I could hear him muttering away and cussing, and it tickled me.

When I realized I couldn't free myself, I hollered: "Joe! Hey Joe! Come over and get this damn bike off me, will you?"

He looked up and wisecracked: "Where you going to be New Year's kid?" Then he went back to work as if annoyed by the interruption.

Utter fury gave me strength I never knew I possessed. I managed to get out from underneath the bike, ran over, and knocked Hennessy ass-over-head.

"What do you hit me for?" he cried.

"You son of a bitch, I'll kill you!" I raged, and he ran to Sergeant Major Steinert and told him that I had hit him for no reason at all. Steinert sent an orderly to bring me to HQ; then he wanted to know what had happened. When I told him, he said, "I don't blame you a Goddamn bit."

When it was Hennessy's duty to drive at night, he'd often claim that his motorcycle wasn't running . . . something was wrong with it . . . he couldn't fix it. Then I or one of the other dispatchers would have to take his duty, even though we may have been working all day.

I'd often carry night orders up to battalions in the lines, then wait until daylight to return with their morning reports; so I rarely got back to HQ until seven, if the roads were good. When I had to pull extra duty because of that goldbrick Hennessy, dispatch riding began to lose its appeal . . . until Billy James was assigned to us and put in charge of the motorcycles.

I was billeted in a hayloft at the back end of the village of Reherrey right on the main street near our regimental HQ and the Officers' Quarters. Returning from a trip one day, I washed up at the watering trough across the street and went up to my billet to rest. There was a stranger in the loft making up a bunk next to mine. We exchanged greetings, and after staring at me intently, he asked:

"Do you have a brother over here?"

"Yes."

"Bill Ettinger?"

"Yes, how do you know?"

"I saw him only a week ago in Paris."

The stranger introduced himself as Billy James. He had been brother Bill's first sergeant, and both had gone to France with the Fordham College Overseas Ambulance Corps.

Billy James was an excellent mechanic. A test driver and mechanic for the Studebaker Automobile Company before the war, he also had been on the Mexican border as a chauffeur for one of our generals down there. When the Fordham Overseas Ambulance Corps was organized, Billy's sister, who was secretary to the president of the college, recommended him as an expert mechanic, and he was made first sergeant of the unit.

After serving in France for several months, Billy was assigned to General Pershing's HQ garage in Paris and promoted to sergeant major. Billy felt like a slacker spending the war in Paris and wanted to get back into a combat area. The general he had chauffeured for on the Mexican border was in Paris attached to Pershing's staff, so through him, Billy got reassigned to the 69th.

At first, Billy became our regimental statistician, replacing Joyce Kilmer, who had been transferred to the Intelligence section. Billy didn't care for that job at all. Who would want to be a statistician in the "Fighting 69th"?

I told Sergeant Major Steinert that Billy was an expert mechanic, and that we needed a good mechanic who could oversee the repair of our motorcycles and enforce assignments, so Steinert had Billy transferred and put in charge of HQ motorcycle detachment.

Billy was a natural leader and the best possible man for the job. Very soon there was an end to grousing about assignments, and all our motorcycles became available at a moment's notice.

Brother Bill and the Fordham Overseas Ambulance Corps

On a hot Sunday afternoon in late May, several weeks after Billy James took over the motorcycle detachment, I was working on my clutch. Billy could have repaired the clutch in less than half the time it took me, but he insisted that I learn how to do these things myself, and he would stand by to offer advice and assistance.

I was on the ground and had the clutch played off and was fooling around with the damn thing, and from time to time Billy would give advice; but I couldn't fix it and was thoroughly exasperated. I asked Billy for a certain wrench, but got no response. I looked up and exploded: "What's the matter with you? Where the hell is that wrench?" And there was Billy staring at someone, not saying a word. So I got to my feet, and the person he was staring at was my brother, Bill! This was the first time I had seen Bill since we left home over six months ago.

Bill Ettinger had been a third-year student at the University of Cincinnati when we entered the war. He immediately returned home and met up with an old friend who was a student at Fordham College. They decided that the quickest way to get into action was to enlist with the Fordham Overseas Ambulance Corps, which was scheduled to go overseas before any of our military units.

In those days, we didn't have any war industry to speak of, but we had the best automobiles and more drivers per capita than any country in the world. Before our entry into the war, pro-Allied Americans had organized the American Field Service, consisting of ambulance units with volunteer drivers attached to the Allied forces. Almost every major American college joined in that effort, and over six hundred college students were driving in France before it became legitimate. After we declared war, this organization changed its name to the United States Ambulance Service.

The Fordham College unit that Bill and his friend had

joined consisted of 140 volunteers plus four Ford ambulances. They trained in Pennsylvania with other college units and sailed to France in late August. Since American troops had not yet arrived, most of the units were assigned to the French Army.[6]

Those ambulances were unbelievable. Like later-day jeeps, they could go across fields pocked by shell holes, or through woods, and those that operated with the French Army would go right up to the front lines to pick up the wounded. In our Army, you rarely saw a motor vehicle within four miles of the lines.

My brother Bill was a high-spirited, excellent driver, and after this particular meeting, he was twice awarded the French *Croix de Guerre* for his dare-devil exploits.[7] (For some years after the war, he continued to drive like crazy, daring police cars to catch him on back-country roads, and after a few drinks, he would weave around 3rd Avenue El pilings, pretending they were shell holes.)

Anyway, here was Bill with his ambulance and a buddy, and I was overjoyed. The day before, he had met a division staff car on the road and, noting the Rainbow insignia, he hailed it down (even though Colonel McCoy was in it at the time) and asked the driver if he knew the location of the 165th Infantry HQ. The driver happened to be a former member of my company, so he told Bill exactly how to find me. Bill hied himself to Deneuvre, ambulance and all, and that's how we were reunited.

Nothing to do, I introduced Bill to Sergeant Major Steinert and got a twelve hour pass. So Bill and his buddy and I piled into the ambulance and traveled about twenty miles to an inn that he knew about, had a great dinner, and spent almost the whole night talking. Bill drove me back the next morning for duty, and he gave me directions to his outfit, which was located about eighty kilometers from our HQ. The very next evening, I took off after chow to visit him and made the distance in no time.

As I entered Bill's barracks, he was sitting on the edge of his bunk strumming a banjo. Bill was a wonderful tenor banjo player, one of the best in the country, and he entertained his comrades throughout the war. I just stood there and marveled. When he looked up and saw me, he let out a whoop. We had a great evening, and I stayed until about eleven before heading back.

Rendezvous with the 15th New York

While flying back along the road, I was flagged down by a black MP in the strangest looking uniform I had yet seen. It was half French Blue Devil and half American. The helmet, blouse, and overcoat were blue, but the pants and leggings appeared to be our issue. The MP just wanted to check my credentials and was with a platoon of men, similarly attired, who were bivouacked around several camp fires. At first, I thought they were Senegalese, but they turned out to be men of the 15th New York, which I had last seen at Camp Mills, so I stopped to chew the fat, and they greeted me like a long-lost brother. They recognized the Rainbow patch, and one of them recalled our assistance at Camp Mills. We yakked about Harlem, where as a boy I had played with my cousins, and then I headed on.[8] Had I only known it, one of my high school chums, Bob Hughes, was a sergeant serving with the 15th in the near vicinity. I only discovered this when Robert and I renewed our friendship after the war.

Kicked Out of Action by a Horse

Between Deneuvre and Reherrey was a charming village (I forget its name) alongside a beautiful little river. En route to Reherrey with a dispatch, I was approaching this village and noticed that a French artillery regiment had pulled into the area. I could see their caissons parked side by side in a field while the men watered their horses. One man would take a span of eight horses, lead them about a quarter of a mile down to the river bank to drink, then guide them back to the escadron where they were tethered. The horses had dripped water all over the road making it as slick as grease.

As I approached, a French artilleryman had just left the river leading a span of horses. The horses were taking up the whole damn road, so I whistled shrilly. (I could whistle through my teeth loud enough to be heard half a mile away.) The artilleryman turned, saw me coming, and yanked on the horses in an attempt to open a space for me. It seemed that he had accomplished about a three foot gap, so I accelerated and started through this narrow opening. That spooked the horse nearest me, which reared, and just as I went by, came down and caught me between the shoulder blades with his left forefoot. Totally unprepared for the blow, I went down, pinned by the motorcycle, and slid about fifty feet along that wet road. Had the road been dry, I might have been killed.[9]

I had lacerations on my right calf, thigh, and elbow; but more serious was the blow between my shoulder blades, and a horseshoe nail had penetrated my back about a quarter of an inch.

As I lay there stunned, French soldiers came running from all directions to help, and a very kind elderly gentleman from a neighboring house insisted that I have a glass of cognac, when available, the primary first-aid treatment in France. For quite a while, I sat on the road just trying to catch my breath. Well, I don't think I'd have made it back to HQ without that cognac. It brought me around, and I was able to get on my feet.

There was nothing wrong with the motorcycle, other than a bent handlebar and footrest, as usual. The French artillerymen washed off my machine and tried to help as much as they could. They offered to take me to their medical detachment, but I refused because I had important dispatches to deliver—which was why I was too hasty in trying to pass those horses in the first place. So I finally cranked up and made it back to Reherrey.

After reporting to Sergeant Major Steinert, I almost passed out, and he told me I was white as a ghost. He knew something was wrong and asked me what had happened. After telling him, he said, "You go back to your billet and lay down, and I'll send the medic up there."

I was barely able to get up the ladder to the hayloft. Shortly later, along came Major Lawrence, our chief medical officer, with two medics. He examined my back carefully, while medics dressed the cuts on my legs and arms.

What worried Major Lawrence was my back. It was completely discolored, and there was a risk of tetanus from the nail penetration. He said he was going to send me to the hospital, but I pleaded with him not to. I knew I'd be all right, if I could just rest a few days. Reluctantly, he agreed to wait four days. If I hadn't improved by then, I'd have to go to the hospital.

Joyce Kilmer

While this was going on, all my buddies were standing around watching, including George Kramer, our mail sergeant, and Joyce Kilmer, at that time a sergeant in the intelligence section.

Joyce Kilmer and George Kramer shared a room adjoining my loft, which evidently had been the sleeping quarters for a groom. It was a neat little room with two beds and a writing table. Joyce Kilmer suggested to Major Lawrence that I use his bed, which would be more comfortable than my straw tick. Lawrence agreed, and the boys helped me to Kilmer's bed.

God! Never before had I experienced such nursing. I had no appetite and was in quite a bit of pain, but George and Joyce would get fresh eggs and milk and make me eggnog laced with cognac, and that helped a lot.

Unable to sleep because of the pain, I'd lay there at night and watch Joyce write by candlelight at his little table. He would compose poetry in his every spare moment.[10] It was fascinating to watch the man. Abruptly he'd scrunch up the paper he was writing on, throw it away, marshall his thoughts, and start again.

Major Lawrence made a daily examination. At the end of the fourth day, I pretended to feel a lot better, so he put me on light duty but ordered me not to ride the motorcycle for several days. After ten days had lapsed, I was still in considerable pain and stiff as a poker; but, damn it, I mounted the motorcycle and could ride it, so I went back on active duty.

Long after the war, X rays revealed that I had suffered a fractured vertebra.

In high school, while editor of the school newspaper, I had started to write a short story about a peasant girl in a French village enveloped by the war. Imagine my trying to write that, never having been there. All I knew about the war was what I read in the newspapers, and my knowledge of France was limited to stories that a cousin, Lou Lambert, who had been born there, used to tell me about French peasant life. Surprisingly, after arriving overseas, I discovered that many of my imaginings were true. It was a corny story, but I brought it with me, intending to finish it "en local."

One evening, shortly before the horse incident, I saw Joyce Kilmer sitting on a bench outside his billet, smoking a pipe. I stopped and chatted and told him that my ambition was to become a writer.

"Fine, wonderful," he said, "keep at it."

"Would you mind looking at a story I'm writing?"

"Why, of course, I'd be delighted; bring it over."

I went up to my billet and returned with the little manuscript. He read it, and although he must have been amused by its naivete, he never cracked a smile.

"Albert, is this your first effort?" "Yes, sir."

"Keep at it," he said. "Keep at it, and furthermore, keep a diary; by all means, keep a diary."

So, I started to keep a diary in a little notebook, and I maintained that diary through most of the war. I carried it in a musette bag over my shoulder, along with toilette articles, a prayer book, letters from home, and the manuscript of that story.

Kilmer and a few of the other men would occasionally get together to discuss religion and philosophy, and Tom FitzSimmons would tip me off so I could listen. The regulars at these sessions, in addition to Kilmer, were Tom and my dear friend John Mahon, a professed atheist.

Now Kilmer was an academician on religion. He was a convert to Catholicism and knew a great deal about the history of the Church and Catholic principles. Mahon and FitzSimmons were also very well informed, and it was a caution to listen to their arguments. No one ever got angry. It was always highly intellectual and most interesting.

Collision with a Railroad Crossing Guard

One evening, there was a lot of excitement at regimental HQ, because we received intelligence reports that the Germans planned to conduct a raid on our trenches the next morning. After reviewing the reports, Colonel McCoy ordered that the 1st Battalion, which was in reserve at the time, get underway at 9:00 p.m. to beef up the lines.

By 7:40 p.m., Sergeant Major Steinert had cut the orders, but they had to be signed and date-stamped by the regimental adjutant, and Captain McKenna wasn't around. Well, I knew where his girlfriend lived and went to her house; and sure enough, Captain McKenna was there. As soon as I reported the emergency, he rushed to HQ. By that time, however, the orders had been delayed about half an hour. Major Donovan was supposed to start moving his 1st Battalion at 9:00 p.m., it was about 8:15 p.m. when McKenna handed me the orders, and 1st Battalion HQ was four miles away in Baccarat.

As I started off, McKenna said: "Red, drive like hell, damn it; get there as fast as you can!" That I did, but I had completely forgotten that, en route, there was a railroad crossing with swinging wooden planks, operated by a woman who lived in a small house beside the crossing. (It was common practice in France to leave the crossing guards down, and lift them only when somebody happened to come along, and the French were very leisurely about it.)[11]

When that damn gate loomed in front of me in the dark, I tried to stand and let the bike escape, but was too late. The plank caught me squarely in the stomach, and I lay in the road semiconscious, while the motorcycle powered under the gate and down the road a hundred feet before turning over with its motor still purring.

As I came to, this lady gate-tender was trying to revive me with a glass of cognac. Well, after a few swallows, I finally got my breath. Oh, my ribs hurt! It's a miracle they weren't broken. That accident must have delayed me another ten to fifteen minutes.

When I got to 1st Battalion HQ, it was about 8:35. I had to find Lieutenant Ames, the battalion adjutant, and neither he nor Major Donovan was at HQ, so it was off to find Ames and rattle him out of his sack. By the time Ames frantically arrived at Major Donovan's billet, it was 9:00, and the troops should have been on the move.

As soon as Donovan entered his HQ, he carefully examined the orders; then turned to me and said, "Ettinger, why was there such a delay in getting these orders to me?"

Estimating time discrepancies as quickly as possible, I replied, "I don't know, sir. I had an accident on the way to battalion HQ. I hit a railroad gate, and it knocked me unconscious for a while. It may have been a half hour before I could get my breath and get back on my motorcycle."

Donovan pierced me through and through with his steely blue eyes. "Ettinger, I believe you when you say you had an accident, but I don't think it wholly accounts for this delay. What time were these orders given to you? It says here eight o'clock. When did you actually receive them?"

"I really don't know, sir; I really don't know."

Boy! He looked right through me and said in words I'll never forget:

"Ettinger, let me tell you something. I know you're trying to protect Captain McKenna, but those for whom you lie to protect would never lie to protect you. Now, remember that. I'm not blaming you, but remember that. You are dismissed."

Encounter with a German Patrol

One night, I was given dispatches to carry to a French regiment on our right flank. It was the first time I had visited this regiment, and the route was a new one, but since the moon was out, it wasn't too bad.

I had to pass through a rugged wooded area to get to French HQ in this village. Coming around a bend, I saw in the moonlight some figures ahead of me on the road. Taken by surprise, they scattered. They were Germans! A German patrol had sneaked around behind the French lines.

My God! It was too late to stop and turn around. Nothing to do, I gave my bike the gun, everything it had, and the flames from its exhaust shot out two feet behind. After I flew by, at least one of them took a shot at me, but missed, and I kept going like a bat out of hell.

French regimental HQ was only a few miles away, and I immediately reported the incident upon arriving. Boy, there was some excitement, and the French quickly dispatched several squads to find this enemy patrol. They found them and killed or captured eight men.

The French colonel in command was very pleased that I

had "discovered" this patrol, and he received me with unbelievable courtesy. He insisted that I stay overnight, saying that his report wouldn't be ready until the next day anyway. They treated me to a great meal and a comfortable bed in a small adjacent house, and the next morning I had breakfast at their officers' mess.

I don't know, the French seemed much better educated than Americans, because every one of those officers spoke English. Hardly any of our officers spoke French.

Their regimental adjutant was a captain. That morning he took me to breakfast. As we passed down a village street on our way to the officers' mess, French soldiers on either side of the street were sitting around, chatting, cleaning their weapons, and this captain would salute and say, "Bonjour, mon camarade," and each would reply, "Bonjour, mon capitaine." There was such a wonderful feeling. We never had that in the American Army. No officer would salute us first and say "Good morning, my comrade."[12]

That camaraderie in the French Army greatly impressed me. Of course, they had already gone through four years of the damn war, and many of their officers had been promoted from the ranks by that time. Most of their original officers had been killed. I guess when you have gone through the kind of slaughter they had experienced, comradeship is about the only thing that can keep you going.

Later that morning, they gave me dispatches to return to our HQ, and their colonel included a nice letter praising my conduct, and this pleased Colonel McCoy.

Hennessy Shoots His Sidecar

Joe Hennessy was something else. What a character! Word got around about my run-in with the German patrol and the fighter plane, so Hennessy apparently decided that it was time for him to establish a positive reputation.

Shortly after my German patrol episode, Hennessy had to carry a dispatch to a French regiment. On the return trip, he ran his bike into a field and, in broad daylight, unlimbered his .45 and emptied it into the sidecar. A dispatcher from the Ohio Regiment was passing by and saw him. Thinking that Hennessy might have a mental problem, the Ohio guy dropped by and told us about the incident before Hennessy returned. Crazy Hennessy shooting his sidecar!

When Hennessy got back, he had a great story about running into a German patrol. For a while, we led him on with all kinds of questions, and he had a beautifully detailed response to every one of them. Then we razzed him and razzed him, and Steinert gave him holy hell. If there hadn't been such a desperate need for dispatch riders, he'd have lost his job then and there. Hennessy just shucked it off as a mere difference of opinion.

Lieutenant Guignon and the Manure Pile

Lieutenant Emile Guignon of our company (later the captain of Company K) was a hell of a good fellow. Considerate, good-natured, handsome, his uniform always meticulous; he was also quite a lady's man. One day he asked a favor:

"Red, I got a pass to go to Tours, and I wonder if you would take me to the railroad station?"—which was several miles away.

"Lieutenant," I replied, "if you want to ride on the back of my solo machine, I'd be glad to take you."

"The hell with that," he said, "but there is five francs for you if you can borrow a sidecar."

So I went over to Joe Hennessy, who drove a sidecar. "Joe, would you lend me your motorcycle for a couple of hours?"

Ever the operator, Joe inquired, "What's in it for me, and what d'you want it for?"

I told him.

Generous Joe: "Well, you can have it for five francs."

Since five francs was all I was getting for the job, I went back to Lieutenant Guignon and told him. He said, "OK, I'll make it ten francs, and you can give Hennessy five."

So Hennessy let me have his motorcycle and sidecar. Lieutenant Guignon got into the sidecar, and we started off down the steep hill leading from Deneuvre. At the bottom of the hill, about a quarter of a mile away, the road dead ended into a main highway, where you had to turn right or left. Going down the hill, Guignon protested:

"For Christ's sake, don't go so fast."

"It's all right, don't worry," I assured him.

As we neared the bottom of the hill, I tried to brake. . . . That damn Hennessy had been working on his brakes and had neglected to connect the rods!

Holy smoke! We were doing about 30 mph and picking up speed, and I knew I couldn't possibly make the turn, either to the right or left. Directly ahead of us at the bottom of the hill was a big manure pile in front of a house. Nothing to do, I headed for the manure pile.

Jesus! I went over the handlebars, did a beautiful somersault, landed right on top of the manure pile, rolled down the other side, and wasn't hurt a bit. It was nice and soft. But Lieutenant Guignon went head first into the manure pile with his spic-and-span uniform. When he crawled out, he was covered with manure from head to foot. Guignon swore a blue streak; then he started to laugh. It was such a ridiculous situation. Oh! how we laughed.

Anyway, nothing had happened to the motorcycle, which had taken a slightly lower trajectory than Lieutenant Guignon. After cleaning out the manure, he got into the sidecar, and I drove back to his billet so he could change his uniform. Then I gave Hennessy holy hell. Fortunately, I hadn't given him the five francs, and he never got it. I found a cushion, lashed it to a board, and secured both to the rear mud guard of my machine. After Lieutenant Guignon washed and changed his uniform, he mounted behind me, and I took him safely to the depot.

Inglorious Departure

Lieutenant Guignon had been shacking up with the best-looking woman I had seen since our arrival in France. When we left Deneuvre for the Champagne sector, we had to go several miles to a railhead to board a troop train. Guignon had not told his woman we were leaving, but she found out. While we were loading our equipment on the train (we had to secure our motorcycles on a flatcar), Lieutenant Guignon stopped by for a chat. Then, behind him, I could see his woman, dressed like a million dollars, driving up to the railhead in a farmer's two-wheeled cart. I told Guignon that she was coming. Jesus! He got down on his hands and knees, crawled underneath the train, and rolled into a ditch on the other side. The woman rushed up to Father Duffy, who was standing nearby, and asked if he knew where her lieutenant was, the Lieutenant Guignon, who had promised to marry her. There was Guignon hiding in the ditch on the other side of the train, and I was afraid the train might pull out any second. Anyway, Father Duffy calmed down the rejected beauty; then he walked over to me and said:

"Albert, I saw you talking to Lieutenant Guignon a short while ago; do you know where he is?"

"No, Father."

Father Duffy fixed me with a visage ever so stern:

"I think you're lying to me, Albert. If I catch that scoundrel, I'll marry him to this woman right on the spot!"

I then finished securing my motorcycle to the flatbed and was distracted by Tony Catrona, but I later was told that Lieutenant Guignon hid in the ditch until the train started to pull out, and then he jumped aboard.

Oh, that was a problem! I liked Lieutenant Guignon a lot, but I worshipped Father Duffy, and how could I confess that lie?

RECONNAISSANCE NO. 6

Shifting the locus of its spring offensive from Flanders in the East toward the Marne River in the South, the German Army launched a furious attack on May 27, 1918 that carried it to Chateau-Thierry, only 50 miles from Paris. There they were blocked, due largely to the valor of the American 2nd and 3rd Divisions, while the 1st Division counterattacked on May 28, taking and holding Cantigny.

The German high command used the last half of June and the first two weeks of July to consolidate its gains and prepare for another southerly blow on both sides of Reims, intending to sever the French and British armies.

Again, Pershing had no choice but to commit additional American forces to the defense. Although he now had over 500,000 combat troops in France, only the 26th and 42nd Divisions were sufficiently experienced to add to his premier troops then in combat.

—ABMC, *op. cit.*, pp. 29–33.

"The 42nd, having proved its value in the Baccarat Sector, was promptly asked for by the French and placed in reserve of Gouraud's Fourth French Army near Chalons-sur-Marne. This was on June 28th and 29th. . . . On the night of July 2nd-3rd, [the Rainbow] moved . . . to the vicinity of Suippes.

"Now . . . they were to face an assault by enemy troops already since early spring twice victorious on a large scale who were certain of a third and even greater victory. This assault had an accompanying artillery and aviation support which in less than twenty-four hours, would rain down . . . more high explosive projectiles, more bombs and more gas than the total which the Division had received during its previous five months service.

"The problem was complicated for the Rainbow because, instead of being able to meet [the attack] bound together as a single division, they were distributed over [a ten-mile] front of two French divisions.

130

"[According to General MacArthur] 'The reason for alternating our units with French units was to allow as many French troops as possible to see American troops in the front position and thus to [counter] . . . German propaganda that the American reinforcement was a myth or greatly exaggerated. . . . The Second Position which . . . would become the line on which they would have to be stopped, was entirely under our command. . . .'

"Since the entry into the line on July 4th, confidence in the French had been increased by the leadership constantly shown . . . by General Gouraud.

"The mere sight of this bearded General, with his alert eyes, his gold braided kepi, worn jauntily on one side of his head, his empty right sleeve, and his lameness [both incurred through war wounds] inspired liking and confidence. . . . The men and officers were one hundred percent for him and proud to serve in his Army.

"Primarily on the 15th, the day of the main attack, but also including the lesser fighting on the 16th, the Division was to lose 1,567 killed and wounded. . . ."

—Henry J. Reilly, *Americans All—The Rainbow at War,* pp. 244–248.

6

Champagne Sector

★ ★ ★

For the great Gaels of Ireland
Are the men that God made mad
For all their wars are merry
And all their songs are sad.

—Chesterton, "Ballad of the White Horse."

Cognac in the Caboose to Champagne

After my disturbing role in "l'affaire Guignon," I completed securing my motorcycle on a flatcar of the train that was to take the regiment from the Baccarat sector to its unknown (to us) destination in the West. As I started to look for the boxcar assigned to the dispatch riders, Tony Catrona, an old buddy from the pioneer platoon, hailed me and, with an air of profound conspiracy, declared: "Red, I just found a great way to travel." "What's that?" I asked. "Come with me," said Tony, and he led me to the rear of the train.

Here was a tail-end caboose unlike any I had ever seen. It was attached to a boxcar by steel girders, and it extended above the roof of the car, a ladder providing access from the outside.

Tony hastened me on as though fearful that someone might reach our destination before us. "Come on, come on; I want to show you." I climbed the ladder and, boy! Inside was a neat little room with a bench, a potbelly stove, and a floor covered with nice fresh straw. Triumphantly, Tony said, "Isn't this better than riding in one of those damn cattle cars?"

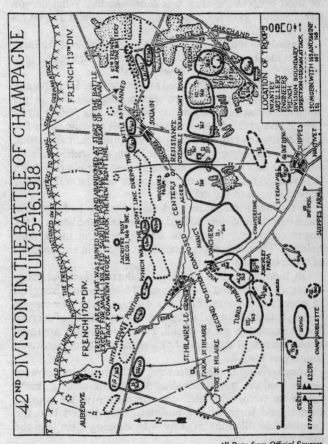

All Data from Official Sources.

Tony was an Italian boy from Brooklyn, and he could speak pretty good French. "I was talking to one of the trainmen," he explained, "and he told me that it wouldn't be used because the crew was short-handed. What do you say?" What was to say, other than to compliment him on his ingenuity?

I called to Fred Young, who was passing by, and the three of us made the journey, about two days and nights, riding in style in this caboose. Oh, it was great!

The first day out, we stopped at some village for water and wood for the engine. There was a long platform at the station, and at one end of the platform was freight to be shipped out, including several hogsheads of wine and a few smaller twenty-gallon barrels. As we pulled into the depot, these barrels were right in line with our caboose, so I suggested that we requisition some wine. We jumped down the ladder, grabbed one of the smaller barrels, and quickly horsed it up into the caboose.

In the meantime, other guys along the line had also seen these barrels, and they flocked out, broke in the heads of the larger casks and started to drink the wine using their helmets. Then the officers stalked off the train and shouted at them to desist.

Oh, there was hell to pay. Some of the men were put under arrest; and here, Fred and Tony and I had this little barrel all to ourselves. We thought it was wine, but when we tapped into it, it turned out to be cognac! Twenty gallons of cognac! We proceeded to get so drunk, I don't remember anything about the rest of the trip. That was the most unmemorable journey of my life.

After arriving at our destination in the middle of nowhere —none of the men, including the junior officers, knew where we were—we filled our canteens with the cognac, then tipped some of our buddies. They rushed into the caboose and filled their canteens by dipping them into the open barrel.

I don't know how I got my motorcycle off the train, but somehow we made it about six miles to an encampment at Breuvery. This, we discovered, was nine miles south of the city of Chalons-sur-Marne. [The date was June 24, 1918.]

Hennessy and the Stone Wall

The roads in the Champagne sector were made of chalk, because the country thereabouts is one great chalk plateau; mining and processing the stuff was the biggest industry in the province.

The second night after our arrival was so beautiful I went for a pleasure-ride on my motorcycle. The chalk road actually gleamed in the moonlight and extended to the horizon like a silver arrow. I knew from a map that the road came to an abrupt end, and you had to turn either right or left, but what I didn't know was that at the end of the road was a wall made of chalkstone, white chalkstone that was virtually invisible against the white road.

From a distance, the road appeared to extend straight ahead, but the first thing I knew this wall loomed directly in front of me. I missed the turn, but luckily was able to stand up and let the machine go the last couple of feet before it crashed into the wall, then had to scramble out of the way as it bounced back, the front wheel busted all to hell; and the nearest repair depot was about ten miles away. While not injured, the thought of having to push that monster ten miles with a dead front wheel was depressing, to say the least. Then I was startled by hearing laughter![1]

Over in the field, only a dozen yards away, was Hennessy working on his motorcycle. He had hit that same wall only a few minutes before! The son of a gun had seen me coming and hadn't warned me. Oh, I was furious! I called him everything in the book, but it was just like water off a duck's back with Hennessy. He thought it was a good joke.

Well, I started pushing my machine back down the road, and soon a French camion came along. Fortunately, the driver stopped and took me back to the repair yard, where I was able to replace the wheel. Hennessy didn't get back until the next morning. Served him right!

Assisting MacArthur in the Champagne

Following my first meeting with General MacArthur at division HQ in Luneville, I saw him many times in the course of dispatch delivery. He always remembered me by

135

name, and of course, that was the biggest thrill a kid could have; I just worshipped the man. I was also very fond of Major Walter Powers, the division adjutant, who had been my company commander. He was a great soldier and a splendid person. Then I had other friends at division, who had been transferred from our regimental HQ. Dan Hennessy, former chief clerk for the New York City Board of Education and an admirer of my father, was now there as a sergeant major, so I always looked Dan up and chewed the fat whenever I had the time.

During the Battle of Chateau-Thierry, at the Ourcq River, MacArthur was promoted to brigadier general and placed in command of the 84th Brigade of the Rainbow. The division had two infantry brigades, the 83rd and the 84th, each consisting of two regiments plus a machine gun battalion. My regiment was in the 83rd Brigade, so later I didn't see as much of MacArthur as I would have had he commanded the 83rd Brigade.

We were at Breuvery, just south of Chalons-sur-Marne, only a few days and were just beginning to relax when orders arrived to force-march by night to Camp de Chalons, which was about 25 miles north of Chalons. [Actually, 15 miles.] That required two nights of slogging for the line companies, but I was lucky, spending most of my time scouting the roads en route on my motorcycle.

During the day, there was a lot of air activity, by far the most we had seen since arriving in France. The sky was filled with German and Allied planes. That's why our troop movements had to be made at night, to prevent detection.

The second night of the march [probably June 28] it rained like the dickens. I was ahead of the regiment because I knew our destination and wanted to arrive first in order to find a good billet. While zipping along, I came to a fork in the road and, checking my map, discovered that the road from the left fork was more direct than the other and that both roads converged several miles farther on. Taking the left fork, I hadn't traveled very far when I came upon a dramatic scene.[2]

A large truck convoy carrying ammunition was stalled at a place where the road went alongside a ravine. Because of the rain, the lead truck had skidded into this ravine, and the front wheels of the second truck were off the road, the chassis half suspended, teetering over the ravine.³

As I arrived, the driver of the third truck in line got out a chain, hitched it to the truck ahead, and put a strain on it so that the men inside could crawl over the back to safety. Then the problem was getting it back on the road. A single truck couldn't move it because the stranded one was supported by its chassis on the rocky edge of the embankment.

Well, there was a great hell of a hullabaloo. A captain in charge ordered other trucks to chain up, and there was a mad scramble that completely blocked the road. It then occurred to me that our regiment wouldn't be able to get by, so I decided to return to the fork and wait there to warn our boys about the problem.

On the way back, I saw a motorcycle sidecar, and on its seat was a beautiful sheep-lined, knee-length corduroy coat. Well, you know what they say: "All's fair in love and war," especially in war, where theft is often justified as a requisition. So I examined this coat and decided to requisition it. There were captain bars on the shoulders, which I took off, then put the coat on, returned to the fork in the road, and hunkered down in the rain to wait for the regiment. That coat was warm even when wet.⁴

Not long after, I could hear troops coming up the highway, and out of the mist and the rain, a column appeared with three officers in the lead, the one in the center obviously in command. By now it was raining cats and dogs, and this officer was huddled in a great coat, wearing a helmet. It was MacArthur marching at the head of the 84th Brigade—the first and only time I ever saw him wear a steel helmet. It gave him some protection from the rain!

I presented myself, and MacArthur greeted me with surprise. I then gave him the news:

"Sir, there is a blockage down the left fork of this road; truck transports are in trouble down there, and I'm afraid it'll be a long time before the road is cleared. You can take the right fork and arrive at the same destination; it's a few kilometers longer, but. . . ." I brought out my map and showed him with a flashlight.

MacArthur thanked me graciously and commended my having returned to the fork to pass on that information.

Then he ordered one of his officers to drop off some men to notify other troops about the road blockage.

That was the only time I saw a general marching in the rain, but I was later told by 84th Brigade dispatchers that they often delivered messages to MacArthur on the march. That was part of the man's appeal. Whenever possible, he led his men, even in combat.

Well, that was a great occasion, and then, thank God, I could get underway and try to find a warm billet.

Battle Strategy

The battle area for the Rainbow was just north of Suippes, about 30 km north of Chalons. Our regiment was eventually positioned around the villages of St. Hilaire-le-Grand and Jonchery. That entire Champagne front was occupied by the 4th French Army under the command of General Henri Gouraud, a one-armed hero of the French Colonial Army Corps, and, to some, the best strategist in the Allied Army. About 80 miles to the east was the Chateau-Thierry sector.

General Gouraud had reliable intelligence that the Germans were building up a huge army in the Champagne and planned a breakthrough to capture the railhead at Chalons. This would cut the railroad between Paris and Verdun and split Allied forces in the East from those in the West.

Based on that intelligence, General Foch gave Gouraud every bit of artillery and reinforcement he could spare, and Gouraud had the pick of several trained American divisions to assist him. He chose the Rainbow, and we were very proud of that fact. We knew how important it was because General Gouraud sent out a wonderful message to all the troops—including the American troops—explaining why we had to stop the enemy.[5]

We interpreted that message to mean that we were going to stand there and defend that area; we were going to stand or die. That's all there was to it. This was not an order from HQ; it was the determined opinion of the men in small talk. The 69th had never flinched from a battle and never would. We were tired of all that mustard gas shit, and now we could get our hands on those Goddamned Germans. Many of the boys just relished that prospect. Moreover, we would be fighting alongside Alpine Chasseurs, and we knew how good they were and that they wouldn't desert us. Those poor German bastards didn't know what fighting was all about. (That's what we said then.)

Gouraud had new trenches built several miles to the rear of the original frontline trenches, all the work done at night. The French and American artillery was hub to hub—I had never before seen such an enormous display of artillery— and everything was thoroughly camouflaged. The Germans never did discover our preparations.

The Indispensable Ambrose Steinert

Just before the battle of Champagne, orders came for our division to move up to the lines. Sergeant Major Steinert called me in and said that Captain McKenna, our regimental adjutant, had disappeared, and we needed his signature to put the orders through. Steinert thought that McKenna was probably relaxing in Chalons, and he asked me to take my motorcycle and try to find him. My God! how was I going to find anyone in a city the size of Chalons?

I decided the only way I could possibly find McKenna was to drive around until I came across a division staff car and then check around for the nearest party.

Because of the hour—the cafes were closed—I targeted the nearest residential area, going up one street and down another. Sure enough, I finally came across a division staff car, and it belonged to Major Walter Powers, the division adjutant. He and McKenna, and several other officers, were having a party with some ladies and, oh, you might say they had been drinking. They greeted me warmly and invited me to join them. I told Captain McKenna the importance of getting back to regimental HQ, and that sobered him quickly. The news also sobered the other officers; the party broke up immediately, and they rushed back to their respective headquarters and I to mine. As it happened, Sergeant Major Steinert had already signed McKenna's name to the orders for the troop movement because it was essential that they depart and arrive on time.

Ambrose Steinert had been chief clerk in the Controller's Office of New York before the war. He had a brilliant mind and was probably one of the finest regimental sergeant majors in the Army. Sergeant majors run the regiment; colonels come and go, but, thank God, the sergeant major remains to ensure that everything runs smoothly.

In addition to his effectiveness, Sergeant Major Steinert was a peach of a fellow. He was fair and considerate of everyone, an unsung hero, as fully important as the generals for whom they erect statues and name office buildings. I'd like to see a New York City office building dedicated to Ambrose Steinert.

The Battle

A few days before the battle, a French raiding party captured several German officers, and General Gouraud was able to predict the exact time the German artillery barrage would begin; so he had his own artillery commence firing a half-hour earlier, and that took the edge off the German artillery, terrible though it was. Then, just before the German shelling began, he evacuated the original front-line trenches, except for a few sentries who were to signal as the German infantry began to occupy those trenches. Then they had permission to run like hell.[6]

The Germans spent twenty-four hours pulverizing front-line trenches that were almost empty. Also, every identifiable target behind our lines was vacated, and our men took up the new positions that had been prepared. Those old positions were completely demolished by German shells.

Our regimental HQ was in a chalk mine, and our trenches were about two miles ahead in the new front lines, with French units on our left and right flanks.

On the morning of July 15, 1918, after this horrendous enemy barrage, their infantry advanced on the old first line of defense, only to find it deserted. They figured our men had fled or had been buried under the rubble. As soon as they reached it, we redoubled our own artillery fire and wreaked havoc on their ranks, but they kept coming, thinking they would find little infantry resistance.

When the enemy reached our new lines, we let loose with machine guns and mortars, and it was a slaughter. They rarely got into our trenches, and when they did, they never left. But the Germans kept coming. They regrouped and attacked repeatedly during the next 48 hours until, finally, their back was broken. Then the French brought up their Senegalese and Moroccan troops to counterattack, and the enemy retreated. That was the last German offensive of the war.

Our men rejoiced at the victory, but the courage of the enemy was so impressive, we knew it would be no picnic down the road.

The preparations I saw, and the comments I heard, but I learned about the battle later in the "Hopital Militaire" in Chalons.[7]

Blown off the Motorcycle

Our division had arrived on the Champagne front about the first of July, and until the day before the battle, we were busy night and day carrying messages between brigade, division, and regimental headquarters.

On July 12, I had dispatches to carry to Brigade HQ, and since they didn't give me any to bring back, I had a little free time. I knew that brother Bill's ambulance unit was attached to the French 4th Army, and one of the dispatchers at brigade told me that he had just seen one of their ambulances on the road. I decided to drive over toward Fourth Army HQ, where Bill's outfit might be located, on the off-chance I might be able to find him.

German artillery had been incessantly pounding highways leading to the front, concentrating on the crossroads. The French had camouflaged many of these intersections, and as I approached one, I could see the legs of artillery horses coming up under the camouflage netting. Believing that we might converge at the juncture, I slowed down. No sooner did this French artillery piece arrive at that crossroads than a German shell exploded right on top of it.

I was perhaps two hundred feet away at the time, and the concussion threw me off my motorcycle, which was smashed to hell. Somehow, my left knee was split open, and for a while I couldn't stand. Two artillerymen sitting at the front of the caisson were killed instantly. Miraculously, the two blown off the rear escaped injury, and they came over to try to help me. Some of the horses were dead, and others were kicking around, screaming.

French medics arrived, and after dressing my knee, they offered to take me to a hospital, but I refused, saying that I had dispatches to deliver to our HQ, which I hadn't (and, technically, I was AWOL). Just then, an ammunition truck came along on its way to our regiment. I flagged it down, checked in at HQ, and went to my bunk.

Word went around that Ettinger was hurt. Soon, Billy James came along, saw what had happened, gave me hell for not getting medical attention, and called the medics. Then Sergeant Major Steinert ordered me to the hospital. That was it. I had to go. They put me in a French ambulance that sped away to Chalons.

Hospitalization with John McMorrow

The hospital reception center at Chalons was so crowded the stretcher bearers had to leave me on the sidewalk outside the entrance. A few hours later, it began to rain, and I felt like hell. Just as I began to despair of assistance, who should walk by but John J. McMorrow, my former captor, dedicated assassin, and guardian of the still. John, not surprisingly, had been drinking, as had his companion, a crazy French civilian.

"Begora, Red, don't ye know enough ter git out av th' rain?" was his greeting remark.

Indicating my bandaged knee, I explained that I was waiting to be assigned to a hospital.

"Well, ye'll be dead befare dat hapins. Come along wit me an me frien 'til th' rain lets op. He's got an apartmint a block away, an we can sip a bit ter ease yir pain."

So I put my arm over the shoulder of each of the two characters and, hobbling between them, managed to attain our objective—then had to climb two flights of stairs to get to the apartment! Four hours later, I was feeling little pain. It was then that McMorrow confided a little secret: "You know, Red, Oi got ter go ter th' hospitil meself an take care av a little infection."

How we made it down those two flights of stairs and back to the reception center, I'll never know.

The doctor in charge of reception was furious with both of us, because after all that exercise, my bandage was blood-soaked. He assigned us to the Hopital Militaire in Chalons, and two days later, a French surgeon operated on my knee and did a beautiful job. Later I was told that he had a reputation as one of the finest surgeons in France.

That was the night of July 14-15. The Battle of Champagne began just before the doctor started surgery, and during the operation, two German shells fell in the hospital courtyard. Miraculously, they didn't hurt anyone, but they shattered a lot of windows and gave us quite a scare.

After the operation, I was assigned to the American Ward, sponsored by the American Red Cross. The ward was staffed by two lovely and delightful American Red Cross nurses, and it was half full with about twenty doughboys at the time, including McMorrow.

That night we lay on our hospital cots listening to the terrific bombardment from the front, about twenty miles away. The cannonading was awesome. Oh, God! it was fierce. We were all extremely grateful we weren't there.

About two o'clock in the morning, we heard voices outside the dimly lit ward, and in came two fellows carrying a wounded French soldier on a stretcher whom they placed on a cot directly across the aisle from me. The stretcher bearers were speaking English, and one of the voices sounded familiar. Suddenly, I realized it was my brother Bill! As he straightened up, I said, "Bill, is that you?" and he turned around. "Oh, my God," he exclaimed, "what happened to you?"

I had my wounded leg underneath the sheet—it was very warm that night—and my good leg was on top of the sheet. Bill gave one look and thought I had lost a leg. He rushed over frantically, but I assured him that it was nothing serious, and he finally calmed down. Bill told us that the fighting at the front was incredibly fierce.

About daylight, Bill returned with another wounded soldier, and this time he brought a bottle of cognac. I passed the bottle around to the nearest patients, including John and a big black Senegalese trooper who was in the bed next to me. Boy, it didn't take long for us to react to that cognac in the condition we were in, and pretty soon we were joking and laughing uproariously, more in relief of being out of danger than anything else.

After a while, the French head nurse came in. She was a Catholic sister—all the nurses, other than the Americans, were nuns. She scolded us for making so much noise, and she quickly realized that we had been drinking and demanded to know where the liquor was. By that time, the evidence had been consumed, and one of the guys had hidden the bottle. Anyway, brother Bill came back twice again before the battle was over, and each time we managed to have a little chat.

Trophy Ears

About the third day, a pervasive odor emanated from the adjacent bed occupied by the Senegalese soldier. Another fellow noticed it too. Concerned that it might be gangrene, we called it to the attention of Miss Adams, one of our American nurses, and she returned with the Mother Superior, who was the head nurse. The Mother Superior took one sniff and pulled the pillow from under this guy's head . . . and there were eight human ears on a string! They had been separated from German soldiers who had fallen victim to our companion's ferocity.[8] That was the source of the stench.

Oh, the Mother Superior gave him a tongue lashing and confiscated his extra ears. The Senegalese protested volubly and started to cry. Those ears were more than souvenirs; they were his certificates of courage. Some soldiers wear medals as certificates of courage; others find greater satisfaction in the display of scalps or dried ears, which, you must confess, is more compelling evidence of the deed accomplished.

Despite all the suffering that was experienced in that ward, as soldiers do, we found sardonic humor in everything. Anything could trigger it, and again, I think it was mainly relief at being out of danger.

John McMorrow wouldn't tell us the full nature of his

problem; "a little infection" was the extent of his otherwise generous communication.

Every morning, a parade of doctors and nurses made an inspection tour of the ward, and this morning, about the third day we were there, they descended upon McMorrow's bed, and Miss Adams asked to see his wound. McMorrow, terribly embarrassed, refused, whereupon the Mother Superior reached down and ripped the sheet off the bed . . . and here was a bandage around John's penis! He had been circumcised because of the "little infection!" He was so embarrassed. Of course, the guys, some of them so sick they could hardly talk, laughed hilariously.

Two weeks later, I was discharged and rejoined my regiment, which by then had moved on to the Chateau-Thierry front.

Jimmy Wadsworth

Our regiment had about ten horse orderlies who carried messages back and forth in the rear areas, usually short distances between companies, and so forth. One of these horse orderlies was a kid named Jimmy Wadsworth, whose uncle was the United States Senator, James Wadsworth.

Jimmy was an excellent horseman, but his chief ambition was to become a motorcycle dispatch rider. He said that he had had some experience on a motorcycle in civilian life, and he would pester me constantly about recommending him for any opening in our dispatch unit; so I told Sergeant Major Steinert that Wadsworth had motorcycle experience, and should an opening develop, I thought he'd make an excellent dispatcher. Jimmy had his chance, because he took my place as a dispatch rider.

Before the Champagne Defensive started on the night of the 14th, our regiment had five motorcycle dispatch riders, and soon after it began, two of them were wounded, and Hennessy was badly gassed. That left only Billy James and Jimmy Wadsworth to carry dispatches, and they were working around the clock.

The second day of the battle, the two men arrived at regimental HQ simultaneously. They parked their motorcycles under some trees across the road from HQ dugout in the chalk mine, then heard German shells coming over. Billy yelled at Jimmy to dive into a nearby ditch, but Wadsworth panicked and started to run across the road. Billy James dashed out, tackled him, and knocked him down, but it was too late. A shell landed alongside them and blew off half of Jimmy's head, and Billy got four pieces of shrapnel in one shoulder and several pieces through his left knee. Nevertheless, he managed to carry Jimmy into the dugout. Although medics were there in an instant, Jimmy was dead.[9]

They rushed Billy back to the base hospital, and the chief surgeon wanted to amputate one of his arms and a leg. He said it was hopeless. Fortunately, a young medical officer on duty by the name of Carroll pleaded with the head surgeon not to amputate; he was certain he could save Billy's arm and leg. The chief surgeon acceded to Carroll's request, and Billy became his patient.

According to Billy, Carroll told him that he would suffer the agony of hell, but that he could save his limbs. And, indeed, Billy did go through torture, because every morning, Dr. Carroll would pump his arm and leg up and down, and the pus and blood would pour out. A fellow who had been in the same ward with Billy later told me it was terrible to hear my friend scream when he went through these motions. He said that after a few of these sessions, Billy would faint in dread of the agony as soon as Dr. Carroll came into the ward. But, by golly, he saved both of Billy's limbs.

And Then There Was the "Blighty"

Our regiment had gone on to the Chateau-Thierry front by the time I was able to walk, and for three days and nights I was transported there on a troop train containing wounded British soldiers returning to their outfits in Belgium. I was put into a compartment with a crazy Scott, a big oaf of a Yorkshireman, and a Cockney from London. The Cockney was constantly teasing the Yorkshireman because of his broad accent, while no one could understand the Cockney.

The Scott of the trio was a member of the Seaforth Highlanders, one Donald Ross Thurston, a lovable rascal of

19 who had already experienced three years of combat. Like Donald Adair, this Don's father was a Presbyterian minister, and Don had run away to enlist at the age of 16. He was some kind of guy with a great sense of humor. He had been wounded, machine gun bullets through both legs, and he told me he had been so anxious to get home for a while that he had deliberately waved his legs in the air, hoping to get a leg wound and a "blighty" home.[10] He got more than he hoped for and was mad as hell, because instead of getting a blighty home, he was being sent back to his regiment. So the crazy guy had tied copper coins to his wounds with a bandage hoping to get an infection, and hopefully, a blighty.

Don and I became good pals during the trip and exchanged addresses with promises to write to one another. Shortly after I had been discharged and was home, I received a letter from Don, which he had addressed to our regiment in France, and it was three months getting to me. It was from a hospital in Leeds, and in it he said:

"Red, I finally got my blighty. Two weeks after rejoining my regiment, I lost my right leg. A Hun shell got me, and here I am in a bloody hospital, and the damn war is over. It will be two months, they tell me, before I can go home."

I had a good cry over that letter. He was such a good kid and so full of fun. I wrote back immediately but never did get a reply.

RECONNAISSANCE NO. 7

After the German "Peace Offensive" collapsed east of Chateau-Thierry along the Marne River (courtesy of a green, but tactically astute and determined, 3rd Division), at Belleau Wood (where Marines of the 2nd Division set an exceedingly costly standard for a strategically useless objective), and in the Champagne, General Foch launched an attack to wipe out the Marne salient. Three French armies and eight American divisions were committed.

Ten days after their victory in the Champagne, troops of the Rainbow trucked through rubble strewn Chateau-Thierry on July 25 and relieved the 26th "Yankee" Division, which had suffered 5,000 casualties in getting to the Foret de Fere, south of the Ourcq River. As the battle progressed, our right flank was first supported by the 28th Pennsylvania Guard, and later by "Red Arrows" of the 32nd Division, whose German-speaking lads from Wisconsin and Michigan could confound the enemy with intelligible insults. Their left flank was protected by elements of a war-weary French Army.

The 69th had it relatively easy in approaching the Ourcq, but the Alabamians and Iowans had to take two fortified farms, without artillery support. This was the first offensive engagement of the Rainbow Division, and its bloodiness presaged the future.

The all-stone Croix Rouge Farm, which blocked the main road North, was defended by an estimated 350 veterans of the 4th Prussian Guard, with about 32 carefully registered machine guns within and around part of its perimeter. Two battalions of the Alabama regiment and one battalion of the Iowas (3,000 men) launched the attack at 5:15 p.m., and within two hours had secured the farm, but at a cost of 800 casualties, 225 of them fatal! Almost an entire battalion had been put out of action by a skillful rear guard, a fraction of their strength in number. The following morning, 283 German bodies were counted, all those in the Alabama sector with bayonet wounds. No prisoners had been taken.

148

This resulted in a formal German protest against the division and an investigation. While Alabama's Colonel Screws had pleaded in vain for artillery preparation prior to this assault, or a delay, if necessary, to provide it, division staff demurred in deference to American First Army Corps orders. Four days later, the 84th's brigadier, an utterly exhausted General Brown, was relieved and replaced by MacArthur.

As the division neared the river on July 27, it was subjected to heavy artillery fire from high ground beyond the Ourcq. Much of that fire was concentrated on the village of Villers-sur-Fere, which was regimental HQ for the 69th during the battle, and almost as many casualties were sustained in that village as on the battleground.

From Villers-sur-Fere, wheat fields sloped down to the Ourcq, exposing the ranks to artillery harassment. Then, across the stream, the ground rose 200 feet in a shallow, concave fashion to create the Ourcq Heights, the Germans' main defensive line. To even get there, the Rainbows had to overcome dozens of well prepared machine gun nests in patches of woods, the villages of Sergy and Seringes-et-Nesles, hill salients, and the Meurcy Farm. These obstacles covered every conceivable approach to the Heights and were mutually supportive, while the Heights, because of their concavity, afforded an enfilading defensive fire as the advance got closer.

On July 27, the division received an I Corps order to attack at night, using only bayonets, and with only ten minutes artillery preparation. New York's Colonel McCoy vociferously protested, at first to no avail. I Corps claimed it was responding to Sixth French Army pressure. Finally, the constraint against using fire was lifted.

The main assault began at dawn on July 28, when all regiments stormed across the Ourcq. On the right, the 168th Iowa captured Hill 212 and fought its way into Sergy; then was forced to withdraw from both. Repeated attacks were repulsed by the Germans. The men of New York and Ohio barely made it to the Ourcq Heights, only to be forced back down. On the following day, the 84th Brigade was reinforced by two battalions of the 4th Division, one of which waged a bitter struggle for possession of Sergy, without success, the other relieving a devastated Alabama regiment in a push for the Heights between the Meurcy Farm and Sergy. That same day, July 29, the 69th took Colas Woods, which supported Meurcy Farm on the West, while the Ohios drove the enemy out of pivotal Seringes-et-Nesles on the left flank. Then the New Yorkers took and lost Meurcy Farm. On July 30, at heavy cost, and after see-saw possession, the 69th finally captured that bloody farm, while Sergy was similarly occupied by a battered battalion of the 4th Division, and Hill 212 taken by the Iowas.

The Rainbow was checked on the 31st with the arrival of a new Bavarian division of veterans. Their counter attack on Sergy was beaten off by remnants of 4th Division men, with assistance from two companies of the Iowa regiment. After another day of intense fighting, the Germans began a retreat to the Vesles River, under cover of darkness. On August 2, the Rainbow raced forward four miles, taking the towns of Nesles and Mareuil-en-Dole. The action closed only five miles from the Vesles River. The next day, after nine days of continuous combat, the 42nd was officially relieved by the 4th Division.

The Rainbow's losses were incredible. The four infantry regiments as a whole had suffered 57% casualties—6,500 men. The Alabama regiment headed the list with 70% casualties!

—Sources: James, *The Years of MacArthur*, Vol. 1. (Boston: Houghton Mifflin Co., 1970), pp. 181–187; Reilly, *op. cit.*, pp. 305–331; Bach and Hall, *The Fourth Division* (published by the division, 1920), pp. 97–104; and American Battle Monuments Commission, 42d Division, *Summary of Operations in the World War*, 1944.

7

Chateau-Thierry
& St. Mihiel

★ ★ ★

*. . . Our own machine guns, the Wisconsin
lads manning them, had followed the advance,
the gunners fighting with desperate courage. The
ammunition was carried up by their men and
ours at a frightful cost. Five feet or so a man
might run with it and then go down. Without a
moment's hesitation, some other soldier would
grab it and run forward to go down in his turn.
But the guns had to be fed and still another would
take the same dreadful chance. . . . Finally the
guns were put out of action by German shell
fire . . . and there they stood uselessly, their gunners lying dead around them.*

— *Father Duffy's Story*, p. 192. Sunday, July 28, at
the Ourcq River.

After discharge from the hospital, I rejoined the regiment
above Chateau-Thierry, at Villers-sur-Fere on the River
Ourcq, where we had driven the Germans back about nine
miles, but I only got in the last two days of the drive.

Fighting around the Ourcq had been brutal, and all the
Rainbow had suffered terrible casualties—more than the
Germans, because they had carefully prepared defensive
positions and their artillery and machine guns had wreaked
havoc with our advance. Half of our 3rd Battalion, the

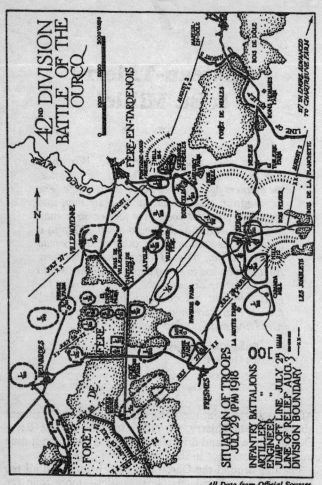

42ND DIVISION
BATTLE OF THE
OURCQ

FÈRE-EN-TARDENOIS

N

SITUATION OF TROOPS
JULY 29 (P.M.) 1918

INFANTRY BATTALIONS [□□
ARTILLERY   "
ENGINEER   "
JUMP-OFF LINE JULY 25 ▪▪▪▪▪
LINE OF RELIEF AUG. 3 ━━━━
DIVISION BOUNDARY   ─XX─

All Data from Official Sources.

Shamrock Battalion, had been put out of action. Some companies had been devastated, with just thirty men or so left out of the original two hundred and fifty.[1] Still, we had taken the measure of the cream of the German Army, elements of four divisions, including the famous Prussian Guard Division, and we had them in retreat.

When I got back, they didn't have a solo motorcycle to replace mine yet; my regimental adjutant, Bill McKenna, had been transferred; and I didn't care for the new regimental adjutant.[2] He was a pretentious officer who insisted that I ferry him here and there in a sidecar. I didn't know how long it would be before they got a solo machine for me, and I was sick and tired of being a nurse to this new adjutant.

Transfer to Intelligence

Finally, I went to Sergeant Major Steinert and told him I wanted out. He asked me where I wanted to go. "Intelligence," I replied. "Will they take you?" he asked—a reasonable question, since I had no particular qualifications for intelligence work—I had more luck than brains. But two of my buddies from the pioneer platoon, Fred Young and Don Adair, were now in the intelligence section, and I greatly admired its commanding officer, Captain Basil Elmer, whom I had already sounded out about the possibility of a transfer. Since he had been agreeable, Steinert made out the papers on the spot.

My first job was to escort German prisoners from the front back to regimental HQ for interrogation. It was a good starter because my leg still bothered me. Now I could exercise it without having to walk too fast, and I didn't have to carry a pack, only a rifle. Don Adair and I would just grab a detachment of prisoners and leisurely march them back to HQ. They were relieved to be out of the fighting, and I had seen enough dead bodies by that time to share in their relief. At the same time, I felt guilty about having been out of it. I had yet to experience active combat, and a number of men I deeply cared for were now dead.

Death of Jack Perry and Joyce Kilmer

Soon after reporting to HQ at Villers-sur-Fere, I tried to locate my old friend Jack Perry, who was a number one gunner with Tom FitzSimmons' Stokes mortar platoon.

I was too late.

During the first day of the battle, the mortars laid down a covering fire for the first wave of infantry crossing the Ourcq River. Then they proceeded to follow the infantry and were about to cross the river when ordered back. Jack was already in the water when he was hit in the stomach. Tom was at his side in an instant and got him back. Tom told me that, while putting him on a stretcher, Jack whispered, "Tom, I hope I didn't let the fellows down."

Stretcher bearers had just got Jack to the aid station located in the schoolhouse of Villers-sur-Fere, when a German shell demolished it. They managed to dig out all the men, and Jack was still alive, but he died before an ambulance could take him to the rear.

God, I loved that kid.

Another great loss at the Ourcq was Joyce Kilmer, beloved by everyone who knew him. The men were still talking about it when I got there. He was such a gentleman and a true patriot. He didn't have to go to war; he was too old for the draft; he was not the physical type; he was a scholar, a student, a writer; he had been an editor of the *New York Times Book Review* and had a brilliant career ahead of him; he was a kind and loving man in every respect.

When Joyce originally came to us, he had a bulletproof job as the regimental statistician, and he detested it because he wanted to share the risks of the doughboy. After persistent effort, he succeeded in getting a transfer to the intelligence section.

On the second day of the battle at the Ourcq River [July 29, 1918], Lieutenant Oliver Ames, Major Donovan's battalion adjutant, was killed at Donovan's side. Joyce begged to take his place, because Donovan was always in the eye of the storm, and the two men greatly admired each other. Donovan agreed, and the very next morning, Joyce, too, was killed by a sniper.

At the time this happened, Joyce was less than a hundred

yards from his dear friend, who was equally exposed. Fate chose between the gifted poet and the born leader. I've often wondered at the outcome if that sniper had sighted in on Donovan rather than Kilmer. At the Argonne, we regarded Donovan as indispensable. Can you imagine how he must have felt with two of his dearest friends killed within a day of each other?

For both Donovan and Kilmer, "The Peacemaker," written by Joyce in France, had an intensely personal meaning:[3]

> *Upon his will he binds a radiant chain.*
>   *For Freedom's sake he is no longer free.*
> *It is his task, the slave of Liberty,*
>   *With his own blood to wipe away a stain.*
>
> *That pain may cease, he yields his flesh to pain.*
>   *To banish war, he must a warrior be.*
> *He dwells in Night, eternal Dawn to see,*
>   *And gladly dies, abundant life to gain.*
>
> *What matters Death, if Freedom be not dead?*
>   *No flags are fair, if Freedom's flag be furled.*
> *Who fights for Freedom, goes with joyful tread*
>   *To meet the fires of Hell against him hurled,*
> *And has for captain Him whose thorn-wreathed head*
>   *Smiles from the Cross upon a conquered world.*

Tom Shannon Was Never a Coward

The motion picture "The Fighting 69th" involves an eight-ball portrayed by Jimmy Cagney, who runs from his position, is court-martialed and sentenced to death. The story then describes Father Duffy's attempt to intercede and have his sentence commuted. Before that is resolved, with the regiment under artillery fire at the Battle of the Argonne, Cagney breaks away and, singlehanded, blasts a lane through the barbed wire with a Stokes mortar to enable an infantry advance. (All the other mortar men, myself included among them at the time, are supposed to have been killed.) Well, the true story of such an event is more interesting.

155

Early that winter, at a cafe in Longeau, I met a likeable guy from one of our line companies by the name of Tom Shannon. Tom had transferred to our regiment from the 9th Massachusetts, a regiment as Irish as our 69th. As a matter of fact, during the Civil War, the two regiments were brigaded together under General Meagher and were known as Meagher's Irish Brigade.

Shannon wasn't very tall, but he was stocky and strong as an ox. He had bright red hair, blue eyes, a busted nose, and a cauliflower ear; one tough-looking hombre.

I'd gone into a cafe for a couple of beers—only had a quarter in my pocket. The place was crowded, but I noticed a table for two with only one man sitting there. He saw me at the same time and waved me over. "Sit down, Red, and have a drink with me." It was in the nature of a command, and he further insisted that I share a meal with him. We divided a dozen-egg omelet with french fried potatoes; then he ordered a bottle of cognac.

Before the night was over, we were both pretty much over the hill, but I remember Tom telling me stories about his boyhood in Ireland. At age seventeen, he came to the United States, settled in Boston and soon made a fairly good living as a brick mason. He also took up boxing, and he said he was a pretty fair club fighter, making anywhere from five to fifty dollars a fight.

We had a grand evening, and I liked the guy very much. Later on, from time to time, we'd bump into each other and shoot the breeze over a few drinks. Then I got some terrible news.

One bitter cold night, Tom had been on guard duty in front of a parish house in Baccarat, and the kindly priest offered Tom a glass of cognac. That was a serious mistake because Tom was crazy about liquor, and before long, he knocked on the door of the parish house asking for another drink. After obliging him with another glass, the priest refused to give him any more. Tom pushed the priest aside, found the liquor, and as he came out, saw the priest running down the street yelling for help. Drunk as he was, Tom took several shots at him but, thank God, missed.

Shannon was court-martialed for deserting his sentry post and attempted homicide and was sentenced to death by a

Albert M. Ettinger in his Doughboy uniform.

Major General William A. Mann, first commander of the 42nd Rainbow Division, and his Chief of Staff, Colonel Douglas MacArthur, at Camp Mills, Long Island, 1917.

Major William J. Donovan after the battle of the Ourcq River in which his 1st Battalion was decimated. Soon promoted to Lieutenant Colonel, Donovan had field command of the Regiment during the Meuse-Argonne offensive.

George Heilman and Red Ettinger at "Bunk Fatigue," Camp Mills. (*)

"Irish Jig" dancing, boxing, singing, and shooting craps were the preferred recreational activities of men of the 69th at Camp Mills, Long Island, New York, 1917. (*)

Doughboys packed into "40 and 8" boxcars that could transport 40 to 50 men or 8 to 10 horses.

Cook J. A. Miller, HQ Company, 69th Regiment, preparing a stew. Bulligny, September 7, 1918. According to Red Ettinger, "we were stewed to death."

Indian motorcycle, used by most Doughboy dispatch riders. Note lack of headlight.

"Our Chief of Staff has pushed himself into raids and forays in which, some older heads think, he had no business to be. . . . His admirers [approve]. Colonel McCoy and Major Donovan are strong on this point. Donovan says it would be a blamed good thing for the army if some General got himself shot in the front line. General Menoher and General Lenihan approve in secret of these madnesses; but all five of them are wild Celts, whose opinion no sane man like myself would uphold."—Father Duffy

Father Duffy shows the strain of four battles. Taken at Brieulles-sur-Bar in the Ardennes, November 4, 1918.

A French 75 in action with American gunners at St. Mihiel. The Rainbow's 149th Illinois Field Artillery used 75s to such effect that, according to Red Ettinger, "the Germans thought we had invented automatic cannons."

Men of the 1st Division dodge shells in Exermont, October 5, 1918. One week later they were relieved by the 69th.

Sergeant Joyce Kilmer, beautiful person and poet. (*)

Cpl. Harry McLaughlin of the 69th visits grave of his brother, Daniel McLaughlin, at American military cemetery, Suresnes, November 30, 1918.

**Victory March of the Fighting 69th up Fifth
Avenue, April 28, 1919. With Colonel Donovan in
the lead, the men marched from Washington Square
five miles up Fifth Avenue in cadence with "Garry
Owen" and "In the Good Old Summertime." New
York City was ecstatic. (*)**

firing squad! Both the parish priest and Father Duffy testified for Tom, pleading that he was not responsible because of the drink and offering in extenuation his excellent combat record. Well, Father Duffy saved his life, at least for several months. The court-martial board commuted Tom's death sentence, but on condition that he remain constantly in the front line until the end of the war.[4]

At the Battle of Champagne, Tom made quite a reputation. He was too short to fire from the trenches, so he jumped on top of a parapet and lay there exposed, shooting at the enemy as they advanced. The word got around, and everybody was rooting for him, hoping his luck would hold. The men tried to make his life as tolerable as possible at the front by smuggling cigarettes and liquor to him.

Then came Chateau-Thierry and the Ourcq River. The very first day of action, both Tom and his buddy were hit by a machine gun, so they dressed each others wounds with their first-aid equipment and continued fighting for three days. Then a medic noticed their tattered bandages and the purple discoloration around their wounds. He immediately had them evacuated, but they were in the hospital only a few days before both died of gangrene. Their surviving buddies were heartbroken, and I grieved it very much because I was very fond of Tom Shannon. He was something else.[5]

Bootz and Quirt at the Ourcq River

Not long after I had transferred out of the Pioneers to motorcycle dispatch, Lieutenant Quirt was assigned to Company C of Donovan's 1st Battalion. Company C was under the command of Herman Bootz, and Quirt was now responsible for a combat infantry platoon. This was hugely ironic because of Quirt's distrust of anyone with a German name, and Papa Bootz spoke with a marked German accent.

On the third or fourth day of the battle, Bootz led an attack on the Meurcy Farm, a German stronghold. During the assault, which failed, Bootz took machine gun bullets through both shoulders. The first one knocked him down, but he got up and continued to lead until the second bullet put him out of commission.

Quirt's platoon lost over a dozen men, half of them killed

by machine gun fire while trying to rescue their buddies.[6] Where was Quirt? According to one of the guys who was there, Quirt was totally useless, so far behind, the men didn't pay any attention to him. Soon afterward, he was transferred back to HQ Company as a liaison officer.

Well, I'll never forget the names of the Ourcq River and Meurcy Farm, because our boys, having a problem with the French pronunciation, always referred to them as the "O'Rourke" River and "Murphy's" Farm.

The Ourcq River was really nothing but a stream, maybe twenty feet wide and a foot deep, and Father Duffy told of having come across Jack Finnegan, who had been wounded and was lying by the bank of the stream. Father offered him a drink from his canteen. Now Jack always had a great thirst, but it wasn't for water, so he immediately asked, "An' what d' ye have in der, Fader?" "Why, it's water, my boy," the good Father replied. "Water!" Jack exclaimed. Then, with typical Gaelic flair, Jack extended his arm toward the stream and said, "Give. it ter the O'Rourke, Fader. It needs ut more den I do."

Although a great story, it has a sad ending. Like many of our grand boys, Jack died of his wound.[7]

R & R in Paris

After the battle, the regiment spent about a week in the Foret le Fere, and everyone received a complete new issue of clothing. Then we marched through Chateau-Thierry and encamped a few miles outside the city on the banks of the Marne River. [At Soulchery, August 13-16] We were there a few days, and the whole regiment, or what was left of it, could rotate to Paris on leave.

This was a Godsend to the fellows in the line. None but a few officers had previously had a chance to see Paris, and most of them hadn't been with a woman since arriving in France. As soon as we would move into a particular area and the local bordello would get all spruced up and ready for action, the MPs would either close it down or put it off limits. That was grossly unfair, because the officers would find billets with the local inhabitants, and some of them ended up cohabiting in every sense of the word, while the enlisted men of the line companies either spent their evenings in a lousy dugout or, if in reserve, they were lucky to find themselves in a barracks. So this trip to Paris was the greatest social event of the war for many of our doughboys.

Now Don Adair was so afraid of missing the trip that he went to Captain Mangan with a great story. It seems that Don's maternal grandparents were from Alsace Lorraine and had emigrated to the States, but a few of their relatives still lived in or around Paris, so Don told Captain Mangan how imperative it was that he visit his "cousins" in Paris. Well, Mangan put him on the first shift to go, and Don buddied up with Unc Shannon for the trip. Needless to say, he had not the slightest interest in visiting his "cousins," nor did he have the remotest idea where they lived. He and Unc spent the first day just looking for female companionship, to no avail. Then they discovered how it was done. They conveyed their desire to the bellhop of their hotel, and he fixed them up with two young ladies. "They were beautiful girls," sighed Don, "and they smelled so good."

Big Jim asked me to join him for the trip, but I had missed the paymaster again and was broke. Besides, it was so beautiful around the river, I enjoyed just lounging around, sleeping, and taking a swim now and then, and my leg began to feel much better.

Bootz Rejoins the Regiment

Heaven was interrupted when the regiment marched back to Chateau-Thierry and entrained to a village [Goncourt] just south of Neufchateau. There we stayed in tents and barracks for about two weeks while training replacements. This was about the middle of August. [August 18-28]

It was there that I next saw Herman Bootz, who had been wounded at the Ourcq. He was being sent from one hospital to another in the south of France for convalescence when his train stopped at this little village to take on water, and there was the 3rd Battalion encamped in a field on the outskirts of the village.

Out of curiosity, I had gone down to the station when the train came in and joined a group of fellows. A familiar head and powerful shoulders protruded from a window of one of the coaches, and damned if it wasn't Captain Bootz. He shouted to us: "Is this the 69th?" He had seen our flags.

(The men from Ireland carried small Irish flags, the old green flag with a golden harp, which they displayed on top of their pup tents. When Herman Bootz looked out of that train window and saw those flags, he knew he was home.)

I said, "Yes, sir, it sure is." "Where are we?" Bootz asked. I told him, and as he clambered off that train with one of his arms in a sling, he was crying. I carried his gear, and he followed me to HQ and reported for duty.

Well, Colonel McCoy gave him holy hell. "Are you crazy, Bootz? You can't even carry a side arm." But Bootz was determined he wasn't going to any rest area. "There's nothing wrong with me. This sling will be off in a week." And, by golly, the Colonel let him stay on.

Shortly thereafter, the line companies had to undertake a series of night marches north, ending up not far from Seichepre in the St. Mihiel sector, and that was to be the scene of our next battle.

Vietnamese Truck Drivers

HQ Company was able to make part of this trip in French camions, but, although more comfortable, that truck ride was definitely more dangerous. These trucks were driven by French colonial troops from Vietnam, which was part of French Indochina in those days. They were a crazy bunch, who drove those trucks like madmen, wrecked a couple on the way, and scared the hell out of us.

The trip took several days because of the road traffic, and when nightfall came, we would disembark and set up our pup tents in the nearest field. It was interesting the way these Vietnamese set up their camp fires, gathered around to boil their rice, and chatted away in their singsong language. They seemed a happy lot.

One of our replacements in the pioneer platoon had been a Chinese boy—Lee was his name—from Miami. Quirt gave him such a hard time that he deserted and joined a group of these Vietnamese truck drivers. I know this, because one night on my motorcycle I joined one of their bivouacs while they were eating, and there was Lee sitting by the fire. I started to talk to him, but he put his finger to his lips and pleaded with his eyes for silence, so I didn't say a thing. We both knew and had suffered under the same bastard. That's the last I saw of Lee.

By the time we got to the St. Mihiel sector, Colonel McCoy had been promoted to brigadier general and was slated to leave the regiment after the battle. This news worried me until I found out who our new colonel was to be—Harry Mitchell, a very fine, experienced, and considerate officer.

At St. Mihiel, Donovan retained field command of the 1st Battalion, with Major Anderson heading the 2nd Battalion, and Major Reilley commanding the 3rd Battalion in reserve.

Intelligence Work at St. Mihiel

As the St. Mihiel campaign was launched [early on the morning of September 12], our regiment was flanked by the Ohios on the left and the Alabamas on the right. That first day we advanced almost ten miles, occupying the villages of Essey and Pannes. There was relatively little resistance, and our units were ahead of schedule all the way.[8]

Don Adair and I were assigned to search all the houses in Essey along a little stream to recover any correspondence or reading material left behind by the Germans.

It was a madhouse. French civilians wept joyously and offered what little provisions they had to our men, doughboys liberated whatever Boche beer they could find, and we had problems with both civilians and our own men. We had to assure the inhabitants that we were not trying to steal their household belongings, and we had to repel souvenir-hunting doughboys. Order was restored later in the day as the 2nd Battalion moved in, and our liberators of the 1st Battalion moved on to Pannes and beyond.

I found the intelligence work fascinating. Two days later, we were well established at our final objective, St. Benoit, and we set up a listening and observation post out in front of our lines. There we would watch German movements through field glasses and report them back to HQ by telephone. Our primary job was to locate their artillery positions by gun flash or smoke, and one of the men had to count the number of German shells that came over.

Collintine and the Cabbage Patch

Big Jim Collintine arrived in Essey right on the heels of Donovan's 1st Battalion. Don Adair and I saw him there with his ammunition wagon, watering his mules, waiting for the artillery to arrive! In the meantime, he had already selected his billet. He had found a house formerly occupied by the Germans, and in the backyard they had planted cabbage, radishes, and onions. He staked out his claim, which no one in his right mind would violate, and a day after the smoke had cleared, he sent out the word:

"Wir goin' ter have a party, an' th' min are t' bring thir own beer an' corn beef."

Jim had found a big kettle, which he filled with cans of corned beef and "his" cabbages, and about fifteen of us sat around to a dinner of corned beef, cabbage, and liberated German beer.

Two days later, the Germans shelled the village and blew the cabbage patch all to hell. Oh! Jim was mad. First he blamed ME because I had permitted it to happen. Wasn't I supposed to have identified the damn German artillery? Then he was ready to attack Metz single-handed. "Why'r we foolin aroun here, annyway, fir Crist's sake? Whyrn't we chasin thim damn Germans!"

The Colonel's Equerry

One day, after bringing in a report from our observation post out in No Man's Land, Colonel McCoy saw me and hailed me over:[9]

"Ettinger, do you ride a horse?"

"Yes, sir."

"I want you to go back to Ansauville and bring up my horse. You go back and tell my horse orderly, Corporal Gavellis, that you are to ride my horse up here, and bring Gavellis back with you."

"Yes, sir."

I made my way to the rear through a traffic jam, hitching

rides now and then, got back to Ansauville late that evening, found Gavellis, and gave him the word. He looked at me with disgust.

"What the hell do you know about horses?"

"I can ride a horse all right."

"This is a particular horse, a gift to the Colonel from President Roosevelt. Up to now, the Colonel wouldn't allow anyone but me, or himself, to ride it."

"I can't help that. That's his order. He wants me to bring his horse up, and you're to come up also."

Well, Gavellis didn't like the idea at all, but we waited till daylight the next day, then saddled the horses and started for St. Benoit.

The road was so clogged with transport we had to take to the fields. The fields weren't much better, littered with barbed wire, and strewn with all kinds of rubble, destroyed trucks, and artillery caissons. It's difficult to ride a horse under those conditions. We especially didn't want to cut their fetlocks on the barbed wire.

On the way up, I saw Jim Collintine with his mule team and big combat wagon bogged down in the road traffic. When he saw me, he gave a holler to come over; he wanted to talk to me. I was too busy handling the horse and yelled: "Sorry, Jim, I can't stop now," and kept on going.

When we arrived in St. Benoit, the Colonel's horse was fine; there wasn't a mark on him, and Gavellis was tickled to death. We pulled into a little courtyard where the stable sergeant had some kitchen mules, and the first thing I knew, one of the damn mules kicked the Colonel's stallion in the ribs.

Jesus! Gavellis was horrified, and I felt like a fool because I didn't realize we were so close to the damn mule. We worked on that big bay for an hour at least, rubbing him down, and rubbing him down to erase the hoofprint on his ribs. Fortunately, the kick hadn't broken the skin. We kept grooming him and applying liniment, and finally there wasn't any trace of a mark. The horse didn't seem to be hurt otherwise, so we continued on to regimental HQ and reported to Colonel McCoy, who immediately came out to examine his prize possession. He rubbed and petted him all over; then he complimented me:

"Ettinger, thank you; you did an excellent job."

I nearly fainted with relief. Gavellis, who was cursing under his breath, never spoke to me again.

That evening when I met Jim Collintine, he said:

"Red Ettinger, ye may tink yir' a gintleman ridin' th' Colonel's horse, but let me tell 'e dis. Whin Jim Collintine wants ter talk with 'e, he means ut."

He then grabbed me in a bear-hug and bit me on the cheek. By God, he drew blood! Oh, then he was mortified. He took a chew of tobacco out of his mouth and slapped it on the cut:

"Thir, lad, that'll take th' pison out."

It evidently did, because the cut rapidly healed.

Capture German Patrol

One night, it was very foggy at the listening post, and we heard noise out on the wire. We suspected it might be a German patrol. A young liaison corporal from I Company said, "If someone will join me, we'll see what the hell it's all about." So, I volunteered.

The two of us went out through the wire into an open field and were prowling around when, suddenly, we heard voices. We froze. The voices got closer and they were German. We got ready, and three guys on patrol walked right up to us. When they got within a few feet, we hollered, "Hände Hoch!" They put up their hands. Nothing to it. We searched them for concealed weapons, tied their hands with their belts, and started back to regimental HQ, which was about a mile to the rear.

When we arrived, we thought we'd get a nice commendation. Instead, we got hell because, on the way back, an uninvited escort had taken a wallet from one of the prisoners for a souvenir, and he didn't report it when we returned. When the prisoners were interrogated by the interpreter, the victim complained about his wallet having been taken. You're supposed to take their wallets, but of course, they have to be turned in for whatever paper they may contain.

Major Anderson was there, and he reduced that poor kid to tears. And who else was there? Lieutenant Quirt! Captain

Elmer had been promoted to major in command of brigade intelligence, and Quirt had been transferred to our HQ's intelligence section.

As fast as I could, I went to Sergeant Major Steinert and told him what had happened. "I've got to get out of here; I don't care where; I've just got to transfer. I don't want any part of Quirt."

Stokes Mortars Under Tom FitzSimmons

Tom FitzSimmons had several times said he would be happy to have me in his mortar platoon, where he was the senior non-commissioned officer. I checked again with Tom—"Yes, indeed"—told Steinert, and within a couple of hours, I was transferred to HQ Company Stokes mortar platoon.

Tom FitzSimmons hailed from South Orange, New Jersey, and had just graduated from law school when we entered the war. He wasn't very tall, about 5'9", but there was no fat on him, and he had the map of Ireland all over his face, except for the eyes, which were steely blue like Donovan's. Also, like Donovan, he was fearless and highly intelligent.

Tom had enlisted in L Company of the 7th Regiment, as had I, and together we transferred to the 69th under the same unique circumstances. Although by-passed by the lottery that had made the original selections for transfer, Tom and I had volunteered to replace two sets of brothers who would have been separated by the lottery.

Far wiser than I, Tom did not volunteer for the pioneer platoon and was assigned to HQ Stokes mortar section. Along came Lieutenant Mike Walsh who, quickly recognizing Tom's potential, promoted him first to corporal and then to sergeant. Mike drilled him in the use of the mortar until confident he'd never have to worry about that platoon as long as Tom was its top sergeant.

Tom was one of those natural leaders whom men would follow anywhere because they knew he'd never let them down. He always made certain that his men had dry quarters, plenty to eat, and that their boots and uniforms were in good condition. He established a slush fund to which the whole platoon contributed on payday, and now and then they used it to throw parties. I believe the idea behind this was to promote good fellowship among the men.

In combat, Tom was as cool as a cucumber and was always out front directing the mortar fire. Sometimes, to better spot the target, he'd stand up in an open field and miraculously survive. He was courageous, intelligent, considerate of his men, and lucky—an unbeatable combination.

This almost nonchalant attitude toward death was a characteristic that Tom shared with Bill Donovan and Joyce Kilmer, and like both of these men, Tom was a deeply religious person. No show, mind you; all deeply considered and committed. He would often meet with Kilmer and John Mahon, our company atheist, and they would have the most fascinating conversations about faith, truth, and skepticism. Tom would alert me when they had these meetings, and I would listen spellbound, because I had never before heard my religious principles questioned; as a matter of fact, I didn't even know what they were.

In joining the mortar platoon when I did, I was lucky. I had only one battle to survive, whereas at least half the original members of the platoon had by now either been killed or seriously wounded. During combat, the mortar men and the machine gunners were always the first target of the enemy because of the damage they could do, but while I often thought of my dear friend, Jack Perry, who had a premonition of death, I never really thought I'd be killed. I saw it as a matter of luck. After all, most of the original dispatch riders I had known were out of action by now. I had been lucky and I felt lucky.

On to the Argonne

It was a five-day journey from the St. Mihiel sector to the Argonne. The first part of the trip was by camion with Vietnamese drivers. As usual, they drove like madmen, and several trucks went off the shoulder of the road into the ditch. A number of the men were injured by this crazy driving.

After the first day, we camped out in a field in our pup tents. The Vietnamese built little fires along the edge of the highway and gathered around to cook their rice and enjoy the comfort of the fire. In an effort to conceal the extent of our movement, we weren't permitted to build fires. The following day, we drove about four hours, then left the trucks and started to march. The next two nights we slogged through cold rain and mud up to our ankles, days spent in tents hidden by woods under dripping trees.

On the third night, as we passed through a village, we noticed a Red Cross hut and a YMCA, and we hoped the officers would call a rest so we could get some cigarettes and cognac or wine, but we trudged on through and kept going another seven miles or so until we reached the high ground of Montfaucon. There we camped across from an observation tower that had been used by the Crown Prince of Germany a few years previously. It must have been beautiful country at one time, but the trees had been splintered all to hell by shell fire, and now it was a Godforsaken field of mud holes.

When the word came down that we were to rest there all day and the following night, Unc Shannon ambled over with a proposal.

"Hey Red, we're going to have this time off; are you game to go back to that village we passed through and try to pick up some cigarettes and cognac?"

"Sure," I agreed without hesitation. (Unc was the Fordham fullback who, at Camp Mills, had conned Joe Hennessy into thinking I was the greatest motorcycle racer in the world.) God knows where we got the energy, having marched that whole night, but we took up a collection among our buddies, sneaked through the woods as though going to the latrine, then circled around until we came to the highway.

After hiking back to the village, we went straight to the Red Cross for cigarettes, but they would sell us only a single pack each. And when we went to the YMCA, it was the same story, even though they had hundreds of cartons on the shelves. But that's the way they were. Disgusted, we went into a cafe to try and buy cognac.

Hank Gowdy and Charles MacArthur

Two American soldiers were drinking at a table, and Unc recognized one of them as Hank Gowdy, a famous catcher for the Boston Braves, now a color sergeant of the 166th Ohio Infantry. Unc hailed him, and we were invited over. Gowdy's companion was Charles MacArthur of the 149th Illinois Field Artillery, a former newspaper reporter and a hell of a nice fellow. We hadn't heard of Charlie MacArthur, but he later married Helen Hayes and became a famous playwright. He and Ben Hecht wrote *Front Page Story*. He also wrote an uncensored, hilarious account of the 149th Field Artillery in France called *War Bugs*.[10]

(That artillery, which was part of the Rainbow Division, was not amusing to us. It was incredibly effective, a God-send, the only artillery we could really count on. Most of its gunners had been college boys from the University of Illinois, and they could fire those French 75s so fast the Germans thought we had invented automatic cannons.)[11]

When Unc told Gowdy and MacArthur about our need, Gowdy said, "Oh, don't worry, I'll fix you up. Give me some money and I'll get the cigarettes." He went out and shortly returned with twelve cartons of cigarettes in a burlap bag. In the meantime, we asked the proprietor, an old man behind the bar, if we could buy some cognac. "Certainement." But when we asked for twelve bottles, he threw up his hands: "Oh, non, non, non." Then MacArthur spoke up, and he surely rated around there; tout de suite, the proprietor came up with twelve bottles of Hennessy Five Star.

It was dark before we started back, but we hitched a ride in a French camion for about half the distance and arrived at the bivouac about two o'clock in the morning. Promptly, we distributed the liquor and cigarettes, keeping a carton and a bottle each for ourselves.

Tom FitzSimmons was on the lookout for us, and he was furious. Boy! did we get a lecture!

"Don't you realize we might have pulled out? You should have known that nothing is certain around here. Luckily, we didn't leave tonight. But you didn't think about that."

He busted Unc from corporal to private first class. I was a private first class, but I guess he didn't want the indignity of having a buck private in the mortar platoon, so he didn't bust me, but he put us both on duty for the rest of the night to guard the kitchen.

Unc and I foraged around to see what we could steal from the kitchen to eat. All we could find was a couple loaves of bread and some brown sugar. Everything else was locked up. So we ate the bread covered with brown sugar, and at daybreak Tom returned and told us we could hit our sacks. Thank God we didn't move out that day; we were so exhausted we never could have made the march.

The following day, the regiment marched west to the village of Exermont, a few miles behind the front lines, where we relieved the 1st Division.

Singing on the March

The most depressing part of those night marches was a prohibition against singing. Our regiment loved to sing on the march. To say our songs were risque would be putting it mildly. They were as bawdy as the collective imagination of 3,000 horny men could conceive.[12]

On the last day of our journey to Exermont, the sun came out, and we were able to march into our staging positions during the late afternoon. To bolster our morale, I suppose, the officers let us sing. It was quite a sight to see the whole regiment under march singing away at the top of their lungs. As a dispatch rider, I used to be able to watch them, but this time I was in the ranks with the mortar platoon. I happened to look up, and there was Father Duffy standing on a bluff at the side of the road, giving his benediction to the troops as we were "banging away on Lulu" under full field pack and full throat. He didn't care what we were singing, as long as we were alive and singing.

Some weeks later in the hospital at Allerey, I picked up an issue of the *Literary Gazette,* and there was a beautiful photograph of Father Duffy with arms outstretched in benediction as the regiment filed below. The caption read:

"Father Francis P. Duffy, regimental chaplain of the 165th New York Infantry, blesses his troops as they march into battle singing 'Onward Christian Soldiers'."

Oh, God, I laughed—a Protestant hymn, no less!

RECONNAISSANCE NO. 8

"Within the German lines were two important railways which ran northwestward from the area around Metz and roughly paralleled the battle front. These railroads were practically the Germans' only lateral communications between their forces east and west of the Meuse. . . .In the vicinity of Sedan and to the southeast they ran through a narrow strip of territory which lay within 35 miles of the [Allied] forward positions. . . . It was apparent that an Allied attack in the vicinity of the Meuse River which penetrated far enough to gain control of the lateral railways . . . would divide his armies . . . [and] he would be unable to maintain his forces in France and Belgium. . . . The German High Command clearly appreciated this and had made elaborate preparations to prevent any Allied advance on that front.

"The nature of this region [south of Sedan, between the Meuse and the Argonne Forest] was such as to provide a series of strong defensive positions [and also] furnished splendid sites from which the country to the east and west could be covered by artillery fire. The woods and underbrush of the broken hills of the Argonne Forest had been organized into an almost impregnable position by the addition of machine guns, artillery, trenches, and obstacles of all kinds . . ."

—American Battle Monuments Commission, *op. cit.,*
   pp. 167–169.

To accommodate Allied planning, General Pershing had agreed to a September 26 starting date for the Meuse-Argonne campaign, yet the St. Mihiel offensive was planned to begin on September 12 with most of his experienced divisions. Hence the nine American divisions (almost 220,000 men) that kicked off at the Argonne along a 24 mile front consisted, for the most part, of green troops, only later to be relieved by veterans from the St. Mihiel campaign. Although the attack caught a relatively small German defending force of 61,000 troops completely by surprise, within a few days American casualties had climbed to 23,000, and the attack bogged down in confusion as units got lost, and the only four muddy roads that paralleled the line of advance became clogged with men and material. It was a logistic nightmare. An average of four miles had been gained, the Germans had rapidly reinforced their effective defensive positions, and the main defenses of their powerful Hindenburg Line were not even reached until October 9. At this stage of the offensive, most of the American veterans from St. Mihiel arrived on the scene. Before the end of the campaign, over one million American troops would be combat committed; over 75,000 would be casualties.

—For detail, consult ABMC, *op. cit.*, pp. 171–340, and Stallings, *op. cit.*, pp. 223–256, 280–305. For critical analysis, see Rod Paschall, *The Defeat of Imperial Germany, 1917–1918*, pp. 181–192.

8

Battle
of the Argonne

★   ★   ★

They will tell of the peace eternal,
And we would wish them well.
They will scorn the path of war's red wrath
And brand it the road to hell.
They will set aside their warrior pride
And their love for the soldier sons.
But at the last they will turn again
To horse and foot and guns.

> —Douglas MacArthur, Rainbow Division
> Reunion, 1935.

The Rainbow's first objective during the Battle of the
Argonne was to capture the village of Landres-St. Georges.

On October 11, we relieved the 1st Division, which
had suffered terrific losses in taking two high ridges
from the Germans on the outskirts of Exermont, a village
about five miles south of our objective. On both of
these ridges, the enemy had machine gun bunkers
made of concrete, and their dugouts were also framed
in concrete, with electric lights and telephones, and
over the four years of their occupation, some even had
running water installed. Their defenses were superb. It
was amazing that human flesh could endure what had
been inflicted on the Big Red One in capturing these
positions.

172

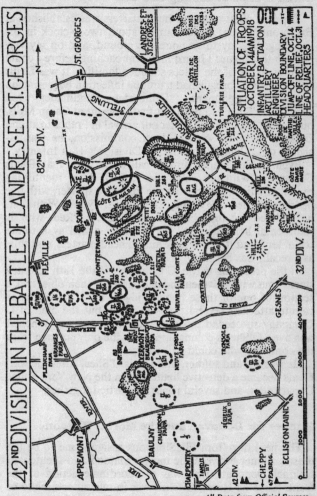

42ND DIVISION IN THE BATTLE OF LANDRES-ET-ST.GEORGES

LANDRES-ET-ST.GEORGES

ST.GEORGES

N →

82ND DIV.

STELLUNG

CÔTE DE CHÂTILLON

TUILERIE FARM

BOIS DES HAZOIS

SOMMERANCE

KRIEMHILDE

CÔTE DE MALDAH

BOIS DE ROMAGNE

GESNES

CÔTE MADAME

FLÉVILLE

HILL 243

151 ALG.

BOIS DE MONEY

HILL 235

MONTREFAGNE

PETIT BOIS

HILL 255

HILL 212

NEUVILLE-LE-COMTE FARM

BOIS DE GESNES

GESNES

32ND DIV.

COURTRE CR.

EXERMONT

EXERMONT

BEAUREGARD FARM

AL INFERNO

NEUVE FORGE FARM

TRONSOL FARM

PLEINCHAMP FARM

GRANGES FARM

APREMONT

BAULNY

CHAUDRON FARM

SERIEUX FARM

ECLISFONTAINE

CHARPENTRY

LANDI ST.PADRIG

42 DIV.

CHEPPY
ST.PADRIG.

SITUATION OF TROOPS
OCTOBER 14 JAN. 1918

INFANTRY BATTALION
ARTILLERY
ENGINEER
DIVISION BOUNDARY
JUMP-OFF LINE, OCT. 14
LINE OF RELIEF, OCT. 31
HEADQUARTERS

1000   2000   3000   4000 YARDS

All Data from Official Sources.

Denis O'Shea of the Big Red One

The first night after our headquarters was established at Exermont, I went to the latrine about two o'clock in the morning. Fog lay thick upon the ground, and on my way back to the dugout I heard men approaching before I could see them. One of the voices sounded familiar. It was Denis O'Shea, whose brogue had a unique inflection bordering on a speech impediment. ("Dime dem handinades, Dod damit!") O'Shea had been our first sergeant at Camp Mills, but he had left us shortly after our arrival in France to attend Officers Training School. Upon commission, he was assigned to C Company of the 1st Division's 18th Infantry.

Even before seeing him, I called out: "Is that Denis O'Shea?" "Who are you?" he replied. After identifying myself, Denis emerged from the fog like a specter, with five bedraggled men. "My Dod, Red, how are you?" With that, he grabbed me in a bear hug and asked: "Red, whir is redimental headquarters? We're havin' a hell av a toime tryin' ter foind it." So I took him to headquarters, and this, as I recall, was his story.

In the preceding battle, C Company of the 18th Infantry started out with 250 men and had captured their objective, a section of one of those hellish ridges. Then the Germans counterattacked several times in force, but the men of C Company succeeded in defending their position. When it was over, O'Shea's companions were the only six men from the company who could still walk.

He was a grand soldier, that Denis O'Shea. After the war, Denis became a detective lieutenant in the New York Police Department, and several times we partied together.

Runner for Donovan and the Mortar Platoon

The next day, Tom FitzSimmons assigned me to be the liaison runner between the mortar platoon and Lieutenant Colonel Donovan, who was to coordinate action at the front. (Colonel Harry Mitchell was in overall command of the regiment, with HQ in Exermont.) Tom told me to find Donovan and request orders concerning the mortar section; what position we were to take, and so forth.

I found Colonel Donovan on the first ridge that the 1st Division had captured. He was sitting in a shell hole, cool as a cucumber, while his barber tried to shave him with a straight razor. The barber was shaking like a leaf because shells were falling all around. Only about a hundred yards away, one of them hit a mule drawing a heavy machine gun and blew the mule and machine gun to pieces. I think the men survived, although one or two were wounded.

After wiping the lather from his face, Donovan said:

"All right, Ettinger. Tell Lieutenant O'Donnelly and FitzSimmons that I want your section to follow the men of the line by about a hundred yards, and be on the alert should they need you to blow up machine gun nests. Stay a hundred yards behind until we reach our objective." [Lieutenant "O'Donnelly" is a pseudonym.]

Then he had me walk with him from the first ridge, across a valley, to our front line on the second ridge, where the 3rd Battalion under Major Reilley was in place waiting for the attack.

You had to do some fancy footwork to avoid stepping on the dead that covered the ground. I had never before seen so many bodies. There must have been a thousand American and German dead in that valley between the two ridges. They were an awful sight, in all the grotesque positions of men killed by violence.

Once I looked down and was terribly shocked. There was a young German soldier with red hair and freckles, eyes staring at the sky—and he looked just like me. Midway through this gruesome passage, Donovan stopped and exclaimed, "Oh my God! What a waste of lives. What a waste! What a waste!"

Tom had already preceded me to the second ridge. After reporting Donovan's message, we spent a sleepless night in foxholes waiting for our attack the following day.

Headquarters' mortar platoon consisted of three sections, four mortars to a section, three men to a mortar. When we attacked this time, only one section went forward; the other two were held in reserve for relief or to repel a German counterattack.

Twenty men from one of the line companies were assigned to help us carry ammunition, and we had twelve ammunition carriers of our own. The mortar shells were carried in satchels, like suitcases, two bombs to each, plus the detonators in a separate compartment.

At that time, our twelve regular carriers were Pawnee Indians. These were replacements, who had been assigned to us the previous month from the Oklahoma National Guard. For the most part, the ones assigned to our mortar section were a sorry lot, quite unlike the fighting Indians you read about. There were three outstanding men among them, however. One, John Robertson, was a graduate of Carlisle; another, Young Eagle, was the son of a tribal chief; and the third was Joe Leader, a big, fine-looking fellow—a very brave and good man. When we got to use our mortars in combat, only two of those three were able to help us, because John Robertson had been wounded on the way up.

Attack

We took off from the second ridge at eight o'clock on the morning of October 14, 1918. On our left were the Ohios, brigaded with us under General Lenihan. On our right advanced the Alabamas and Iowans, under General MacArthur. The Rainbow's front was about five miles wide. [Actually, 3 miles]

That morning, we had been issued extra water canteens, but these arrived without covers and they were bright aluminum or tin. With the sun reflected on them, they made great targets, so Donovan passed the word to throw them away and everyone did. Ironically, soon afterward, the sky darkened, and it rained almost constantly for the next two weeks we were there.[1]

There was fierce resistance from the enemy at first, but then the German infantry was driven back, and we captured several hundred of them. However, German machine gunners, concealed in wooded areas, kept to their posts and poured a devastating fire upon our advance, inflicting many casualties. Because our mortar section got lost, we weren't available to help take out the machine gun nests; the men had to do it with rifles and hand grenades, but they managed to sweep away that resistance and advanced to within four hundred yards of the defenses in front of Landres-St. Georges. There we ground to a halt on rising ground leading to the enemy wire. This was about two miles from our kickoff point, and it took us the better part of the morning to get there.[2]

The Lost Mortars

Shortly after starting our advance, I heard a whirring sound from a clump of bushes on my left. I swung around with my rifle, about to fire, when a guy stepped out and shouted: "DON'T SHOOT! WE'RE CAMERAMEN!" Sure enough, there was their signal corps insignia. They were taking pictures of the advancing troops, and they gave me quite a shock, because I damn near shot into those bushes.

We kept going, and I noticed that we were drifting to the left. I expressed my concern to Tom FitzSimmons, and he passed it on to Lieutenant O'Donnelly, but O'Donnelly dismissed it, and sure as hell, he got us lost. We ended up way off to the left, behind some woods.

The Germans spotted us and started to lay down a box barrage. That is to say, they'd lay a line of artillery fire in front of you, then behind you, then on either side of you; then they would slowly converge the pattern. Those shells were getting closer and closer, and O'Donnelly didn't know what to do.

(We used to call him "Desperate Desmond O'Donnelly," after a movie matinee character of the time, because of his turned-up, waxed, black mustache. He was a good-looking guy about six foot four, unafraid of anything, but he wasn't very bright and had no sense of command.)

Tom FitzSimmons saved our hides by persuading O'Donnelly to hustle off to our right as fast as possible, taking a chance on a few of us getting killed, rather than await the convergence of those shells. Fortunately, we all made it.

Then O'Donnelly said to me: "Ettinger, do you think you can find Colonel Donovan?" I told him I would certainly try. He wrote out a message, and I started off.

Because we had drifted to our left, I went to the right and came out into an open valley. Here the artillery and machine gun fire were intense. My God, it was terrible! Every few minutes, the bullets sounded like a swarm of bees.

Mike Walsh in the Argonne

Men in squads or platoon formation were rushing hither and yon; nevertheless, there seemed to be an orderly process in everything they did. Darned if I didn't come across Mike Walsh, then captain of I Company of the 3rd Battalion. I asked Mike if he knew where Donovan was, and he exploded:

"I don't know, and I don't give a damn. The son of a bitch has me here in this cleaning-up operation. The best company in the whole regiment, and he uses me to clean up."

Walsh was madder than a wet hornet, but his men were doing a terrific job routing out whatever Germans were hiding in the wooded areas left behind by our advance, and I could see groups of prisoners being taken to the rear.

I told Captain Walsh about the problem with our mortar section, and he cursed, saying, "I'll send somebody to rout that bastard out and get them up there, believe me."[3]

I continued trotting along, trying to get my bearings, and recognized a big, long-legged fellow running toward me. He was a lieutenant from one of the line companies, but he didn't have any insignia, just wore a regular doughboy uniform and carried a rifle. He called out: "Where the hell do you think you're going?" I told him I was trying to find Colonel Donovan. "Well, you're going in the wrong direction. If you keep on as you are, you'll be in enemy territory in no time. Our right flank is exposed, and the Germans are over there, about a half mile away. Donovan is in that direction," he said, pointing toward the north.

I thanked him and started off again at a lope, but my pack and musette bag were slowing me down too much, and I needed a breather. I took them off and set them in a small shell hole that I identified with shattered tree branches, planning to retrieve them after the action.

Apparition in the Sky

Suddenly, I heard an approaching scream and knew damn well that shell was going to land close. (You can tell by the sound.) Jesus! There was a big shell crater only about ten feet away. I gave two leaps and went head first into a pool of mud at the bottom of the crater. Just then the shell exploded. The concussion was awful! It tossed me about two feet into the air, and when I came down, I didn't know whether I was dead or alive. It was a while before I regained any sense at all. I just lay there on my back, terrified, looking up at a cloudy sky misted by light rain. Then I saw something I have told only a few people because I was afraid of being thought crazy or a liar, but I want you to know.

A light in the sky came floating toward me from the north, and as it slowly approached, it became a figure of Jesus pointing to his heart, which was exposed. (At home, we had built a Catholic church—the Church of the Sacred Heart—and my mother had donated a beautiful statue to the church called "The Sacred Heart of Jesus." This vision resembled that statue, but it seemed so real.) The figure hovered directly over my head, looked down on me with great compassion, then slowly receded in the same direction from which it had come. I lay there feeling so peaceful and watched it float toward the north. Before disappearing, it seemed to stop for several seconds and brighten, and I thought to myself, that's where Colonel Donovan is. I picked myself up and no longer felt any fear.

The shell had totally destroyed my pack and musette bag. All that remained of my novel and diary were tatters of charred paper; and my rifle, which I had set down while marking the location of the pack and musette bag, had been blasted in half.

I started off in the direction indicated by the apparition, looking for another rifle. There were rifles all over the field, but most were useless. I finally found one that looked good, but it was a Canadian Enfield that had been issued to our replacements, and it wouldn't take my clip. Eventually I came across a Springfield in good condition, tried it out, and kept it for the rest of the war.

Pushing on, I met more and more troops and asked each

group where they thought Donovan was. Invariably, I'd get different directions. Then, down in a gully, I came across a dry stream bed filled with wounded. The medics had set up a dressing station there, because willow trees protected it from German observation. At one side, I saw almost fifty men from a machine gun company crouched in a shallow trench. To catch my breath, I dove into this trench and landed alongside Sergeant Mike Donaldson.

"My God, Red, what are you doing here?" he exclaimed. I told him I was looking for Colonel Donovan. "He's up there on that ridge, but you can't get up there; you just can't make it. Stay here for God's sake. Stay here!" He grabbed my arm . . . but I had to go, broke away from him, ran up the slope, and found Donovan.[4]

Donovan in Command

Colonel Donovan was in a shell hole about 200 yards down from the top of a rise, in front of which were the barbed wire approaches to Landres-St. Georges. He had a telephone in there, runners all around, officers standing by, and so forth. I handed him the note Lieutenant O'Donnelly had given me. He read it, then looked at me in bewilderment:

"What the hell is this all about? Where are the mortars?"

"Back toward the rear, sir. We lost direction."

"If you got up here, why couldn't the rest of them?"

"I don't know, sir."

"You go back and find Lieutenant O'Donnelly and bring him up here at once."

Jesus! Now I had to return through all of that damn shrapnel and machine gun fire. Fortunately, I had gone only a short distance when I saw our boys trooping along, Fitzie in the lead. I told the lieutenant that Colonel Donovan wanted to talk to him, led him to the command post, then returned to the section. I don't know what happened between him and the Colonel, except that when O'Donnelly returned, he told Tom that the Colonel wanted to see him, and FitzSimmons was put in command of the mortar section. Donovan temporarily relieved O'Donnelly of his command but ordered him to stay around.

Slaughter at the Wire

The regiment was stalled on this slope. Four hundred yards in front of us were acres and acres of barbed wire, laced with pill boxes and machine gun nests, which barred us from taking the village of Landres-St. Georges.[5] The problem was lack of adequate artillery support to blast a path through the wire. Our own precious Illinois Field Artillery was being used to assist the 84th Brigade to capture the Cote-de-Chatillon, the high ground to our right that was sweeping us with machine gun and artillery fire. All we had to cope with the wire at our front was heavy artillery, which was way in the rear, and our own shells landed on us as much as on the Germans. Their hits on the barbed wire were rare and incidental.

Several times, our infantry advanced to that wire, seeking a passage, only to be mowed down by German machine gun fire, which was positioned to sweep the front of it. By early afternoon, half of the 3rd Battalion had been put out of commission and was replaced by the 1st Battalion.

Some of our regular engineers tried to cut a passage through the wire, covered by riflemen and several of our machine guns. But the Germans were firing from concealed pill boxes behind the first belt of wire and from the high ground of the Cote-de-Chatillon, and our men couldn't see them to do any damage. Their machine gun fire killed or wounded all those engineers.

Colonel Donovan told me to have FitzSimmons send a barrage of mortar shells into the wire to see what effect it would have. Well, we tried our damndest. My God, I don't know how many hundred shells we sent into that wire. The mortars had pretty good effect in small areas, but there was just too much territory to cover. Donovan finally concluded it was useless, and he ordered the mortars to cease fire; so we had to stay there and wait for the artillery support and tanks that were now promised to us.[6]

By the end of the first day, our mortar section had suffered eight casualties—two men killed and six wounded, most of them ammunition carriers. Jim Terrill, a gunner on our Number 4 mortar, was among the wounded, so Tom assigned me to take his place. My job was to screw the detonator into the mortar bomb and pass it on to the Number 2 man, who slid it down the barrel of the mortar, while the Number 1 gunner squatted on the base plate to operate the range mechanism.

Eventually, I had three regular details, because Tom kept me going back and forth to Colonel Donovan; then, beginning on the fourth day, I had to travel three miles to our kitchen in the rear, pick up a detail of the fellows, and bring up hot food carried in huge thermos containers. Each container would be slung on a pole, a man supporting each end on his shoulder. Every evening, we brought up two thermos cans of stew and two of coffee. I believe that ours was the only unit to get hot food regularly. Tom made this assignment because I was pretty fast on my feet and had a good sense of direction. In those days, I could walk and run all day long.

Sherwood Orr Learns to Shovel

After the first day's action, our mortar section dug in about fifty yards down the slope from Donovan's command post. I chose as my buddy Sherwood Orr, a fellow transfer from the 7th Regiment. Sherwood was a sweetheart of a fellow, a junior at Dartmouth when he enlisted, but he was one of the most helpless guys I ever knew.

Although a gunner on the Number 1 mortar, and an excellent gunner at that, I don't think Sherwood had ever dug a hole before, because when we started to enlarge a shell hole, he just didn't know what to do. He'd put one foot on the shovel, then try to push it with the other foot. I actually had to show him how to use a shovel.

After completing the foxhole, we dug a little trench toward where our feet would be so the rain water would drain off. Then we spread our shelter halves over the foxhole and weighted their edges with clods of mud to hold them tight. After several hours, the rain developed a pocket in the center of the shelter halves, and Niagara Falls came flooding in. God, we had to do it all over again. Fortunately, the rain let up, and our shelter held the rest of the night.

The Mortal Remains of William Sheahan

Early the next morning [October 15], Sherwood and I were reminiscing about home. I wanted to smoke and had plenty of tobacco and paper for making cigarettes, but, damn it, I didn't have a match, and Sherwood didn't smoke, so he didn't have a match. Consequently, I went over to the next foxhole to get some matches.

In this foxhole was our color sergeant, Bill Sheahan, and another doughboy I didn't know. I got some dry matches from them and squeezed back into our foxhole. No sooner had I rolled and lit a cigarette than there was a terrible explosion! Both Sherwood and I were stunned and buried in mud. We managed to dig ourselves out of our hole, heard shouts, and discovered that the shell had landed in the adjacent foxhole where those two men had been. There was no sign of Bill Sheahan, and the other fellow had both legs blown off. He was being carried down the slope to the aid station, but you could tell it was useless.

Everyone was mystified as to what had happened to Sheahan. I told Tom FitzSimmons he had been in that hole, because I had spoken to him only a few minutes before the shell exploded. At dawn, we looked around and soon came across what appeared to be a piece of roast beef strapped by a web belt, and the initials "W S" were burned into the belt. Those were the mortal remains of Bill Sheahan.

Twenty years later, in 1938, we held a service in the 69th Regiment Armory in memory of our comrades who had been killed during the war. A beautiful plaque was unveiled on which were engraved the names of the men who had died in France. A man sitting next to me introduced himself as the brother of William Sheahan; then he introduced me to a woman next to him, who was Bill's sister. They had traveled all the way from Ireland for this occasion. I was nonplussed when he told me that, during the war, Bill's body had been returned to his hometown in Ireland for burial. I wondered what in God's name had been returned. Then his brother confided:

"You know, Father Duffy told us that he was killed by shell concussion, and there wasn't a mark on his body."

Although shocked, I managed to reply, "Father was right, Sir, that's what happened."

Then I just sat there full of sorrow. It had been so thoughtful of Father Duffy to tell his family that. And the story was believable, because, during the war, many men had been killed by shell concussion alone, without any appearance of a physical wound.

The Second Day

Soon after dawn on the second day, we heard a clanking noise and, looking down, saw a column of eight tanks coming up the gully that traversed our field. It was the damndest thing you ever saw. At the front and on the flanks of these tanks were several officers guiding them! The drivers' vision must have been very restricted. These were small French [Renault] tanks with American crews. We cheered like crazy. "GO GET 'EM, BOYS! GO GET 'EM!" we yelled. We thought they would break through the wire without stopping. God! They got within a hundred yards of that wire when the Germans let loose and blew one of those tanks all to hell. The rest of them just turned around and clanked back, and we never saw them again.[7]

(Tanks were laughable in our battles, although larger English and German tanks made a big difference on the British front, which had more open fields. German tanks almost wiped out my old Company L of the 7th Regiment, which was part of the 27th New York Guard Division now fighting with the British.)

Tom FitzSimmons sent me to Colonel Donovan for orders as to the placement of our mortars. As I arrived at the command post, Captain Flynn of our Wisconsin machine gun battalion was talking to Donovan, who earlier that morning had been wounded with a bullet through the knee. As I stood behind Flynn, waiting my turn, several machine gun bullets whacked into his legs, crippling him for the rest of his life. That command post was becoming a hell-hole because the Germans had spotted the traffic around it and were trying to register in from both the front and the right flank.[8]

As the medics carried Captain Flynn down the slope, I

saw someone waving a handkerchief on the end of a bayonet about a hundred yards to our right. I called it to the Colonel's attention, and he ordered me to investigate. As I ran forward, a big, nervy sergeant from the Pennsylvania machine gun battalion joined me. We arrived to find two wounded doughboys in a shell hole. The one who had waved the handkerchief was the cooler, although the more seriously wounded of the two. The other guy, who had a minor flesh wound, was hollering as though he were going to die. These fellows told us they had seen German troops a thousand yards or so to the right of our position emerge from a wooded area, cross an open space, and enter another wooded area on our right flank. While the sergeant called for medics and remained to render assistance, I ran back and passed the word to Colonel Donovan.

Mortars Save the Day

Anticipating an enemy counterattack, Donovan immediately ordered the mortar section to take up a position on our right flank to cover an opening between two wooded areas. There was a slope over there beyond the sunken road, and we set up our four mortars on the reverse side of this slope.

Tom FitzSimmons crawled about a hundred yards forward to a concealed position at the top of the slope, and we waited . . . and waited . . . and waited. Finally, a large group of Germans appeared from a corner of the woods and started toward our position intending to cut off our front line. Tom didn't make a move, and as the seconds passed, we were terrified they were going to overwhelm us. At last, he gave a signal to fire one for effect at three hundred yards. The range was perfect, and he quickly signaled: "Rapid Fire, Rapid Fire!" and we rained shells on them with devastating effect. But they still kept coming. Then some Pennsylvania boys rushed up with two machine guns, and with our combined effect, the Germans broke. They came back once more, and we broke them up again.

During their second attack, our mortar bombs ran low, and we yelled at the Indian carriers to bring up reserves from a large shell crater, where they had been stashed a hundred feet away. They were too terrified to move and sat huddled in the crater with blankets over their heads. Tom, who had worked his way back to our position, threatened to shoot them, but still they wouldn't move. I guess they figured they were going to die anyway and stood a better chance with Tom than the German artillery, which had begun to seek us out.

I dashed over to pick up bombs for our mortar, and just as I turned with a case under each arm, a German shell landed right in front of our mortar. Poor Gus Cosgrove was blown away with his chest torn open, while John Taylor was stretched on the ground. He wasn't wounded but was unable to speak for at least an hour. I dropped the bomb cases and ran over to Gus, but there was nothing anyone could do. He died as I reached him. The shell had also split open the barrel of our mortar and had twisted the base plate like a piece of paper. It was a miracle that Taylor had survived; and if those Indians had been doing their job, I might have been killed because I would have been at Taylor's side.

As the German artillery fire increased, and with no indication of a renewed attack, Tom ordered us back to the sunken road. Colonel Donovan was pleased with the action because, had the German attack succeeded, our frontline troops could have been in jeopardy.

Tom FitzSimmons was awarded the Distinguished Service Cross for fearlessly exposing himself to enemy fire while directing the mortars. That decoration was richly deserved, because Tom was the bravest and coolest man under fire that I ever knew, apart from Donovan, who received the Congressional Medal of Honor for heroic conduct in the battle. (See Reconnaissance No. 10.) And do you know what Tom did? He put me in for the DSC, and according to one of the clerks at HQ, Quirt, who was standing in for the regimental adjutant, threw it in the wastebasket. When Tom received the medal, he gave me the ribbon saying, "You deserve it, Al, as much as I do." That wasn't true, but that was a measure of the man.

The Third Day

The next day, our Alabama and Iowa regiments of the 84th Brigade, under MacArthur, took the Cote-de-

Chatillon. Then these men repelled repeated enemy counterattacks. In so doing, our gutsy comrades broke the last heavily fortified German position in the Argonne. This straightened our line, which was a tremendous relief. The Germans kept constant artillery pressure on us, but now it was all coming from the front, and they didn't have the accuracy of observation afforded by the Cote-de-Chatillon.[9]

The most damage I witnessed during the battle at any one time came from our own heavy artillery, whose shells fell short and killed or wounded eight of our men. I was only a hundred yards away at the time, and it was an awful sight. When the regiment finally pulled out of the lines for a few days' rest behind Exermont, we came across that artillery outfit—not the 149th Illinois. The men were so furious that some of them threw their rifles at these fellows, and others rushed over and threw a few punches.[10]

We named the slope we were on "Donovan's Ridge" in his honor, because he was up there continually before he was wounded and for five hours after his knee was shattered. Finally, under direct order, he was evacuated. Four men carried him off that hellish slope in a blanket, one being wounded by machine gun fire in the process.

During all this time, ammunition had to be hand carried from a cache two miles behind the front up to the lines. The bulk of our ammunition was transported to this cache by Jim Collintine in a big combat wagon drawn by two mules. In previous battles, he had brought our ammunition right up to the lines, but at Landres, because of the intense artillery fire, he was ordered to leave it within two miles of the front. So Jim transported it to a wooded area, and every day, our men had to trek back two miles to pick up the ammunition. Even so, Jim came up at least a mile farther than any other ammunition wagon in the regiment.

During the two weeks that we were before Landres-St. Georges, it rained almost constantly, and it was cold. We were miserable, soaked to the skin without winter underwear or overcoat, with only one soaked blanket, and at night, our rest was broken by artillery fire. At least half the men had severe colds; some could hardly drag themselves around.[11]

After the battle, we were relieved by troops of the 9th

Infantry from the 2nd Division, and we headed back to Exermont, about five miles to the rear, where there were barracks built by the Germans that had comfortable bunk beds and wood-burning stoves.

Joe Leader, That Son-of-a-Pawnee

Tom had put me in the lead for the return trip, but our section hadn't gone very far over the shell-shattered fields when we were immersed in a dense fog. It was so thick I completely lost my orientation and had to stop. That's when Joe Leader proved himself.

"Red," he volunteered, "I can find the way back."

"My God," I replied, "how can you? The fog is so thick we can hardly see our feet."

"I know, but I can get us back."

"Be my guest," I said, and that son-of-a-Pawnee led us to our destination as straight as an arrow.

Both Joe and I knew the lay of the land, he from his daily retrieval of ammunition, and I of food, but I needed some visual reference, while he seemed to have a compass implanted in his brain. Never was a guide so aptly named.

In Exermont, we had the luxury of a hot shower, shave, a good meal, and a great sack. I slept for thirty-six hours.

After four days of rest, we were assigned a position formerly held by the Alabama regiment on the Cote-de-Chatillon, and we were held there in reserve for about a week until the third phase of the battle was launched through our lines by the 2nd Division.

The Mac and the Mick

After the episode at the forked road in the Champagne, I didn't see MacArthur again until September, after we had consolidated our position in the St. Mihiel sector.

One day, I had just delivered an intelligence report to regimental HQ, when up drove the general to pay a courtesy call on Colonel Frank McCoy. The room was crowded with brass, and I was ready to leave when MacArthur barged in. Much to my surprise he recognized me, hailed me by name, and asked if I was still that "demon dispatch rider." "No sir," I replied, "I have been transferred to the intelligence section." "Good for you; good for you," he said, and passed on.

I didn't see him again until just before the third phase of the Argonne offensive in late October. We had lost 50% of our men, killed or wounded. [Actually, 44%] Now we were securing replacements and resting in the line while the 2nd Division prepared to resume the attack.

Our mortar crew had set up a position in a shell crater on the Cote-de-Chatillon, and we were sitting around cleaning our weapons on one of those rare bright sunny days with just desultory artillery from both sides interrupting the peace. Who dropped by but Frankie McGuire, my old buddy from the pioneer platoon.

Frankie was a great comedian and a magnificent mimic, always full of hell and good humor. He invariably boosted our morale with a wisecrack when things were blue, when we were homesick, or just plain scared. When he saw me, he jumped down into the shell hole, and we merrily yacked away until I looked up, and here coming toward us was Major Alec Anderson, now commander of our 2nd Battalion, and . . . Douglas MacArthur! As usual, MacArthur was sporting his fancy rakish officer's hat and had a corncob pipe clenched between his teeth—and the Germans were only a ridgeline away. Anderson was conducting him on an inspection tour of the front lines, although MacArthur, having just captured this position, undoubtedly knew it better than Anderson.

When Major Anderson was captain of our company, he would constantly shout at the men: "PUT THAT HELMET ON, SOLDIER!" even if we were miles from the front. He caught me once when I was shaving, using water from a small shell hole in a field. At first he shouted: "PUT THAT HELMET ON, SOLDIER!" Then he bawled me out because I was shaving with field water which, he said, must be full of all kinds of germs and contamination.

Anyway, the two officers came up to the shell crater, and MacArthur greeted us warmly and commented on our mortar action of the previous battle. He said it was a great bit of action, and we deserved to be congratulated. That was nice. Then he bid us adieu, turned around, and the two officers had walked off only a half-dozen yards when crazy McGuire, imitating Anderson's voice to perfection, shouted: "PUT THAT HELMET ON, SOLDIER!"

If only the earth could have opened and let me drop in. I was thunderstruck and terrified because I was facing them (McGuire had turned away), and when Anderson wheeled around, livid with anger, he was looking straight at me. Oh God!

"WHO SAID THAT!" he bellowed.

Well . . . MacArthur paused for a second . . . then slowly turned . . . and with a grin on his face, flipped us a jaunty salute and quipped, "I'll consider that, soldier." Then he steered Anderson by the arm, and away they went.

I called McGuire everything under the sun and concluded:

"You son of a bitch, don't you ever come back here again!"

"What the hell," replied McGuire, totally unconcerned.

"What the hell? I'll tell you 'what the hell.' When Anderson gets back, you won't be here. You'll be back with the lousy pioneers, but I'll be here, and the rest of us will be here. God knows what he'll do to us!"

Oh, McGuire shucked it off, I calmed down, and fortunately, Anderson didn't return. The following day, the battle resumed, and we were too busy to worry about it. But that was MacArthur for you. He was something else. I just worshipped the man.[12]

Third Phase of the Argonne Offensive

In preparation for the third phase of the Meuse-Argonne offensive, they wheeled up every gun in France that wasn't absolutely needed on the other fighting fronts. My God, it was almost like the Champagne Defensive over again—hub to hub. Oh, that we had had such artillery support!

There were not only our own artillery regiments, there were also French batteries present. The Marines, who had a full brigade in the 2nd Division, had their own artillery there as well, and woe betide any "friendly fire" that fell short on them! They would probably charge back on the offending artillery unit.

When that artillery barrage lifted, it had pulverized, not only the acres of barbed wire that had frustrated our advance, but also the entire village of Landres-St. Georges. For the 2nd Division, it was a damn foot race with virtually no opposition.[13]

Gassed at the Argonne

The following day, Lieutenant O'Donnelly had me and a fellow named Baker accompany him to relocate our mortar position. Baker was a nice little guy, but he was a replacement with very little training. We went on up and met a lieutenant of the Alabamas, who showed us where they had placed their mortars, and O'Donnelly decided that was good enough for us.

When we started back, we had to go through a little valley, and I noticed there was smoke with a bluish tinge to it, hanging close to the ground like a fog. I could smell that it was gas, and I warned O'Donnelly that it was gas. It was only about four feet above the ground, and he was well over six feet tall, so he went right through it and left us there. Later, we found out that, upon returning, he had told the medics he had been gassed, and they sent him to the hospital.

Here we were, and Baker didn't know how to put on his gas mask, so I took mine off to show him. By that time, we had swallowed a considerable amount of gas. After we made it back, both of us were violently ill, but after puking a lot, I didn't feel too bad and thought I had it out of my system. However, Baker had inhaled more than I. The medics packed him off in an ambulance. Later I learned that he died before reaching the hospital.[14]

The next day, I became terribly ill, and Tom FitzSimmons assigned two men to assist me to the first-aid station. There, some careless medic tagged me: "F.O.U." (Fever, Origin Unknown.) A mule ambulance rattled my bones four miles back to Exermont, where my stretcher was placed on the cement floor of a former German barracks with about a hundred other wounded men, there to await motor transport to a field hospital. It was dark as pitch in there, no medics, and the cries of the wounded were awful. An ambulance driver would come in with a flashlight, check the tags on the men, decide which were the most seriously wounded, and have half a dozen picked up to be placed in the ambulance.

Saved by a Buddy from Home

God, it was cold in that barracks, and I was sick as a dog. Not knowing how I had been tagged, I couldn't understand why I wasn't picked up. I began to feel hopeless, when suddenly a flashlight focused on my face, and I heard a voice shout: "Hey! That's Al Ettinger."

"Who are you?" I asked.

With surprise, the voice queried, "Don't you recognize me?"

"I can't see you with that flashlight in my eyes."

Then the voice identified itself: "I'm Eddie Ruckles."

Oh, my God! Eddie Ruckles had been a caddie master at the White Beeches Club in Haworth, New Jersey, where I had caddied as a boy. At the outbreak of the war, Eddie enlisted with the 165th Ambulance Company from Red Bank, New Jersey, and they had become our regimental ambulance men.

Eddie grabbed his partner: "Here, let's get Al the hell out of here, right now." They picked up my stretcher, put it in the ambulance, and bounced back to a British field hospital several miles to the rear, where they gave me some kind of medication and hot tea, but neither could I keep on my stomach. Later that evening, I was stacked in another ambulance and driven to a hospital train.

It was so wonderful just to be indoors. I was placed in a bunk but soon felt terribly ill again. Tried to get to the toilet, but Jesus! the door to the toilet was locked . . . and I fainted.

The next thing I knew, I was in a hospital ward on a stretcher, and someone was about to roll me onto a bed. I looked down, and the sheets were so filthy my stomach revolted, and I vomited on them. Fortunately, they then changed the sheets. Later, I was told that a patient had died only twenty minutes before on those damn sheets. Then I discovered I was in a base hospital in Allerey, an enormous medical complex, with 35,000 other casualties from the Argonne campaign.[15]

RECONNAISSANCE NO. 9

"The exposed positions and the close proximity of the opposing lines were responsible for a number of casualties, and many effectives were also lost through evacuation because of influenza and exhaustion from exposure and the hard service. Living conditions were unbelievably bad, and men existed in 'Fox Holes' half filled with water for days at a time. The weather added to the natural discomforts with almost continual rain and cold."

"As the weather grew colder, discomfort and even suffering was caused by the lack of winter underwear and overcoats. This, coupled with the hard continuous service of the division in the open, was inevitably taking its toll."

—From Maj. Harry D. Jackson and Capt. Thomas K. Lewis, "Medical History of the 42nd Division." Quoted in Reilly, *Americans All,* pp. 726, 727.

"In the woods the mud was almost knee-deep. Gas saturated the air above from continuous bombardment of the enemy. . . . So impassable were the roads at the front that relays were necessary in transporting patients from the lines. Often they were carried on the shoulders of the litter-bearers through the muddy, shell-raked woods, for two or three miles. There they were taken back in mule ambulances to the more solid roads where they were consigned to motor vehicles for a still longer ride. Many were carried a hundred miles before they were at last in clean, soft hospital beds. At the best speed possible, it was hours before wounded men could have efficient treatment."

—From William T. Lampre, "Tulsa County in the World War." Quoted in Reilly, *op. cit.,* p. 728.

"During periods of great activity when the casualties were many, each first line division established a sorting and diagnosis station which drained in an hour glass fashion the wounded from all the battalion and ambulance stations of the Division. It was the most forward station established by a divisional medical unit at which all casualties finally arrived. It was known as a Triage. It was usually located in a central position on the natural line of drift or evacuation of the wounded and at a distance of from three to five miles from the front line. It was established and operated usually by a field hospital company."

—From Colonel Fairchild's summary of the Division's medical operation. Quoted in Reilly, *op. cit.*, p. 765.

9

Allerey Hospital & Stockade

★　　★　　★

Have you forgotten yet? . . .
For the world's events have rumbled on since those
　　gagged days,
Like traffic checked awhile at the crossing of city ways:
And the haunted gap in your mind has filled with
　　thoughts that flow
Like clouds in the lit heaven of life; and you're a man
　　reprieved to go,
Taking your peaceful share of Time, with joy to spare.
*But the past is just the same,—and War's a bloody
　　game . . .*
Have you forgotten yet? . . .
*Look down, and swear by the slain of the War that
　　you'll never forget.*

　　　　　　　　　　　—Siegfried Sasson, "Aftermath."

The ward I had been assigned to was jam-packed, mostly
with patients who had the flu or had been gassed. Later,
I was told I had been unconscious for the better part
of three days. Now, flat on my back, I was sick as a dog,
and over the next two days, several of the patients died,
choking in their own phlegm. Our only treatment was
to drink as much fluid as possible, and most of it I just
threw up.

Fortunately, a new doctor came on the scene who changed
things around, but fast. He was a young captain from

Chicago by the name of Schneider or Schroeder. He took one look at me and yelled at the nurse: "My God, woman, don't you know how to take care of a gas patient? This man has been gassed!" He then propped me up in bed and tightly wrapped a bandage around and under my chest to support my lungs and help me breathe. Apparently, he was one of the few doctors in the hospital who knew how to treat gas patients, and he seemed to take a personal interest in my survival. Had he not been in attendance, I may not have made it, but under his treatment, I quickly began to improve.[1]

Description of the Camp

The American high command had planned a major offensive long in advance and had anticipated many casualties, so they rushed to completion the largest hospital center in all of France just prior to the Meuse-Argonne Offensive. This was constructed on the outskirts of the village of Allerey in eastern France, not far from the Swiss border— on a clear day you could see Mont Blanc in the distance. The nearest city of any size was Chalons-sur-Saone (as distinct from Chalons-sur-Marne, which is farther north on the Marne River) about 35 miles from Allerey.

Allerey and the nearby villages were charming, the countryside was beautiful, the local people most pleasant and hospitable. The camp itself, however, was terrible.

The very size of this hospital complex created problems. Some convalescent patients had to walk almost a mile in the mud to get necessary medication and they couldn't get liberty. It was a God-forsaken place, and I doubt that anyone who was a patient there could ever forget the misery of it all.[2]

First, morale was very low among the hospital personnel. While I was there, the Armistice was signed, and the only thing the hospital staff thought about was getting home because the war was over. Staffers actually became negligent in their duties. Naturally, this became a problem with the troops. On top of that, the food was awful, and you had to wait in line for hours, three times a day, if you could stomach that food three times a day.

There were no hard-surface roads in the camp. During the fall rains, the streets were quagmire mud, then slush when it began to snow. This condition was relieved only when it got cold enough for the mud to freeze. To cope with the mud, duckboards were constructed—sidewalks made from slats of wood. Stepping off the duckboards, you'd sink over your ankles into the mud.

If we'd had passes to visit Chalons-sur-Saone or the neighboring villages, it wouldn't have been so bad, but off-base leave was generally reserved for medical personnel and other members of the staff. Instead, we had a YMCA barracks and a Red Cross hut, both of which charged for everything they dispensed. The only place you got anything free was the Knights of Columbus hut. Naturally, I gravitated there and met Father Bannahan, the chaplain in charge.

Father Bannahan was a wonderful man. He was over seventy years old and reminded me a great deal of Father Duffy. In his "K of C" hut, you could always get free cigarettes, hot chocolate, candy bars, and reading matter, and it was the most enjoyable place to visit in the camp. About a dozen convalescent patients from the 69th gathered at the K of C hut almost every evening.

Rubin Bernstein and the Armistice at Allerey

On November 11, 1918, while still in the treatment ward, we heard a lot of shouting and singing outside. Raising myself in the bed, I could see out the window, and there was a rag-tag parade coming down the street with this tall, lanky guy leading it carrying an American flag. It was Rubin Bernstein, my old buddy from the pioneer platoon! Oh, how I wanted to join and embrace him. It turned out that the Armistice had been signed, and everybody started to celebrate; but at that moment, all I cared about was rejoining my buddy. After leaving the treatment ward, I tried several times to locate him, without success. By that time, he had been discharged, and it wasn't until several years later that I met him again in the States.

Sergeant Green of the 92nd Division

One of the patients next to me in the ward was a Negro sergeant, John Green by name, and he was quite a guy with a wonderful sense of humor. Green was from the 92nd Division, which was all black except for the officers. It was from him that I learned something about the problems that division had experienced.

The 92nd Division, unlike the black 93rd Division, consisted of drafted troops, and they were not nearly as well-trained as the National Guard units of the 93rd Division. The 92nd also had to cope with the prejudice of the American general staff, as well as the Germans, whereas the 93rd Division had been assigned to the French Army, which fully appreciated their services and didn't have that kind of prejudice. Finally, the black officers of the 93rd were as well-educated as white officers anywhere.

To illustrate the difference in education between the two divisions, John related how he had become a sergeant.

After induction, the draftees were lined up in some camp in the South (he was from Tennessee), and a regular Army sergeant inquired if anyone had previous military service. No one had. Then the sergeant asked, "How many of you boys can read and write?" John was the only one to raise his hand, so this old sergeant asked his name. "Well, Green," proclaimed the sergeant, "you, too, are now a sergeant."

John told me that he was in a reserve battalion in the Argonne, and battalions in front of them broke and ran from the Germans. He said his battalion stood fast for a time, but after a while, "I was heading for home. I wasn't going to stand there alone!"

The 92nd Division had been rushed into the Argonne Offensive with only one month's experience in the lines, and then without adequate training; naturally, with sad result.

The 93rd Division, on the other hand, and the black New York and Chicago National Guard units in particular, were excellent. It was all a question of better training, better motivated volunteers, and better leadership.[3]

The 15th New York Regiment (369th U.S. Infantry) had an excellent combat record. It was about a mile to our right during the Battle of the Champagne, went over the top near

Chateau-Thierry and at Belleau Wood and served with great heroism in the Argonne Offensive. Its troops never retreated an inch throughout the war and saw more action than most regiments of the A.E.F.

Larry Collins—Partner in Crime

Shortly after transfer from the hospital ward to a convalescent ward, I was making up my bunk when a young fellow, sitting on the adjacent bed, introduced himself as Larry Collins from New York. He was a member of the engineer battalion that had worked on the hospital barracks. One day he fell off the roof of one of the barracks and broke his leg; that's why he was in the hospital. When I introduced myself, he said:

"Ettinger? Are you any relation to Dr. Ettinger, the superintendent of schools in New York?"

"Why, yes, he's my father."

"Oh, my God! Do you know Tom Churchill, president of the Board of Education?"

"Sure, I know him."

"You should, because I've heard about you and your brothers since I was knee high to a grasshopper. My mother is Tom Churchill's sister."

It was quite an event, and we quickly became good friends.

As a convalescent patient, I immediately had two problems. First, I was broke. As a motorcycle dispatcher, I was rarely around when the paymaster made disbursements, and my records had yet to find me at this hospital. Of course, I could have survived at the K of C hut, but that put a definite crimp in my freedom. Second, I wanted to get out of that damn camp and visit around, and for that I needed a new uniform; the one I had was in terrible condition.

An apparent solution to the second problem developed when Larry Collins and I learned how to get out of the hospital center without being observed. There was one particular place that the MPs didn't cover, and fellows had been sneaking out to visit different villages in the area. Then we heard that a member of my regiment was a clerk in the supply barracks; that should take care of my uniform problem. Finally, we learned about a woman in a nearby village who would buy all the American Army raincoats she could get her hands on, because she could make a nice profit by converting them into women's raincoats. To that end, my supply clerk "buddy," as yet unknown, might prove cooperative.

Larry and I hied ourselves to the supply barracks, and sure enough, the clerk's name was Callahan, and he had been one of our company cooks. The last Cally was seen, he was disengaging from the front on the back of a kitchen mule! I never did like the man; no one did; he was a surly guy. Even so, I thought, he had been in the same company of the same regiment; why, I'd be treated with a little consideration. Not so. When he refused to give me a uniform, I was mad as hell and called him all the names I could think of. ["Callahan" is a pseudonym.]

In the meantime, Larry Collins located the counter where these slickers were stored. After we got outside, he said, "Hey, Al, this is going to be a cinch."

"What do you mean?"

"Hell, we can get all the slickers we want. You know that back door? It has an ordinary key in the lock and a rope tied to the door handle, with the other end nailed to the floor. We only have to break one of those little panes of glass in the door, reach in, cut the rope, turn the key, and there you are."

Talk about crooks planning a job.

That night, after dark, we spent an hour scouting this supply building. There were no guards of MPs to be seen, and the building was dark, evidently no one inside. So, the following night, Larry and I went over to execute our first act of grand theft. I covered my fist with a handkerchief and broke a pane of glass. Larry reached in, cut the rope, turned the key, and we walked in. Each of us then appropriated a case of a dozen slickers, beat it out of there, and stashed them under some loose floorboards of an empty barracks adjacent to our own. We had a safe cache.

Well, the following evening, we each put three raincoats over our uniforms until we looked like fat generals. There was over a foot of snow on the ground, but we made it to this village about five miles away, entered the only cafe visible, and asked the owner if she knew a woman who bought

American raincoats. "Oui." "How can we find her?" The proprietress dispatched a small boy, and pretty soon the enterprising dressmaker arrived. We negotiated a price that came to ten francs a coat; about a dollar fifty each. Well, a dollar and a half was a dollar and a half. We were broke.

When the business deal had been completed, we each had 15 dollars, contingent upon delivery of the remaining coats. That was the most money I'd seen in a long time. We were able to live it up from then on, as we made many a trip to this village.

The more adventurous patients would sneak away to different places for enjoyment, many getting as far as Chalons-sur-Saone. Some of them were caught by the MPs and slapped into the stockade. Others just kept going and got back to their outfits, but the 69th was in Remagen, Germany, and I had no idea when they were going to pull out for home.

One night, Larry Collins, another fellow, Vallentine, and I went to a cafe in a village we hadn't seen before. We ordered wine, an omelette and french fries, and as we chatted away, I spotted a bottle on a shelf that looked like cognac. Pointing it out to the others, I suggested that we buy it, but we weren't particularly flush at the moment.

Vallentine said, "Red, you talk to the woman, and I'll get that bottle of cognac." So I engaged the lady proprietor in my best conversational French, which was awful, while my comrade in crime sneaked around, grabbed the bottle off the shelf and slipped it in his overcoat. Shortly later we said "bonsoir" and started to leave; but the neck of the bottle protruded from Vallentine's coat, and the proprietress saw it and started to yell. Oh God, we ran like hell, and as we ran, we could hear her screaming for the gendarmes.

Down the street was a cemetery on the left, protected by a stone wall. We vaulted the wall, ran through the cemetery, vaulted over another wall, and came upon a pile of crushed stone by the side of a road that appeared to lead back to the hospital. We sat by this pile of stone, and Vallentine fished out the bottle of cognac. But we had no corkscrew, so he took a stone and knocked off the head of the bottle, took a swig, and didn't say anything. Then he passed the bottle to

Collins who took a swig. Collins didn't say anything, just passed the bottle to me. I had a swallow—and then we all laughed. It was grenadine, not cognac, and it tasted awful, like a syrupy wine. Well, the laugh was on us. In the meantime, we could hear the MPs blowing their whistles in the village, but they didn't find us, and we made it back to the hospital.

Looking back, I am awed at what we had done. Stealing from the Army for our own use was one thing; that was regarded as a fully justified requisition. Army supplies were for the Army, and we were part of the Army. But there is little to justify stealing from the Army to sell to civilians. And stealing from the civilian population was just out-and-out theft that we would never have dreamed of earlier in the war.

Double Cross by the Red Cross

One day, a fellow told us that the Red Cross was giving away cigarette tobacco, so Larry and I went over to the Red Cross hut. It was colder than a witch's tit, and we had to get on a long line. After waiting an hour or more, a guy came back and warned us:

"Listen, fellows, if you don't have any money, there's no use going in there, because they're charging seven and a half francs for these little packages."

Fortunately, Larry and I had that much from our loot, so we stayed on the line and eventually bought a small cardboard box that contained a can of Prince Albert pipe tobacco, a package of Bull Durham cigarette tobacco, a package of Duke Mixture, a corncob pipe, and some cigarette papers.

After returning to our ward and opening the packages, we were furious! In each was a lovely hand-written note to the American doughboy recipient, hoping that he would enjoy the contents as a gift from some girls club in Augusta, Georgia.

Can you imagine? These girls had spent hours making up these boxes, then turned them over to the Red Cross, thinking they'd be given to doughboys in France without charge; and here the Red Cross charged seven and a half francs (that was over a dollar) for their charity. From that day to this, I haven't contributed one damn dime to the American Red Cross.[4]

Sometime later, Larry Collins and I were sent to different convalescent wards. He went to one designated for troops to be returned to their outfit for further duty, and I was sent to a class "A" area for troops to be returned to the States, either as unfit for further military duty, or because of our veterans' status.

A Problem with the Supervision

In our first convalescent ward, the medical sergeant in charge was a peach of a fellow, and we did pretty much as we pleased. There was no bed check or extra duty. We swept the barracks, made up our beds, and that was it.

After I was transferred to this class "A" convalescent ward, the picture changed. The supervisory "medic" was a Sergeant Major McCullough, a miserable bastard if ever there was one; and for some reason or other (probably length of service), I was put in charge of the men and held responsible for keeping the place clean.

Many of the men had been seriously wounded, yet all we had for beds was straw ticks on the floor. In the winter, that barracks was never really warm, and the floor was cold as ice. There were two wood-burning stoves, one at each end, but the wood supply was scarce. Sometimes the fire would go out for lack of fuel, and we had a heck of a time replenishing the wood supply.

There were no zippers on our cotton bed ticks. We'd tie the open ends, but the straw would eke out, no matter what we did. Ten minutes after we had swept the ward, there'd be more straw around.

Every morning, McCullough would meticulously inspect the barracks in an attempt to discover stray wisps of straw. If he found one, he'd restrict the men until making another inspection an hour or so later. Oh, he was a miserable son of a bitch.

We heard that he hadn't arrived in France until after the

Armistice, and he seemed to resent the combat veteran; I don't know why. He used to say: "You guys think you're tough just because you've been in combat. What the hell, you're going home now; what're you bitching about?"

Actually, with home and discharge now on the horizon, nobody complained about anything except his conduct. His attitude was so unnecessary. We had a fine group in there.

One memorable Saturday night, we were in the Knights of Columbus hut, when a kid who worked in the medical center HQ rushed in. He was a regular member of our K of C Club and he excitedly announced that my barracks and two others were scheduled for return to the States on Monday. Well, you can imagine the hollering and excitement.

Father Bannahan finally calmed us down and said, "Boys, this is a very happy occasion. You know I've never asked a favor of you before, but I would like to ask a favor now. I wish you'd come to mass tomorrow so we can all pray for your safe return home." Mass was held in the Knights of Columbus chapel. All the guys assured him they'd be there. I don't know whether half of them were Catholic or not; it didn't make any difference in the Army. In my day, where you hung out usually depended on where most of your buddies hung out. It could be a local cafe. In Allerey, it was the K of C hut, although sometimes I liked to get away from all my buddies and just explore by myself.

The next morning, after reveille, I reminded the men: "Don't forget, right after breakfast we'll go to mass as we promised Father Bannahan." (Most of the fellows in my ward had been in the K of C hut the previous evening.)

"OK, we will, don't worry."

They trooped off to breakfast after policing the ward, while I stayed behind with Sam Yarborough, a buddy from Texas, to make sure there wasn't any straw on the floor; but the boys had done a good job, and I couldn't see any straw.

I had just started to put on my overcoat when in walked Sergeant Major McCullough. He looked around and started a most fateful conversation:

"Where the hell is everybody?"

"Well, the men are having breakfast right now."

205

"You better go over to the mess hall and tell them to report back for duty. I've got a duty detail."

"After breakfast, they're going to mass at the K of C chapel."

"Mass, hell, when have you guys become so Christly?"

That was a poor choice of language on McCullough's part, so my reply was somewhat testy:

"Well, Sergeant Major, you know Army regulations as well as I do, and you know that every man is entitled to go to church service on Sunday. Even if in the guard house, he's entitled to go to church services, under escort, on Sunday.[5] What is this detail you want the men to do?"

"You've got to take these bed ticks to the warehouse and leave them there."

"Are we leaving today?"

"No, you're leaving tomorrow morning, but you've got to check in these ticks before you leave."

Now I was really becoming steamed.

"You mean to tell me the men have to sleep on the bare floor tonight?"

"You're so Goddamn tough, what about it? You've been sleeping in shell holes, haven't you? Why can't you sleep on the floor for one night?"

"Simply because some of these men are still too sick to sleep on the floor. They might get pneumonia. They're weak from their wounds, and it'd be criminal to make them sleep on that cold floor."

At that point, McCullough figured I was challenging his authority, and he was right. I was on the absolute edge of killing that bastard; only a spark was needed, and he provided it.

"You're going to take my orders, and them is my orders. And furthermore, you Goddamn Catholics give me a pain in the ass."

Well, that was it. I grabbed his overcoat, pushed him out the door, and started to pound the hell out of him.

Now at that time, I weighed no more than 140 pounds, and McCullough was 185 if he was an ounce, but I had learned one thing in my various scraps in the Army: Fight hard and fast and don't let up. Then, even if you get beat, the guy won't bother you again. This time, I didn't have to think about that lesson. I was so furious, I didn't think at all. I just wanted to kill McCullough with my bare hands. In fact, after knocking him down, which didn't take very long, I jumped on him and beat him as he was lying there on the snow. Never before had I hit a man while he was down.

All this time, Sam Yarborough was behind me shouting: "Get off him, Red! Get off him, and give me a chance!"

Then, somebody grabbed my shoulder from behind, shouting at me to get off the man. I didn't know who he was and couldn't care less. As he bent over, trying to pull me away, I swung my fist around and caught him alongside the jaw, and off balance, he went ass over head in the snow. He turned out to be a medical lieutenant.

Finally, MPs came rushing up, and they dragged me off McCullough. By this time, about a hundred men had gathered around cheering like crazy. "Let 'em fight! Let 'em fight!" they yelled, because everybody hated McCullough's guts. But it really wasn't a fight anymore, and it was fortunate those MPs came along when they did. They dragged both Sam and me off to the stockade.

One of the fellows ran to the K of C hut and told Father Bannahan about the fight, and he immediately came to the stockade. At first, the MPs wouldn't allow him to see me, but Father Bannahan insisted and, as a major in the Army, pulled rank on them. After I told him what had happened, he went directly to the commandant of the hospital, a Colonel Forbes, and tried to intercede for Sam and me.

The Colonel had not yet received a report on the incident, so he contacted the provost marshal by phone, got his version of the event, and Father Bannahan was told that I'd have to stand general court-martial along with Sam Yarborough. Father Bannahan protested that he had received numerous complaints about Sergeant Major McCullough, and were the truth known, there might be justification for my having struck him, but Colonel Forbes insisted that would have to be determined by the court-martial. Father Bannahan explained that Sam Yarborough and I were scheduled to leave the next morning for the States, but old Forbes said that it might be quite a while before we would leave France. However, he agreed to convene the court-martial that very evening so that, should we be acquitted, we could return home with our regiments.

Justice Is Dispensed With

Well, what was supposed to be a general court-martial board was convened that very evening. Colonel Forbes was the presiding officer, and the four other members of the court were all medical officers, no combat officer among them, and I didn't have a defense counsel. It was a farce. They had prepared numerous charges and specifications against me: Assaulting a noncommissioned officer, assaulting a commissioned officer, resisting arrest, and using abusive language are the ones I recall.

Colonel Forbes wanted to know whether I pleaded guilty or not guilty. I said: "Not guilty to most of the charges, sir, but to some of the charges I'd like to plead guilty with an explanation."

Forbes retorted, "What do you mean, 'guilty with an explanation'? You deliberately disobeyed the orders of Sergeant Major McCullough to start with."

"There was some justification for that, if you will let me explain, sir." I began to describe how the sergeant major had insulted my religion, but didn't get very far when Forbes asked:

"Just what is your religion, young man?"

"I am a Roman Catholic."

"That's enough for me," said Forbes. He didn't even confer with the other officers on the board. "Three months at hard labor."

Sam Yarborough jumped to his feet and protested: "I am a Methodist, and my daddy is a Methodist Minister!"

Forbes interrupted: "And three months of hard labor for you, too, young man."[6]

Before Sam and I were carted back to the stockade, Father Bannahan jumped to his feet and strongly protested the conduct of the Colonel and the trial procedure. He called it a "kangaroo court" and said that he was going to bring it to higher authority immediately. Well, two days later, Father Bannahan was shipped back to the States on Colonel

Forbes' orders, but before he left, he wrote a letter to Father Duffy explaining what had happened.

As soon as Father Bannahan returned to the States, he contacted my father, told him what had occurred, and assured him that I was justified in my conduct. Pop immediately went to a friend in Washington, who took the matter before Secretary of War Baker, and I understand that orders were processed from the Secretary for my release. But the red tape in Washington took so long that I was released before his orders were ever received in Allerey.

The Stockade at Allerey

Well, this stockade was something! It consisted of several large, one-story barracks, each guarded by MPs, from which labor details were dispatched daily.

I'd never been in a stockade before. I'd twice been in a company guard house, which was nothing, because there our own buddies were on guard, and we had very light duties. But this stockade at Allerey was all business. It had been run by a provost marshal with a reputation as a sadist of the worst kind. As a matter of fact, his conduct, as well as that of several other provost marshals in France, was later investigated by a congressional committee. (That was quite a hearing, and, eventually, several provost marshals were sent to Leavenworth.) Fortunately, he had been replaced prior to my arrival, but it was still no picnic.

Naturally, I felt very badly. I thought I'd let everyone down, particularly my parents and the regiment. But my spirits soon lifted because word of what had happened spread like wildfire through the stockade, and I was treated as a hero. Sergeant Major McCullough was disliked by more people than I had suspected, and they were delighted that I had trounced him.

The Sheriff

The first man to approach me was a Negro about six foot five. God, he would have made some basketball player. Thin and angular, his chin, which sported a wispy goatee, slanted back up to the front of his skull at a 45-degree angle. He wore a civilian vest over his uniform shirt, and on this vest was a big star, which he had cut off from the top of a mess kit. His name was "Jus call me Sheriff," and it turned out that he was the "Sheriff" of the stockade.

Well, Sheriff was some character! With a lot of crazy language, he announced that I was "Uner Arres" and had to be tried by the stockade court! Until then, both Sam and I were to be in his custody.

As there was some Red Cross stationery in the barracks, that evening I sat down to explain to my father what had happened. Later, I discovered you could write to your heart's content, but they wouldn't post any of your letters.

While writing, Sheriff pulled alongside to shoot the breeze:

"Say, you mus' be ejicated to write like dat."

"Well," I said, "I've got a little education."

"Oh, Ah wisht Ah had. Ah can't read ner write."

"Oh, that's too bad, but it's never too late to learn."

"Yes, indeed. Ah often wisht Ah could read'n write. Ah would 'specially likes to read poetry. Ah also likes to hear a man talk poetry. You know any poetry?"

"Oh, I know a little."

"You tell me some?"

"Sure," I said, and I recited a few verses of "Gunga Din."

Well, you never saw anyone get so excited over a few verses of poetry. He had never heard that poem before and thought it was great.

"Man, you is smart," he said. "You really got an ejication."

"Well, I'm glad you enjoyed it."

"Ah sholy did. De only poem Ah knows, an Ah really likes, Ah can' rememer. Ah used to bum aroun a lot back in d'States, ridin' d' rails here'n'dare. One night aroun a fire in one ob our hobo jungles, der were a fellow who recited a poem Ah sure wisht Ah could rememer."

"What was the poem?"

"Ah jus rememers d' begining ob it. Ah woners if you eber hear ob it."

"How did it start?"

"Well, it began like dis:

> *"Ah trabels dis worl' all over,*
> *Fom Norph an to de Souph,*
> *Ah dined an stayed wif millionaires,*
> *An Ah bums fum han' to mouph."*

"Da's all Ah rememers. You know dat poem?"

"It seems to me I've heard it. (I hadn't though.) Let me try to finish it for you."

"You thinks you can?"

"I'll try."

Well, I postponed the letter to Pop and began an exercise in "creative writing." I can't remember everything I wrote, but we'll give it a try:

> *I've traveled this world all over,*
> *From North to way down South,*
> *I've dined and stayed with millionaires*
> *And bummed from hand to mouth.*

> *I've just returned from Switzerland,*
> *Spent summer on the Rhine,*
> *And hung out on the Bowery*
> *At Tom Lee's "Number Nine."*

> *And then I went to Boston,*
> *Where I had some pork and beans,*
> *And saw the band in Exchange Alley*
> *Way down in New Orleans.*

> *From there I went to Tennessee,*
> *Where I made myself a still,*
> *But the revenues got after me,*
> *So I beat it over the hill.*

> *Then I went on to Chicago,*
> *Took the boat to Montreal,*
> *Got lucky in a craps game,*
> *And set up a monte stall.*

> *I stoked the whale backs to Argentine,*
> *Jumped ship and had a ball,*
> *But when I got back to that beautiful wharf*
> *The ship wasn't there at all. . . .*

and so forth, and so forth; a lot of nonsense. I covered almost every city in the United States and ended the poem like this:

> *But now I'm tired of roaming,*
> *No place to lay my head,*
> *So I'm sitting in the guard house*
> *Eatin' slop and bread.*

Sheriff just went crazy. I gave him a copy of this poem, such as it was, and he thought I was the greatest guy in the stockade. From then on, he made it his business to protect me, and he announced to all and sundry: "Red is uner mah protecshon." Thank God for that. I had established a "rep," and one or two of those inmates might have been tempted to establish a bigger "rep" simply by beating me up. After all, I didn't look very tough, and whoever heard of a tough "poet."

Kangaroo Court

Two nights later, the major domos of the stockade convened a kangaroo court, and Sheriff hauled Sam and me up before the court; but he had already urged the "judge" to take it easy on us because I was his friend and Sam was my buddy. The charge was: "They did break into this stockade without permission of the inmates." That was the charge placed against every new inmate! They had a judge, a jury, a prosecuting attorney, and a defense attorney, and it was the damndest rigmarole you ever saw.

The best part of it was the judge. He was an enormous, powerful Negro, who, apparently, had been in court so many times for various offenses that he could quote and misquote from both the law and the Bible with an incredibly ponderous flow of nonsense. And he behaved with all the dignity of the judges he had been before so many times. Jesus, what a character!

Usually the sheriff and his deputy would search inmates immediately upon their unauthorized entry into the stockade and confiscate all their possessions. A watch or cigarette lighter was especially prized. Inevitably, after an hour of hilarious nonsense, with the "defense attorney" actually sweating on your behalf with points of law, points of order, and points of holy writ, the sentence would be "Guilty as Charged," and the fine was whatever had been confiscated upon your arrival. And if the defendant gave the court any lip, the judge would pronounce him in contempt, and he would be sentenced to so many lashes over his bare, bare ass. The "bailiffs" would take down the guy's pants, and Sheriff would whack him with a strap.[7]

Fortunately, because of my pugilistic and poetic status, Sam and I were only fined a few cigarettes. Then I was made "Foreman of the Jury!" In this capacity, I shared in the loot confiscated from subsequent inmates. Since I had no desire to offend anyone, I made it a point to return my share to the hapless victims.

I met some fabulous characters in that stockade. Most of the inmates should never have been there to begin with. They were fellows who had slipped away to some village without a pass and were unfortunate enough to get caught by the MPs. The judge, however, was waiting to be sent to another jurisdiction for court-martial because he was supposed to have killed a prostitute. I never did learn the outcome of his trial, because he was still at Allerey when I left.

Marines Invade Stockade

One of the inmates was a Marine corporal, whose name was Mike Bond, a combat veteran and a swell guy. Mike had been caught one night without a pass in Chalons-sur-Saone and was accused of robbing the proprietress of a cafe there. It seems that he had got drunk in this cafe and was picked up by the MPs after he left. In the meantime, someone had beaten and robbed this woman. When they brought Mike before her, she swore he was not the man. Despite that fact, he was still confined to the stockade on the AWOL charge.

The stockade was a large barracks guarded by two sentries at the front entrance and two at the rear, day and night. One night, there was a commotion at both doors. From the front, in burst a Marine lieutenant with three Marine sergeants. At the same time, from the back door exploded a Marine sergeant with three corporals. One of them yelled: "WHERE IS MIKE BOND!" Then they grabbed their astonished comrade and hustled him out. They had actually disarmed the sentries on duty. Everybody cheered like crazy!

I thought that was a wonderful example of Marine loyalty, and that's one of the reasons I enlisted in the Marine Corps during World War II. We never did hear from Mike Bond again. But, boy! I'll never forget the way they invaded that barracks.[8]

Dirtiest Detail

The first detail I was assigned in that stockade was the dirtiest job I have ever experienced, and it was shared by almost all the inmates. Every morning, we had to clean out all the latrines for one of the base hospitals and dispose of the excrement.

Each latrine was a long building with about forty holes. Under each hole was a GI can, and the back of the latrine opened so you could remove and replace the can. At least three cans were placed on a long pole, and with a man on each end of the pole, they were carried to an incinerator shed, where there was an enormous bowl that resembled a urinal. The contents of the cans were dumped into this bowl to drain. Straw was then added to the cans, the solid contents shoveled back into them, and the resulting mess then mixed with a stick. Concluding the process, a huge Black would throw the contents into a large furnace.

Soon after the operation began, you were covered from head to foot in excrement. The odor was incredible, and no matter how hard you tried, you couldn't wash off the smell. On the other hand, because I was on that detail, I was freed from the stockade before my three month sentence expired.

One morning, while marching to a latrine, we passed a detachment of the 3rd Engineers, which was tearing down one of the barracks of the medical center. A sergeant from this outfit saw the Rainbow insignia on my shoulder and hollered:

"Hey, Rainbow, what outfit you in?"

I told him.

"Do you know (I forget his name) in 'C' Company?"

"Sure, I do." (But I didn't.)

"Hell, he's my brother. What are you in here for?"

I told him I had mixed it up with this McCullough.

"Oh, my God! I heard all about that. You got a dirty deal. Even my captain thinks you got a dirty deal. Does your outfit know about it?"

Not knowing whether Father Duffy had received Father Bannahan's letter, I replied, "No way to let them know."

"Can't you send them a letter?"

"You can write all the letters you want, but they won't let you post them."

"Oh, hell, you write a letter, buddy, and I'll see it gets posted."

Just then the guard broke up our conversation and ordered me to move on.

That evening I wrote a letter to Father Duffy, and one to Colonel Donovan, explaining what had happened to me and Sam Yarborough. I also mentioned the misadventure of another inmate from the 69th by the name of Gallagher.

The next day I slipped these letters to the sergeant of engineers, who was waiting for me.

"Don't worry, Red," he assured me, "these will be taken care of."

By God, he took care of them all right. His captain gave them a censor stamp, and both Father Duffy and Colonel Donovan received those letters. With Donovan's permission, Father Duffy went directly to General MacArthur and showed him the letters from me and Father Bannahan.[9] MacArthur, bless his soul, immediately started the process to secure our release and return to the regiment.

New Job—"Assistant Butcher"

In the meantime, I met an interesting older man whom I shall call Sam Hart. Before he was wounded by shell fragments and sent to the hospital, Sam had been the mess sergeant of his outfit. AWOL for several days in Chalons-sur-Saone, he was caught by the MPs. In the stockade, he was a butcher for the Officers' Mess.

Sam and I yacked it up on several occasions. Then one

evening he said: "Hey, Red, I think I can get you a cushy job. I'm going to speak to the mess officer about it." By golly, he told the mess officer that he needed me as an assistant because of my previous experience as a short-order cook, which was pure invention, and the mess officer agreed. So I was only on that latrine detail for about two weeks. I then became an "assistant butcher," in which capacity all I did was open cans for Sam.

Sam Hart had owned one of the largest livery stables in Philadelphia, inherited from his father and established by his grandfather. About twelve years before the war, he killed a man he had found in bed with his wife. Sam was tried, found guilty, and sentenced to life in prison.

The case created quite a stir in Philadelphia, because his livery stable used to supply horses to some of the elite families of that city, and he was very popular among them. Several tried to help in his defense, without success.

After Sam was sentenced, one society woman in particular kept pestering the governor about a pardon for Sam, and he showed me an old newspaper clipping that described her efforts to free him. He had served about eight years of his sentence before we entered the war. Then a new governor was elected from the same political party as his benefactress, and he granted Sam a pardon on condition that he enlist in the armed forces. Of course, Sam jumped at the chance.

Sam was not the criminal type at all, but during his time in the Pennsylvania state penitentiary he naturally learned a few tricks from the more seasoned inmates, and one of these was an ability to pick a door lock with a piece of stiff wire.

Well, there was a store room just off the kitchen where we worked, and to get anything from it, you had to notify a guard. He'd open the door with a key, then watch you like a hawk. Sam would have me get into a conversation with this guard; then, in a flash, he'd unlock that door and return with a couple of bottles of lemon extract stuffed in his shirt. We'd go back to the stockade and that evening have a party on the lemon extract. Of course, you cut it with water, but it was awful stuff to get drunk on. Sometimes, Sam would also retrieve several small steaks, and we'd broil these on top of the potbelly stove in the barracks.

Sam made my life tolerable in that God-awful place.

Lem Ford, Grand Woodsman

Another unforgettable character I met in the Allerey stockade was Lem Ford. Lem was a powerful, handsome lad from the backwoods of Kentucky, and he, too, was confined because he had gone to town without a pass and was caught by the MPs. Like most of the other fellows there similarly charged, he hadn't had a court-martial, not even a summary court-martial. That was against Army regulations! Anyway, Lem's duty was to keep our two large potbellied stoves going. He just had to chop wood and feed those stoves. That was a cushy job, but nobody was resentful of him, because Lem was such a good fellow, and nobody could handle an axe the way he could.

No one ever picked an argument with Lem Ford. He'd whet that axe blade as sharp as a razor, take the end of the axe handle between just his thumb and forefinger, hold it straight out from his body, turn the axe with the blade down until it reached his lips, then turn and raise it again. No one in the stockade could duplicate that feat, and you can understand why very few would even try.

Well, Lem and I became good buddies. One day, he abashedly confided in me:

"Red, Ah wants to make a confession. Ah never had no schoolin' and Ah cain't read ner write. Ah got a couple letters from mah Old Lady; would yew read them to me?"

The poor devil had carried these letters in his pocket for months and had been too ashamed to ask anyone to read them for him. They were the dearest letters. His "Old Lady," incidentally, was sixteen years old. They had been married when she was fourteen.

Lem told me about his mountain home in Kentucky, but I have forgotten the name of the nearest city. I wrote it in a little address book but lost the book before I got home. He had a couple of milk cows, some hogs, and a few sheep, and grew tobacco (his main cash crop) and vegetables for home

217

consumption. Lem also had a little still, and he was very cautious about it.

One day, Lem was sitting on his front porch overlooking the road that snaked up from the valley below, and with some apprehension, he saw the sheriff's car approaching. The sheriff greeted Lem, and after an exchange of pleasantries, said, "Lem, Ah'v got a little bad news fer yew."

"What's that, Sheriff?"

"Uncle Sam wants yew."

"Uncle Sam wants me? Yew know, Sheriff, Ah'v not run thet still fer six months."

"Oh, Lem, it ain't about thet old still of yourn. He wants yew to go fight them Germans."

Lem knew nothing about the war. He didn't read, so he had no newspapers or magazines. He didn't have a telephone or radio, and he seldom went to town, which was a good distance away. But there was a hamlet over the mountain called Germantown, which had been settled by a group of Germans before the Revolutionary War, and he thought those were the Germans the sheriff was referring to. So Lem said:

"Hell, Sheriff, Ah don't want to fight them Germans. They is good people. Ah'v got a lot of friens over there. Ah'm not goin' to fight them people. What's the matter with yew? Aire yew crazy?"

"Now, calm down, Lem. It ain't them people who live in Germantown. These Germans live across the ocean, over in Germany, an' they aire a fightin' us. They's a big war going on, Lem, an' Uncle Sam needs yew."

That's how Lem was drafted. He was given two days to pack, then had to leave his young wife behind. My God, the nearest neighbor was a couple of miles away, and here was this sixteen-year-old girl left to cope alone.

Lem had never been outside the state of Kentucky, or even on a train before, so the trip to the Army camp was very exciting. Then, after a month's training, "We got on to another big railroad train, me an' a lot of other soldiers, an' we came to New York to get on the ship to go overseas. We got out there at Pennsylvania Station. Yew know thet Pennsylvania Station?" I acknowledged as how I did.

"Well, Ah'm tellin yew, they's some railroad people. God!

they's some railroad people. Yew know, Ah seen the damndest thing in mah life in thet railroad people."

"What was that, Lem?"

"Ah seen a woman smoking a cigarette."

"Oh, you did?"

"Ah surely did! Ah surely did. Now, mah ol' lady smokes a pipe an' chews tobacco, but by God, if Ah ever seen her smoke a cigarette, Ah'd bust her right in the mouth!"

Another time, he said to me, "Red, the President of the United States is a Democrat, isn't he?"

"Yes, President Wilson is a Democrat."

"Yew know somethin' Ah cain't understain'? They call the United States a republic, don't they?"

"Yes."

"How come we got a republic an' we have a Democrat fer a president?"

Lem had been assigned to the 18th Infantry Regiment of the 1st Division. That's the same outfit we relieved at Exermont. Soon after he arrived in France, the Army realized that Lem was an expert shot and made him a sharpshooter. He had been wounded in both legs by machine gun fire at the Argonne and was lucky to have survived.

Soon after I had been discharged, a man appeared at our apartment in New York City, and our housekeeper, Mrs. Weitz, answered the door. Now, Mrs. Weitz was German born and spoke with a heavy German accent, which was very difficult to understand, especially by someone from the mountains of Kentucky. It was Lem Ford. I had given him my New York address, but none of the family was in at the time. Mrs. Weitz asked him to write a message for me, but of course, Lem couldn't write. She got his name, but I don't know whether she told him I would be home that evening, and if she did, whether he could understand her. When I came home that evening and discovered that Lem Ford had been there without hospitality from any of the family, I almost cried.

I never saw Lem again. I didn't know his address, except that he lived a few miles from Germantown, Kentucky. Every time I went to different veterans' reunions, I sought out fellows from Kentucky and asked them about Lem Ford, but now I'm unable to visit him and don't even know whether he is still alive.

John Hurley, VD Specialist

Another interesting person I met in the stockade was John Hurley from Buffalo, New York. John was a chief pharmacist mate in the Navy and was in charge of Navy corpsmen attached to the 6th Marine Regiment. The Marine Corps had Navy medics for corpsmen.

John had graduated from some school as a pharmacist and opened a little pharmacy in Buffalo, without the extraneous baggage that most drugstores carry having nothing to do with drugs. He kept his store open every evening until midnight, and as most of the other drugstores would close much earlier, he built up a very nice business.

John married a girl he had known in high school. He said that, at first, they were very happy; but he was late getting home at night and had to leave for work early in the morning. As time went on, she took up with someone else, and they were finally divorced. That broke John's heart. He sold his pharmacy, enlisted in the Navy and had served about ten years by the time we entered the war.

John was a specialist in the treatment of venereal diseases. There was a special ward at Allerey for VD patients, and John had been placed in charge. He was such a dedicated guy; but he, too, had gone to Chalons-sur-Saone without a pass, was caught and slammed into the stockade. However, the authorities let him continue his service in the ward because it was so valuable to the hospital.

One Sunday, while talking about his work, he invited me to visit his ward, assuring me that I would find it very interesting. So I spoke to Sam, and he let me have the day off from my demanding duties as "Assistant Butcher."

John Hurley took me over to the VD ward. Oh, my God, they had about eighty patients. I held a tray for him with all kinds of medication, needles, swabs, and what not, as he went from bed to bed giving treatment. It was sufficiently horrible to convince me to take every precaution against contracting venereal disease—except total abstinence. John

Hurley gave me valuable advice on that subject, for which I have always been most grateful.

Sam Yarborough, Buddy from Texas

Sam Yarborough was my best buddy in the stockade. I felt responsible for getting him in that jam in the first place, so we were always pretty close. He was a good-humored, long drink of water from Texas, and he got out when I did, because I had told Father Duffy and Colonel Donovan about his innocent role in the episode, and General MacArthur had included him in the orders directing our release.

After Sam arrived in the States, he, too, came to visit, and again, I wasn't home. But my mother was, and she fixed a lunch for him and entertained him. Unfortunately, Sam had to catch a train that night back to Texas, so he couldn't wait for my return. My mother liked him very much—"Such a fine young man, and a perfect gentleman," she said. Sergeant Major McCullough and Colonel Forbes might be the only two persons in the world who would disagree.

MacArthur to the Rescue

Almost one month to the day after I passed those two letters on to the sergeant of engineers, Yarborough, Gallagher, and I heard our names shouted by one of the guards, and two MPs promptly escorted us to the hospital HQ building. There we discovered that Colonel Forbes had been returned to the States, and we reported to a major who was now in command. Orders had come through from General MacArthur for our immediate release and return to our regiments, with funds for food and transportation. This major was concerned because he had been unable to locate our files. Consequently, he had sent MPs throughout the several barracks of the stockade to locate us, and he was greatly relieved when they succeeded.[10]

221

RECONNAISSANCE NO. 10

Recipients of the Congressional Medal of Honor
Rainbow Division—World War I

July 28, 1918
Sidney E. Manning
Corporal, 167th U.S. Infantry, 4th Alabama

"When his platoon commander and platoon sergeant had both become casualties, soon after the beginning of an assault on strongly fortified heights overlooking the Ourcq River, Corporal Manning took command of his platoon . . . Though himself severely wounded, he led forward the 35 men remaining in the platoon and finally succeeded in gaining a foothold on the enemy's position, during which time he received more wounds, and all but seven of his men had fallen. Directing the consolidation of the position, he held off a large body of the enemy only 50 yards away by fire from his automatic rifle. He declined to take cover until the line had been entirely consolidated with the line of the platoon on the flank, when he dragged himself to shelter, suffering from nine wounds in all parts of the body."

July 28, 1918
Richard W. O'Neill
Sergeant, 165th U.S. Infantry, 69th New York

"In advance of an assaulting line, he attacked a detachment of about 25 of the enemy. In the ensuing hand-to-hand encounter, he sustained pistol wounds but heroically continued in the advance, during which he received additional wounds; but, with great physical effort, he remained in active command of his detachment. Being again wounded, he was forced by weakness and loss of blood to be evacuated, but insisted upon being taken first to the battalion commander in order to transmit to him valuable information relative to enemy positions and the disposition of our men."

October 14, 1918
Michael Donaldson
Sergeant, 165th U.S. Infantry, 69th New York

"The advance of his regiment having been checked by intense machine gun fire of the enemy, who were entrenched on the crest of a hill before Landres-St. Georges, his Company retired to a sunken road to reorganize their position, leaving several of their number wounded near the enemy lines. Of his own volition, in broad daylight and under direct observation of the enemy and with utter disregard for his own safety, he advanced to the crest of the hill, rescued one of his wounded comrades, and returned under withering fire to his own lines, repeating his splendidly heroic act until he had brought in all the men, six in number."

October 15, 1918
William J. Donovan
Colonel, 165th U.S. Infantry, 69th New York

"Colonel Donovan personally led the assaulting wave in an attack upon a very strongly organized position, and when our troops were suffering heavy casualties he encouraged all near him by his example, moving among his men in exposed positions, reorganizing decimated platoons, and accompanying them forward in attacks. When he was wounded in the leg by a machine gun bullet, he refused to be evacuated and continued with his unit until it withdrew to a less exposed position."[1]

October 16, 1918
Thomas O. Neibaur
Private, 167th U.S. Infantry, 4th Alabama

"On the afternoon of October 16, 1918, when the Cote de Chatillon had just been gained after bitter fighting and the summit of that strong bulwark in the Kriemhilde Stellung was being organized, Private Neibaur was sent out on patrol with his automatic rifle squad to enfilade enemy machine gun nests. As he gained the ridge he set up his automatic rifle and was directly thereafter wounded in both legs . . . The advance wave of the enemy troops, counter-attacking, had about gained the ridge, and although practically cut off and surrounded, the remainder of his detachment being killed or wounded, this gallant soldier kept his automatic rifle in operation to such effect that by his own efforts and by fire from the skirmish line of his company, at least 100 yards in the rear, the attack was checked. The enemy wave being halted and lying prone, four of the enemy attacked Private Neibaur at close quarters. These he killed. He then moved alone among the enemy lying on the ground about him, in the midst of fire from his own line, and by coolness and gallantry captured 11 prisoners at the point of his pistol and, although painfully wounded, brought them back to our lines. The counterattack in full force was arrested, to a large extent by the single efforts of this soldier, whose heroic exploits took place against the sky line in full view of his entire battalion."

10

Homeward Bound

★ ★ ★

They shall not grow old,
as we that are left grow old;
Age shall not weary them,
nor the years condemn.
At the going down of the sun
and in the morning
We will remember them.

—Lawrence Binyon,
"For the Fallen"

April had just turned the corner when Gallagher, Yarborough, and I left the Allerey Hospital Complex en route to Brest by way of a replacement camp outside Paris. Before departure, we each received transportation vouchers and seventy-five francs for rations.

For two days, the train huffed and puffed to the replacement center, where we were given a physical examination and deloused—in spite of our protest that we had just arrived from a hospital. Then, having been issued a complete change of clothing, Gallagher and I, along with three other fellows from the 69th, who had arrived from different hospitals, entrained to Brest, with me in charge. Sam Yarborough had to remain behind until they tracked down the itinerary of the 1st Division. It's always hard to leave a buddy whom you have shared so much with, but Sam and I pledged to get together stateside at the first opportunity.

From the railroad station at Brest, we had to hike seven

miles, mostly up a long hill, to Camp Pontanezen, a large rest and relocation center, under the jurisdiction of the Marine Corps, for men embarking at Brest. It was a beautiful warm spring day, but that hill was murder, and by the time we got to the camp, we were pooped.

I went into HQ office and presented our orders to a Marine Corps sergeant major sitting behind a desk. He looked at them, then pronounced in some bewilderment:

"The 165th isn't here."

"I don't know about that," I replied. "All I know is that we have orders to rejoin them here."

He then went into another office and soon returned with good news:

"They ought to be here in a couple of days. You wait outside until I figure out what the hell to do with you guys."

General Smedley Butler Expedites Billet

Outside HQ office was a magnificent lawn, absolutely beautiful—in fact, the only lawn I ever saw in France. I told the guys we had to wait until called, so we unlimbered our packs, lay down on the lawn using them as pillows, and lit up cigarettes. Soon I was sound asleep.

The next thing I knew somebody was booting me.

"GET UP! STAND AT ATTENTION!" the guy was shouting.

Furious, I replied, "Take your foot off me, you son of a bitch, or I'll . . ." Before concluding this threat, I opened my eyes, and there, towering above me, was a huge, scowling, bad-assed Marine sergeant, and standing beside him was a little guy with a star on each shoulder. Jesus! It was like awakening to a nightmare.

I jumped to my feet and saluted. The officer turned out to be General Smedley Butler, Marine Corps commandant of the area.[2]

"Soldier, what seems to be the problem here?" he barked.

"Sir, we have orders to report to meet our regiment, the 165th Infantry. We've just been discharged from base hospitals."

"The 165th hasn't arrived yet. Where are your orders?"

"I gave them to the sergeant major inside, and he told us to wait out here."

"We'll see about that. You come with me, son."

Now, General Butler was only about five-foot-five, but he was a tough, fiery, fighting man through and through. He went in and bawled the hell out of the sergeant major:

"Didn't you receive the travel orders for these men?"

"Yes, Sir; we're getting to it."

"God damn it! Get to it right now! Don't you know these men are just out of a hospital and exhausted from travel? Find them quarters and get them something to eat. Take care of these men right away!"

Holy God! I wonder what he would have said had he known I'd just been released from a stockade. The sergeant major immediately collared another sergeant, who found us quarters in the Marine Corps barracks, then took us to the mess hall, where the cook fried us some small steaks. It was so great just to be able to eat, sleep, and loaf around.

Two days later, the regiment arrived, and I reported to headquarters. Oh, what a reception we got. Wonderful! From Colonel Donovan, Father Duffy, Tom FitzSimmons, and all the fellows. Father Duffy put his arms around me, and I started to blubber like a baby. He knew exactly what to do.

"All right, Albert, forget what has happened, just forget it. Repeat after me: 'TO HELL WITH THEM ALL!'"

"To hell with them all!"

"Fine! That's the spirit. Say it again louder: 'TO HELL WITH THEM ALL!'" So I did. "Good boy! Now, just forget it."[3]

Of course, I never did forget those days in the Allerey stockade, but I felt a lot better about them from then on.

Third Reunion with Brother Bill

I rejoined the mortar platoon, and the next day—I think it was a Sunday—we all looked forward to sleeping the entire morning in the large squad tents that had been assigned to us. At daybreak, there was a racket outside and a repeated pounding that had the tent shaking. I was sleeping next to the entrance, and my tent-mates started to curse the noise, so I got up, stuck my head out of the tent and shouted: "Hey, keep that damn noise down, will you? We're trying to sleep in here!" I saw a guy with a sledge hammer and looked up . . . right into the eyes of my brother Bill. There he was as big as life! We embraced and shouted for joy, and the other fellows came out to congratulate our good fortune in both having made it through the war.

Bill had been assigned to a detail to secure the guy lines and stakes of all the tents in the area. I immediately took him to meet Father Duffy, and then we each wrangled a 24-hour pass to go to Brest. That was no problem because neither of our outfits was due to leave for several days.

We spruced up, hitched a ride to Brest, and put up at a first-class hotel. I was broke, hadn't been paid in months, but Bill was flush, so we took in the sights, had a fantastic dinner; then, instead of doing the town, we took a bottle of cognac to our hotel room and talked the night away. For the first time, I learned about his two *Croix de Guerre*.

One time, up in the Champagne area, the French battalion he was assigned to occupied an old chalk mine. The enemy launched a surprise attack and overwhelmed their position, and there were several hundred men trapped in this mine, including Bill and his medic buddy. The Germans posted machine guns at the entrance and called upon them to surrender. After long pourparler, the French major in command decided to surrender. Bill wouldn't have anything to do with that. After a desperate search, he and his buddy found an exit out of the mine that wasn't covered, and they got out unnoticed. Still, German troops were between them and their own lines.

They started running toward their line and, lo-and-behold, came across one of their own ambulances. There in the front seat sat the driver, Dolan, one of Bill's buddies, with his head almost blown off, and the ambulance was filled with wounded. Bill jumped in and took the wheel. Having only stalled when Dolan was killed, the engine started, and Bill managed to get through the German lines and deliver his wounded to a hospital. That was the occasion of his first award of the French *Croix de Guerre*.[4]

He received it the second time for another act of daring during the Second Battle of the Marne, when his was the last ambulance to evacuate a city with fourteen wounded men in the teeth of a German attack.

He was some brother Bill! He thought I had experienced more combat than he, because I was in the infantry. Yet, he had been under enemy fire as much as I and had to drive over shell-interdicted roads and fields, a nice big target with nothing to defend himself but that red cross.

Now, Germans in World War I would not intentionally target in on an ambulance (ethics counted for more in those days), but neither would they cease fire if there was any other traffic around, and ambulances with the French Army would go right into the midst of a battle.

We returned to Camp Pontanezen the following morning, and Bill's unit pulled out two days later.

Donovan's Last Charge

In mid-April, the day after Bill's departure, our regiment massed in formation, and in line of march, with Co. A in the lead, left Camp Pontanezen for the dockside at Brest. We had proceeded a couple of miles down the long hill toward the outskirts of the city when a captain of MPs, with about a dozen of his men, blocked the road and commanded us to halt. As he did so, several of the MPs, their faces bruised and sporting black eyes, began to walk down the long column, peering intently at our troops as they passed.

Colonel Donovan, who was in the lead as usual, asked the captain what it was all about.

"Colonel," declared the captain, "some of your men were in town last night and ganged up on my MPs and stole their truck and escaped. I demand that they be apprehended and placed into my custody."

"Do you know who they are?" asked Colonel Donovan.

"No, sir."

Donovan was incredulous. "Do you really expect me to conduct an inquiry among an entire regiment stalled on this highway? We have to board ships at Brest this evening."

"I can't help that," replied the captain. "These men think

they can do any damn thing they like, but they can't beat up my MPs and get away with it!"

"Captain," said Donovan, exasperated, "I am ordering you to stand aside."

The silly captain refused to move, although you had to give him credit for guts. Then Donovan wheeled and shouted:

"COMPANY A ... FIRST PLATOON ... ATTENTION!"

"FIX BAYONETS!"

"AS SKIRMISHERS ... FORWARD MARCH!"

And forty-eight Irishmen with bayonets started bouncing down that highway with a gleam in their eye. Of course, the MPs scattered, and we continued our march to the dockside. That was Colonel Donovan for you.[5]

Eleven Months Without Pay

They had a crazy pay system in the Army. The paymaster would come around during the month—you never knew when—and you had to sign the payroll. Then he'd return several days later to pay you off, but you had to have signed the payroll on his previous visit. For one reason or another, I always happened to be absent on one of the two days, either off on the motorcycle or in a hospital. The day I stepped aboard the S.S. *Harrisburg,* I received eleven months' back pay, plus this and that, which came to $400. I was surprised they had my records straight, but soon after boarding the ship, I was ordered to the paymaster's office, and a Navy Paymaster paid me off in 80 five-dollar bills! Never before had I seen such a stack of bills.

There was a regular post exchange on that boat, and first off, I bought a five-pound box of chocolate, which Don Adair and I ate while hiding behind a lifeboat. Then I bought a hat for my mother—supposedly the latest Paris model—and a wallet for my father.

I came home with over three hundred dollars. Some of the men arrived broke because a nonstop crap game was organized immediately upon boarding ship. After several attempts to get me involved, I finally took out fifty dollars and decided that win, lose, or draw, that would be the extent of my investment. As it happened, I was down forty dollars by the time we entered New York harbor.

Catch-up on the Regiment in Remagen

During a joyous two-week voyage across the Atlantic, I was able to catch up on the exploits of my HQ buddies since leaving them in the Argonne.

Fortunately, all those I had been close to had survived the race to Sedan, but during the very last days of the war, patrols from the 3rd Battalion took fairly heavy casualties—over two dozen men—while scouting the approaches to Sedan. Then the regiment got orders to stand down and permit a French division on our left to occupy the city. In a nice gesture of comradeship, the French invited a company from both our regiment and the Ohios to enter Sedan with them. Unfortunately, orders to our fellows got mixed up, so a patrol from Company D of the Ohios were the first American troops to enter Sedan.

While I was fully engaged in the "Battle of Allerey," HQ Company was having a ball in Remagen, Germany. Remagen, I was informed, is a small, beautiful city on the Rhine River, where the whole regiment was billeted for three and a half months.

After the Armistice, the troops had no difficulty arriving there. Hospitality was offered in each village through which they passed. Everyone seemed to be delighted that the war was over; and anti-fraternization orders had to be issued, because it was difficult to be formal and correct conquerors when confronted by smiling children and frauleins. The men even enjoyed swapping lies with German veterans who still wore their uniforms, not having anything else to wear.

The most striking remembrance of the men was their first setting foot on German soil. They crossed a bridge over the Sauer River into Germany, and as they marched down this river road with the band playing "Garry Owen," a beautiful rainbow formed in the sky ahead of them. Whenever we saw a rainbow, particularly before or during a battle, it gave a tremendous boost to our spirits.

Let's face it. We are still superstitious, and good fortune associated with a rainbow is a magnificent superstition because it is so beautiful. Of course, being the Rainbow Division, that vision of beauty had even greater impact. It was part of MacArthur's genius to have so named the division that we love so dearly.

McMorrow and the Boar Hunt

After our troops had settled in, about twelve men of the pioneer platoon contacted the local forest warden to organize a wild-boar hunt. The game warden assembled the men in a field facing a wooded area in a semicircle so they wouldn't shoot each other if a boar did appear. In the meantime, he and his assistants went back in the woods to drive out a boar. Sure enough, a wild boar emerged from the woods across a field and stood there, motionless, looking at John McMorrow, who was his closest adversary.

The fellows shouted: "SHOOT HIM, JOHN. SHOOT! SHOOT!" But John couldn't bring himself to do it, and he and the boar just stood there looking at each other. Then John called out: "Here, piggy! Here, piggy, piggy, piggy!" The boar trotted up to within fifty feet of John, who never even raised his rifle. Finally, John bent over, as though he were calling a dog, and repeated: "Here, piggy, piggy, piggy!" Suddenly, the boar charged and knocked John head over heels. John only fired his rifle in mid-air, and then by accident. The other fellows were laughing so hard they didn't shoot either. Then they heard John call for help and became aware of what it was like to be gored by a wild boar.

That boar's tusks had ripped a sizeable hole in John's thigh! The men carried him to the game warden's cottage, where the warden's wife administered first aid; then they took him to the medics. John recovered all right, but from then on, the guys always said that the reason the boar was attracted to John was because some of its family used to live in his kitchen back in Ireland.

Murry Murchison, Paul LeClair and Jimmy McKic

Murry Murchison had been an All-American fullback before the war, but he was a 250-pound bully as a first

sergeant, and the men despised him. It had taken Big Jim
Collintine to call his bluff on the march to Longeau. For
some crazy reason, the Army sent him to officer candidate
school in France before we went into the trenches. He never
saw any combat with us, but after the troops arrived in
Germany, he reappeared as a second lieutenant. Then he
started strutting around as he had as a first sergeant, and
again he had trouble with the men. ["Murry Murchison" is
a pseudonym.]

Now, there were two fellows from the pioneer platoon
who were particularly tough hombres. One was Paul
LeClair, a longshoreman from Brooklyn, and the other was
Jimmy McKic, our ex-Marine. Both weighed in at about 165
pounds of solid muscle. When Lieutenant Quirt pushed
Paul LeClair that night on the lines of the Rouge Bouquet,
he was lucky that Paul only told him off.

LeClair and McKic were the strangest buddies I ever
knew. When sober, they were pals, but when drunk, they
used to beat each other up. Almost every payday they'd get a
load on, get into an argument, and fight like hell. God, they
had some awful fights. They never fought or bothered
anyone else, and of course, nobody in their right mind ever
bothered them. The morning after payday, you'd see them
both, faces bruised, eyes blackened, just as friendly with
each other as you please. They also got along with everyone
in the outfit, with one exception. Surprisingly, it wasn't
Quirt. I guess they figured they had to live with Quirt as
their platoon commander. Either that, or he was just
beneath their dignity. Their common enemy was Murry
Murchison, whom they hated with a passion.

One day in Remagen, Murchison gave LeClair an order to
do something crazy, and LeClair told him to fuck himself.
Murchison threatened LeClair with court-martial. That
night, McKic and LeClair got pissed but instead of beating
each other to a pulp, they decided it would be more
enjoyable to pound on Murchison, so they ambled over to
his billet, stood under his window, and challenged him to
come out and fight like a man. Then, in a spirit of rare
self-restraint and good sportsmanship, they promised he
only had to fight one of them at a time. Murchison was wise

enough to decline the invitation, but it must have scared the hell out of him, because he never brought charges against either of them.

When the story got around, the other men were tickled to death. As far as they were concerned, it demonstrated that Murchison had a yellow streak, because he was twice the size of either LeClair or McKic.

Don Adair and the Affluent Trio

Soon after he arrived in Remagen, canny Don Adair managed to wrangle a three-week pass to visit the Cote d'Azure of southern France. Moreover, he arranged this trip to heaven with the three more affluent men in Headquarters Company—Ward, Read, and Blake.

Vanderbilt Ward, Bill Read, and Joe Blake were the craziest trio in the Company. All were from wealthy families who kept them well supplied with cash throughout the war, so much so that they used to lend money to some of the lower ranking officers. Consequently, they often received privileges ordinarily denied enlisted men, especially passes to wherever they wished to visit in France. Of course, this was not during combat, and no one resented these favors because these three were so full of fun and were equally disposed to lending money to enlisted men—which was rarely repaid.

In spite of his affluence, Joe Blake was the damndest-looking soldier you ever saw. His uniform coat was always too large and draped over his frame as if it had been donated by some benevolent giant, and his wraparound leggings were so sloppy they gave the appearance of imminent collapse. There may be a moral in this for persons of wealth who wish to retain the good will of their less fortunate companions.

In any case, Don Adair had perfect companions for exploring the fleshpots of Cannes, Nice, and Monte Carlo. According to Don, they had a ball. None of them particularly cared for gambling, but all enjoyed the company of beautiful women who were not averse to sharing their generosity.

There developed but one problem. When it came time to

return to Remagen, all were flat broke. They couldn't afford rail transportation, and they didn't have time to hitchhike.

On the morning of Armageddon, with AWOL staring them in the face, they were pondering their fate on the main boulevard of Monte Carlo, when who strolled by but John Mangan, now a major. Nothing to do, he loaned them the necessary funds for railroad fare and saved their collective behinds.

Jim Collintine's Boat

Now there was nothing special about the *Harrisburg* as a troop transport other than the fact that it was going in the right direction, but to listen to Jim Collintine, you would think it was the grandest vessel afloat. Indeed, as with the cabbage patch in Essey, this was "his" boat, "th' sweetist vissil that iver ploughed th' sivin seas." It turned out that Jim had shoveled coal on the *Harrisburg* when, before the war, she was called the *City of Paris.*

During the early stage of the voyage, many of the men became seasick, and it was a riot to see Big Jim stroll the deck, clap his arm around the shoulder of a green-faced doughboy, and offer reassurance:

"Now me lad, don't woory about a ting. Dis woise ould *City av Paris* won't let ye down. Here, take a chew av this tobacco, an it'll sittle yer stomach."

When the captain of the *Harrisburg* heard about Jim's former affiliation with the vessel, he had Collintine up on the bridge and introduced him to the ship's officers. Jim was in seventh heaven. I suspect those two weeks were the happiest in the old man's entire life, and Big Jim Collintine deserved all the happiness that anyone could bestow, because he was one of the grandest men I ever knew.

Victory March and Discharge

Although brother Bill's boat had departed Brest twenty-four hours before ours, it arrived in New York a day later because of a wicked storm. After we docked on April 21, 1919, our outfit was transported to Camp Upton at Yaphank on Long Island, while Bill had to report to some camp in

Pennsylvania.[6] Nonetheless, we both got leave the same day and arrived home within a few hours of each other. Mom was so happy, she cried almost constantly, and we had the grandest family reunion, and oh! what a feast. We both had to return to our respective camps, but within a few days we were discharged.

In the interval, the City gave the regiment a great welcome-home celebration, and we paraded in full battle-dress from the Washington Arch in Greenwich Village up Fifth Avenue to 110th Street. Colonel Donovan it was who determined that we would wear our steel helmets—"They'll never forget you in those helmets," he said—and he led the van marching on foot, as usual; no silly horse for him.

Hundreds of thousands of cheering spectators lined the avenue, and the roar of welcome was so great you couldn't hear the band—and that was most unusual, because what our band lacked in precision, it made up for in volume and spirit.

I didn't think much about the dignitaries, but our wounded and disabled were something else. Many were there in the reviewing stand, and tears streamed down our cheeks as we honored them in passing:

"EYES RIGHT!"

We dipped the regimental colors and company flags in salute. It was a sad but wonderful feeling. They, and the hundreds we had left behind under the soil of France, were our truest and dearest brothers, and their memory will live until the last of us has passed over the rainbow.

Epilogue

★ ★ ★

From quiet homes and first beginning
Out to the undiscovered ends,
There's nothing worth the wear of winning
But laughter and the love of friends.

—Hilaire Belloc, "Dedicatory Ode."

But what when love was poisoned by the
Brute,
And laughter trampled in the mire?
Sacrifice has been my friends' route
To, wearingly, rekindle freedom's fire.

—A. C. Ettinger

Billy James

Billy James was severely crippled from that shell burst during the Champagne Defensive, and after the war, he spent two years at Fox Hills, a veterans hospital on Staten Island. We were dear pals, and I used to visit him there frequently. Then, after his release, he often stayed with our family in New Jersey until he felt fully confident in going out on his own.

Billy had been quite a golfer before the war. His parents lived near Van Courtland Park, which had a public golf course. After the war, Billy would go there often, trying to swing a golf club. He couldn't do it at first; indeed, he could

237

hardly walk; his knee was so stiff he had to use crutches. Within a year, however, he had worked the stiffness out of both his arm and his leg. One would never guess by watching him that his knee had suffered such terrible damage, although he walked with a slight limp for the rest of his life.

Between jobs, we vacationed together at Redbank, New Jersey, where we made a few hundred dollars rebuilding a couple of boats. We also toured throughout the Northeast with my brother Bill in Dad's Pathfinder automobile. Oh, we had such great times together. We kept in touch until Billy passed away a few years ago.

Tom FitzSimmons

After the war, Tom FitzSimmons went back to law school, graduated, and developed a fine practice. The Ballentine Brewery was but one of his large corporate clients, and he was an attorney for the Bishop of Newark. Tom was also a prominent Democrat and a colonel in the New Jersey National Guard. With these connections, he was appointed a receiver and a guardian of several estates.

In 1930, the skies fell in. Tom had been appointed guardian of a trust fund from a wealthy woman to help stray dogs, and this fund consisted of several hundred thousand dollars in bonds and securities of excellent value. So Tom set up this "Home for Homeless Dogs." Unfortunately, he fell for the line of an investment counselor who touted stock that would double in value in a few months, and he foolishly sold some good securities from the homeless dog trust fund to buy this stock.

Now, it's illegal for the executor of a trust to use its assets for purposes of speculation. The examiners found out about it, and Tom was charged with misapplication of funds and brought to trial. Well, Tom was so prominent a Democrat that he was often mentioned as a candidate for governor of New Jersey in the forthcoming election, and the judge he went before was a staunch Republican. That may have had something to do with Tom's sentence: ten years in state prison.

At Trenton, Tom was a model prisoner, and after seven years, he was paroled, although while in jail, his wife divorced him, which didn't help matters. I wrote to him but never got a reply, and he later told me that he was just too ashamed to keep in touch with old friends.

Upon release, Tom went to Bill Donovan, who was then organizing the Office of Strategic Services, and applied for a position. He said that Donovan led him to believe that he would find a slot for him, but nothing came of it. I don't think the reason had anything to do with Tom's prison record per se. The prison experience had wreaked havoc with his self-confidence (he had acquired a habit of constant talking), and Tom was simply not up to emotionally demanding or security-sensitive work at that point.

J. Peter Grace, a great philanthropist, who was especially considerate of former prisoners, hired Tom as a bookkeeper in one of his Maine lumber camps. After a few years, Grace had him transferred to the legal department of the American Can Company, and eventually, Tom headed the labor-relations office for the Davison Chemical Company, which had large holdings in Florida phosphate.[1]

When I heard that Tom was living in Bartow, Florida, which is only a hundred miles from my home, I wrote to him again, and at least quarterly, Tom spent several days with us in Sarasota, until he died of a heart attack in 1970.

My wife, Ardel, and I attended his funeral services in Bartow. The funeral parlor was jammed with workers from the plant, most of them native Floridians. It was obvious that Tom had been as popular with the workers of Bartow as he had with the men of his mortar platoon. It was a bittersweet ending for a beautiful person and a genuine hero.

Rubin Bernstein

After the war, Rubin Bernstein joined the New York City Police Department and became a skilled motorcyclist; so much so, he organized a special unit that entertained with trick riding at affairs like the Sugar Bowl and the Rose Bowl.

One day, there was a bank robbery in the Bronx. Bernie was on Moshulu Parkway, and a car came by at terrific speed. The alarm had gone out, and Bernie knew it might be the holdup men, so he took off after them. As he pulled alongside, they swerved and knocked him off the shoulder into a ditch, but not before he managed to shoot the driver of the car. The crash broke his leg, messed up his back, and damn near killed him. Meanwhile, the car went off the road and was soon surrounded by the police.

Bernie was given a physical disability discharge from the police force, and he and his wife moved to Miami. Since his son-in-law was an expert baker from Switzerland, Bernie bought a bakery and developed it into one of the largest in Miami, serving the most famous hotels in the area. Our wives were as fond of each other as we were, and we visited each other at least once a year. Then Bernie's wife died, which was quite a blow, but we continued to visit until he passed away in 1979.

Herman Bootz

The first time I met Bootz after the war was at a Rainbow Division reunion in Washington, about 1925. Billy James and I were standing at the bar of the hotel's taproom when someone shouted: "HEY RED! RED!" At first, I didn't recognize them in civilian clothes, but there were Lieutenant Colonel George Mitchell and Colonel Bootz sitting at a table. (Colonel Mitchell had been at Headquarters with Colonel Barker when I first reported to drive the motorcycle. He was our lieutenant colonel through most of the war, was in command at the Argonne, and was an excellent officer.)

Colonel Mitchell called me over and asked Bootz if he knew me. Bootz said, "Sure, I know that red-headed kid, the one on the motorcycle; he drives like the devil." Anyway, old Colonel Mitchell invited Billy James and me to share their table, and he and Bootz reminisced about the war.

I didn't see Papa Bootz again until the Rainbow met in Baltimore back in the 50s. He had just retired from the Army and invited a group of us to his room. There, we drank his good whiskey, while he regaled us with tales of his experiences in the war and the Cavalry. We sat there, hypnotized.

I next met Bootz at a Rainbow veterans' reunion in Miami. He had moved to Pompano Beach and immediately joined the Rainbow chapter in Miami. We became close friends and exchanged numerous visits until Herman passed over the rainbow a few years ago.

James Collintine

Poor devil. The dearest man I knew in France had such a tragic end. He came home without a scratch and was in a veterans domicile in Bath, New York. One payday he went to town in the evening and evidently got tipsy. On his way home, he was waylaid, stabbed in the back, and robbed by some cowardly bastard. They found his body in the road the next morning. It was a sad passing for such a good man as James Collintine.

Father Duffy

Shortly after the regiment's return from France, Father Duffy was appointed pastor of Holy Cross Church in Manhattan. Holy Cross is in Hell's Kitchen, near the center of the theater district, and many actors and actresses attended mass there. They all loved Duffy because he understood theatrical people and their problems.

Father Duffy died in 1932 from colitis and infection of the liver. An attendant problem was eczema. Uncle Tom Churchill, a close friend of Father Duffy, often visited him in the hospital. I shall never forget his telling me about one of those visits. He asked Father Duffy how he was getting along, and Duffy cracked: "Tom, I'd be fine if it weren't for this son of a bitch of an itch."

We erected a statue to Father Duffy, most of the donations coming from members of the old 69th; but many men of the Rainbow from all over the country also contributed. The statue is an excellent likeness of this great man and stands at the intersection of 7th Avenue and Broadway, two blocks above Times Square. The little plot of ground that supports the pedestal is dignified as *Father Duffy Square,* and every year, representatives of the 69th veterans held services there. They also went out to St. Raymond's Cemetery in the Bronx and conducted services at his grave site. His memory is very dear to all who knew him. Very, very dear.[2]

John J. McMorrow

One afternoon, on the way back to his office at the Board of Education, my father noticed a man peering at the names on the office doors. Asking this person if he sought anyone in particular, the man replied in a rich Irish brogue that he was looking for Albert Ettinger. Pop was dumbfounded. "Well," he explained, "Albert is not here, but I'm his father." "Oh, indeed you are," said this fellow, and he introduced himself as John J. McMorrow, a close buddy of "Albert." (John had never before called me Albert, only "Red.")

My father was thrilled. He invited John into his office and sat him down, whereupon McMorrow proceeded to tell the grandest lies. He told Pop that I was the bravest man he ever knew. Then . . . "He saved me life wan time. He dashed trew shot an' shell, an' dragged me out av a dangerthus pothison. Oi was wounded an' couldn't move, but Albert carried me back t' whir th' medics were."

That was a wonderful lie; it never happened, but of course, Pop didn't know.

My father told John that I was working in New Jersey and asked him how he was getting along. McMorrow avowed, "Well, Sor, hard time has been upon me, an' Oi can foind no work." Pop interrupted: "Just wait a minute now. What have you done in civilian life?" "Well, Sor," John replied, "Oi work on th' railroad, an' Oi was a stoker on a stheemship."

That's all Pop needed. He called the head custodian of the Board of Education and asked him if he had an opening for a fireman in one of the larger school buildings. As it happened, there was such an opening, and Pop got McMorrow a job as a fireman at pretty good pay for those days.

Pop kept him on the job, even though several times John went on a drunk and wouldn't show up for a day or two. The custodian of the school where he worked complained, but Pop pleaded with him to try to straighten John out, so he could continue to hold his job.

One payday, John went off and never returned. That was the last that we heard about John J. McMorrow. I've often wondered what happened to the dear scoundrel.

Tom O'Kelly

After the war, Tom O'Kelly opened a saloon on 34th Street, between 8th and 9th avenues, only a few doors from my office at 461 8th Avenue, and I'd stop by occasionally after work to share a drink with him. Tom was a delightful Irishman, with a beautiful command of the English language. He was a graduate of the University of Dublin, and the graduates of that university speak the most beautiful English of any group in the world. It was sheer pleasure to listen to him, even though his voice was slightly hoarse from the gas, and poor Tom, who had been a tenor with the Chicago Opera Company before the war, was never able to sing again.

Red Casey

Speaking of Tom O'Kelly reminds me of another veteran who became a bar manager. Let's just call him "Red Casey."

Red was manager of a famous night club in New York called the Pre Catalan, a favorite rendezvous for alumni and football fans of Harvard University. It was a very nice place, dignified by being called a "cabaret," rather than a bar, a cafe, or even a nightclub. The food was excellent, the entertainment was good, and after-hours it was a favorite rendezvous for show girls from the Broadway theaters. Indeed, I almost married Veronica La Hiff, a beautiful, vivacious show girl whom I met at the Pre Catalan. She later became a famous movie actress under the nom de plume, Nancy Carrol—but that's another story.

After the war, many of our veterans used the Pre Catalan as a hangout, and for about a year, all was well. Then we got stuck with prohibition in 1920, and revenue agents closed it down, along with most of the other cafes in the city.

Shortly after this disaster, I got word that Red Casey was running a speakeasy in the East 50's, so I went over there one evening, and he greeted me warmly. The clientele was mostly theatrical people. It was very pleasant, and I was a steady patron until it, too, was closed down.

Red then moved his business to the basement taproom of the Markwell Hotel on 47th Street, just off Broadway, and I'd often stop by, especially after attending an event at Madison Square Garden.

During prohibition, every establishment had contacts with one or another bootlegger to keep supplied with liquor. Bars had been outlawed, and you were not supposed to be able to buy alcohol over the counter. Customarily, you brought your own hootch to a favorite restaurant, and they would sell whatever you desired in the way of a mixer; and indeed, unless the proprietor knew you, that's the way it worked. If he knew you, or if you could be vouched for by another patron, and if there weren't any suspicious-looking strangers around (who might be Treasury agents), he would serve you bootlegged liquor, and believe me, some of it was really terrible. Even then, that was supposed to be a private drink on the house, later to be recompensed by means of a "tip" carefully calculated in advance.

Now, Red's bootlegger was the famous, or I should say infamous, Lucky Luciano, who, at that time, was involved in a gang war with another bootlegger, Dutch Schultz.

One night, about one o'clock in the morning, I walked over to the Markwell from Madison Square Garden. Much to my surprise, when I walked in, the only persons there were Red Casey behind the bar and three hard-looking guys drinking at a table. Usually, there would be a waitress on duty as well as another bartender. Moreover, Red wasn't the least bit hospitable this evening, and he seemed rather nervous. He told me that he had to close up early and that I'd only have time for one drink. Foolishly, I insisted on another drink, and the next thing I remember was being unloaded from a taxi at our apartment, sick as a dog. That jasper had slipped me a mickey finn.

The next morning, there was a front-page story about some gangsters, who had entered the taproom of the Markwell Hotel and killed three members of the Dutch Schultz gang sitting at a table. Well, I didn't see Red Casey again for a long time, but I later found out that he was a member of the Luciano gang, and his job was to organize the different speakeasies that the gang controlled in Manhattan.

In other words, Red knew that killing was in the works, and he probably saved my life by getting me out of that bar when he did. I don't remember whatever did happen to Red Casey.

Joe Blake and Jack Ryan

You may recall my account of the "affluent trio"—Ward, Read, and Blake—and my meeting with our former 1st sergeant, Jack Ryan, in the Argonne. Well, a couple of months after the war, Leonard Beck organized the Joyce Kilmer chapter of the American Legion for the members of Headquarters Company, and we met at the Pre Catalan.

At our very first organization meeting, someone asked, "Did Jack Ryan know about this?" Another commented, "We definitely have to send him a notice." We all knew Jack worked on the police force, and Joe Blake inquired as to the location of his beat. I had run into Jack only a few days before, so was able to tell Joe that our friend's beat was on Second Avenue between 32nd and 28th streets. Damned if Joe didn't immediately hop into his car, track Jack down, and drag him to the meeting—in spite of the fact that Jack was still on duty!

Of course, we had a grand reunion, and everyone got plastered. As the party broke up, Joe grabbed Jack by the arm, then turned to me and insisted: "Come on. You and Jack are going to stay over with me tonight. You've got too damn far to go." (I lived in the upper Bronx at the time.) So we started out in Joe's car with Jack in full uniform, standing on the running board, vigorously blowing his whistle to clear traffic.

We went way over to West 58th Street, where Joe kept his car garaged. As we got out of the car, Jack complained, "Those lights (the garage lights) bother me," whereupon he unholstered his revolver and shot out a half-dozen light bulbs. Considering Jack's condition, that was damn good shooting, but he not only frightened us, he scared the hell out of the garage man, who threatened to call the police. "I am the police, you numbskull," declared Jack. "Don't you recognize this uniform?" "You're drunk as a skunk," mumbled the attendant," and he scooted off like a rabbit, no doubt fearful that Jack might switch to human target practice.

"Goddamn it, Jack," I said, "let's get out of here before he does call the police and get you fired." So we ran out of the garage, flagged down a cab, and hied ourselves to Joe's palatial home in the West 50's. We put our hats and coats on a rack in the front hall, to which Jack added his police club; then Joe escorted us to a guest room and said that he'd call us for breakfast.

Joe left early for his office, and no one called us, so we didn't wake up until ten o'clock in the morning, when the butler stuck his head in the door to inquire if we were ready for breakfast. As we engaged a magnificent multi-course breakfast, Mrs. Blake entered the dining room and introduced herself. Joe hadn't even told her we were there. She was absolutely charming, but noting Jack's uniform, expressed concern for her son's welfare. She had passed Joe while he was leaving and asked him about the policeman's coat and billy club on the coat rack. Joe replied, "I had an argument with a cop last night, beat him with his own club, and took his overcoat." Needless to say, she was somewhat confused, but after we explained that the coat and club actually belonged to one of her house guests, she was perfectly composed. Apparently she was used to her son's repeated hijinks.

Jack Ryan was transferred to Staten Island, a rural area in those days, as punishment for being AWOL. But a few months later, Jack Mangan, who had been promoted to major before leaving France, was appointed deputy police commissioner. He immediately collared Jack Ryan, and to keep him out of trouble, transferred him to the "Lost and Found" office of the Police Department. There Jack reigned for the next nineteen years, a veritable fount of information and assistance for his buddies of the regiment. And we were all happy for him, because we loved the guy so much.

Nick Harris

After the war, I often palled with Nick Harris, an old buddy from the 7th Regiment. Nick's cousin, Captain

Nicholl, had prevented his transfer to the 69th, thinking he'd be safer in L Company of the 7th. Ironically, L Company was almost wiped out while fighting with the British at the Saint Quentin tunnel complex. Fancher Nicholl, twice decorated, was killed leading an attack against enemy machine guns.

One November in the late '20s, Nick Harris and I spent a couple of weeks at Clayton, New York, [this son's hometown] hunting ducks and pheasants along the Saint Lawrence River. Nick was a very good shot, and we got more than our share of birds.

On the return trip, we left Clayton about four o'clock in the afternoon, expecting to arrive at Nick's home outside Newburgh by midnight, but we soon ran into a severe rainstorm, and then a dense fog rolled in. It was the first and only time I ever saw heavy rain combined with fog. Driving conditions were terrible. Nick and I would spell each other at the wheel every few miles because of the intense concentration needed to drive.

A few miles outside Watertown, a horn blasted from behind, and a bread truck went by. Fortunately, that driver knew every twist and turn of the road, and all I had to do was camp on his taillights. At Utica, the fog lifted, and we arrived in Albany about half past one in the morning.

Both Nick and I desperately needed a break. We went into an all-night diner for coffee; then inquired where we might imbibe of stronger stuff. The counterman advised us that all the bars were closed, but he called over a taxi driver who assured us that he knew of a place. "Just follow me," the driver said. He led us to a place called the Shamrock Club on the outskirts of Albany. Remember, this was during prohibition, and here they had a wide-open bar in operation. Adjacent to the bar was a large dining room, where an excellent floor show was in full swing. It was truly amazing to see an elaborate floor show in such a remote location. I would say that it rivaled any I had seen in New York City. They had a superb chorus line and a full range of entertainers.

Nick and I sat at a table and ordered drinks, but I never drank fast enough for Nick, so while I would sip mine, enjoying the show, he would periodically slip out to the bar to augment his intake.

There appeared to be a charming woman heading the chorus—by far the best looker of the bunch—so I had the waiter go over and ask her if she'd care to have a drink with me. After she came to the table, I said, "I've been admiring your performance. Would you care to join me for a drink?" "Sure I will," the glamorous creature replied, "but you know, bud, I'm a female impersonator." My God, I was embarrassed. Oh, well, we had a drink and an interesting conversation; then he rejoined the other entertainers.

Shortly later, a group of seven men arrived and sat together at one of the head tables. They were all well-dressed but a hard-looking bunch, and I thought to myself, brother, I wouldn't want to walk into any of you fellows in a dark alley. I figured them to be bootleggers. Then the bartender came over to me and whispered, "Listen, Red, I wish you'd get your friend out of here. He's causing a problem at the bar insulting people, and we don't want any trouble. You know, this place is owned by Lucky Luciano. That's him over there at the head table."

Now, when Nick Harris was sober, he was a prince, but when carried away with alcohol, he went through two stages of intoxication. At first, he would assume a highly dignified pose—the very prince of his baronial manor on the Hudson. Then he would become intolerably abusive to any and all around, except me. By this time, Nick had progressed to stage two, and this time, I was included among the enemy.

I took him by the arm and warned: "Nick, we've got to get out of here; it's getting late, and we've overstayed our welcome." "Oh, hell," he replied, "I'm having a good time." I pulled more firmly: "Come on, Nick, we have to go!" At that, he muttered a few epithets; then took a healthy swing at me and missed. Nothing to do, I applied a short jab to his jaw and connected. Nick reeled back and indignantly exclaimed: "My God, Al, you hit me! You hit me, Al!"

Apparently the blow sobered him enough to introduce reason. With assistance from the friendly bartender, we managed to maneuver him downstairs and into the car, and I lost no time in getting out of there. If that bartender hadn't been so tactful, we might both have ended at the bottom of the Hudson River, because if Nick had got into a serious fight, I'd have been obligated to help him.

Nick married the daughter of the Cuban ambassador to Spain, grew oranges in California, then settled down with his second wife in Sarasota, Florida, where I went into business with him running a villa on Siesta Key.

Joe Hennessy

About a year after our return from France, I saw Joe Hennessy in his uniform selling pencils on Broadway. I was shocked at his appearance, and he had a hacking cough. I hadn't seen Joe since the Champagne Defensive, where he was wounded and severely gassed shortly after I landed in the hospital.

I took him to dinner and learned that he had only recently been discharged from a veterans hospital and had been unable to find a job. Joe suggested that we team up with Billy James as our mechanic and race motorcycles professionally, but I could see he really wasn't up to it. Moreover, I had a good construction job at the time and was no longer interested in motorcycles.

What a tragedy! Joe had been a scheming rascal but always self-confident, and I had liked him in spite of our petty disputes. Now he was a beaten man, and it broke my heart. Not long afterward, he passed away, and I always felt a little guilty about that, because maybe if we had raced motorcycles, he might have got back on his feet . . .

Robert Hughes

I met Bob Hughes my very first day at Dewitt Clinton High School. We were in the same class and had adjoining seats. Robert had just arrived from North Carolina, where his mother was a sharecropper. Bob's father having disappeared when he was a little shaver, his mother took over the farm and operated it herself. In those days, there weren't any high schools for Blacks in North Carolina, so when Bob became of high school age, his mother sent him to live with his grandmother in New York City. For years, his grandmother had been a cook for a wealthy family and had been able to save enough money to buy her own home in Harlem.

Bob Hughes and I became friends immediately. In this big New York high school, I was as green as he was, having graduated with only eight others from our little elementary school in Haworth, New Jersey. Now, here we were in classes with fifty or sixty kids. I was scared to death and felt like a fish out of water. Moreover, the New York kids were about six months ahead of me in mathematics. That was a serious handicap, and Bob was very good at math. He quickly caught on to the algebra and helped me all he could. On the other hand, I was far ahead of the New York kids in history and English literature, and Bob was a little behind in those subjects, so I was able to help him also.

We became good friends, stuck together, usually ate lunch together, and went to the movies when we had the money. I had dinner at his house three or four times, and he came out to Haworth to spend several weekends with us, and we had a great time. Then we lost touch as I transferred to a different school.

I didn't see Bob again until after the war. I didn't know that he had enlisted in the 15th New York, where he did a lot better than I, becoming a sergeant in no time. Had I known that, we could have buddied at Camp Mills, and I'd have been all over the countryside in France looking for him. He might have been just a mile or so down the road from where I met those other fellows from the 15th.

Bob was severely gassed during the war and spent four years at a V.A. hospital in the Adirondacks, and because of the gas, he developed tuberculosis. While there, he took college correspondence courses and graduated with a degree.

In the summer of 1934, during the heart of the depression, we renewed our friendship when I went to the Solvay Chemical Company to sell them some advertising and found Robert at the reception desk. Eventually, he was promoted into the advertising department, but the poor fellow died during the 50s. I don't think he ever recovered from the poison gas that seared his lungs.

Robert Hughes was better educated than I, and he had to

struggle harder than I, but he never surrendered to the obstacles of bigotry placed in his path. He was a man of great courage, intelligence, and integrity.

William J. Donovan

After discharge, I didn't see Bill Donovan again until 1932, during his campaign for governor of New York State against Herbert Lehman.

Although always a Republican, Dorothy[3] had joined the Jackson Heights Woman's Democratic Club. She had a great friend in Margaret Burns, who lived across the street, and Margaret, who was president of this club, had persuaded Dorothy to join, which she did for the fun of it rather than any political conviction. When Dorothy later became the Republican Mayor of Clayton, I sent her a congratulatory note, promising that I would never squeal on her previous indiscretion in having joined a Democratic club.

When Donovan ran for governor on the Republican ticket, Dorothy persuaded many of the women in the club, most of them Irish, that they should vote for Donovan. She and Margaret then organized another club, "Women Democrats for Donovan."

Donovan was campaigning in New York City at the time, so I called his headquarters, said that I had news for him, and asked him to call me back. That evening he did so, and I told him about these women Democrats who had formed this club to support him, how my wife was responsible for it, and how they would appreciate having him as their guest speaker. By golly, he agreed to do so. The women hired the Knights of Columbus hall a few blocks away, made a specific date, and that evening, the Colonel and several of his entourage came out and he delivered a fine address to a packed house.

Dorothy was tickled to death. He was so charming, and he said a lot of nice things about me to the assembly: I was one of his boys, blaa, blaa. He laid it on thick and made me feel pretty good, but that was the last I saw of Bill Donovan until our regimental reunion in 1940.

William Donovan was not cut out to be a politician. I could tell that after the meeting, when many of the women wanted to talk to him. He was a famous and handsome man, and they just wanted to shake his hand and flirt a bit, but the Colonel couldn't wait to get away. A good politician would have made the most of it. But Donovan was of great value in providing foreign-policy advice to several presidents; and during World War II, as head of the Office of Strategic Services, he was responsible for establishing our foreign intelligence network.

Douglas MacArthur

In January of 1940, the entire regiment was invited by Warner Bros. Studios to preview their new movie, *The Fighting Sixty Ninth,* at the Waldorf Astoria in New York. Needless to say, I attended and sat at a table with some of my old buddies from Headquarters Company.

On the dais were James Cagney, Pat O'Brien (who played the role of Father Duffy), George Brent, Bill Donovan, Alec Anderson (then Colonel of the regiment), and Governor Herbert Lehman, the guest of honor. However, there were actually two guests of honor at that affair. The second was General Douglas MacArthur, who spoke to us by radio from Manila.

Also on the dais was a gorgeous redhead in a green gown. Much to my astonishment, she turned out to be my old girlfriend, Nancy Carrol, then a star at Warner Bros. I had no idea she was going to be there, and she took my breath away. God, she was beautiful. I mentioned our former relationship to the fellows and got a predictable response. "Oh yeah, and I'm Clark Gable," one of them quipped. Nothing to do, I walked up to the dais to greet her. She saw me coming, jumped up, screamed out my name, ran around the table and threw her arms around me. Oh, it was wonderful! And when I returned to my table, the fellows were sitting there with their mouths open.

Well, that was the highlight of the evening, as far as I was concerned. MacArthur's speech and the movie were definitely anticlimactic. Of the two, MacArthur's speech was superior.

We laughed through much of the movie, it was so corny. Today, the General's speech would also be considered corny, but he best expressed what most of us believed. Don Adair recently sent me a copy of that speech, which he had saved all those years:

No greater fighting regiment has ever existed than the One Hundred and Sixty-fifth Infantry of the Rainbow Division, formed from the old Sixty-ninth of New York. You need no eulogy from me or from any other man. You have written your own history and written it in red on your enemies' breast, but when I think of your patience under adversity, your courage under fire, and your modesty in victory, I am filled with an emotion of admiration I cannot express. You have carved your own statue upon the hearts of your people, you have built your own monument in the memory of your compatriots.

One of the most outstanding characteristics of the regiment was its deep sense of religious responsibility inculcated by one of my most beloved friends— Father Duffy. He gave you a code that embraces the highest moral laws, that will stand the test of any ethics or philosophies ever promulgated for the uplift of man. . . . The soldier, above all men, is required to perform the highest act of religious teaching— sacrifice. However horrible the results of war may be, the soldier who is called upon to offer and perchance to give his life for his country is the noblest development of mankind. No physical courage and no brute instincts can take the place of the divine annunciation and spiritual uplift which will alone sustain him. Father Duffy, on those bloody fields of France we all remember so well, taught the men of your regiment how to die that a nation might live. . . . Somewhere in your banquet hall tonight his noble spirit looks down to bless and guide you young soldiers on the narrow path marked with West Point's famous motto—duty, honor, country.

We all hope that war will come to us no more. But if its red stream again engulfs us, I want you to know that if my flag flies again, I shall hope to have you once more with me, once more to form the brilliant hues of what is lovingly, reverently called by men at arms, the Rainbow.

I never saw MacArthur after the war, but I am infinitely proud to have known him. In my opinion, he was our most brilliant military commander and one of our greatest Americans.

Donald P. Adair

After the war, Don Adair completed his education by going to night school at New York University, and he worked at various jobs around the city. We went out on the town several times with my brothers, and Don hit it off with Bill and Churchill right from the start. Indeed, Don and Bill would party together when I'd be away on one job or another. When in town, I dated Veronica La Hiff, whom I had met at the Pre Catalan, and she had a girlfriend who was crazy about Don, so we would often go out as a foursome.

After I married Dorothy, Pop gave me the old house in Haworth, New Jersey. Don and his wife would visit us there, and we would usually share the same table at various reunions of the regiment. But our greatest diversion was Madison Square Garden. Don knew Harold Dibley, manager of the Garden at that time, and he could get free tickets from Dibley to any of the events there.

Don eventually got a good job with the Universal Atlas Company selling cement and ended up as their district manager in Connecticut. After his wife died, Don moved to a nursing home at Cromwell, Connecticut. In the early '70s, we renewed our friendship through correspondence, but darn it, we haven't seen each other in years.[4]

William J. O'Day

A. Churchill Ettinger: I researched the following information from court-martial documents on file at the Federal Records Center in Suitland, Maryland.

At the court-martial of William O'Day, Corporal Robert

Taggart was the key witness other than Lieutenant Quirt. The only other witness called was the platoon bugler, who had been at the opposite end of the barracks and had seen and heard very little. The officer assigned to the defense had inadequately prepared his case by failing to call other witnesses to develop the extenuating circumstances that led to O'Day's threat to shoot Quirt. O'Day, himself, was less than eloquent. Taggart's testimony supported Quirt, who portrayed O'Day as an incorrigible rebel. Unfortunately, Lieutenant Walsh was not a member of the court-martial board, and Lieutenant Bootz, who was a member, had excused himself.

The precipitating incident, as described earlier by my father, differs from that presented in the court-martial record, where there was no reference to a coil of barbed wire, or to O'Day having been kicked on the barracks floor by Quirt, although no one rebutted O'Day's testimony that Quirt had knocked him down outside the barracks while O'Day was carrying a full pack. My father was adamant as to his version, and it is possible that both events occurred. The record did mention bread as having been involved, but only to the extent that O'Day had thrown his ration away.

O'Day escaped three times from the Fort Leavenworth Disciplinary Barracks and was recaptured, adding three-and-a-half years to his sentence. Each time, he refused to testify in his own behalf, and the defense was perfunctory. After the third escape attempt, he was transferred on May 24, 1919, to the U.S. Disciplinary Barracks at Alcatraz, from which he also temporarily escaped on September 16, 1919. O'Day's conduct in confinement, as noted in court-martial records, deteriorated from "Fair," in the beginning, to "Very Bad" at Alcatraz.

A tragic irony revealed by the O'Day file was an attempt by the Judge Advocate's office to seek clemency for O'Day and to reduce his sentence to one year, but this was aborted by another futile escape. I surmise that O'Day had no knowledge of this clemency effort and could only imagine years of intolerable confinement dictated by an unjust and capricious system.

Under military law, the mere verbal threat to kill an officer constituted "lifting a rifle against one's superior officer," and that damning charge repeatedly appeared on the face sheet of the trial records that were to plague this illiterate, inarticulate, embittered young man for years.

Advised by Michael Knapp, archivist in the military records branch of the National Archives, that Alcatraz military prisoner files in deposit at the Archives were destroyed in July of 1983 (under disposition authority NC2-407-83-1), I was unable to pursue O'Day's fate to a conclusion.

Foolishly, I related this information to my father, who was under the impression that O'Day had died in 1918 en route to Leavenworth. All he could think of was the lost opportunity to free O'Day through the combined efforts of his buddies after the war, and my father's wife told me that he would cry at night in recollection of the tragedy.

Albert M. Ettinger

A. Churchill Ettinger: Following the war, my father's greatest ambition was to become a writer. With encouragement, he might have had something quite similar to this book ready for publication in the early twenties. After an initial attempt, however, Dr. Ettinger firmly discouraged Albert's pursuit of a literary career. "Nobody writes like that. You just can't publish that kind of language. Go to college and learn how to write properly."

That was devastating advice. Red had no desire to learn propriety from people who had not shared the intensity of his war experience. If he couldn't write, he would pursue another avenue, one that he had learned well in France, working outdoors with men he could understand and respect, many of them veterans.

There ensued a series of construction jobs as a crew boss, building bridges and roads—usually in the New York metropolitan area, so he could socialize with his veteran buddies from the regiment.

Occasionally, Albert would vacation with his family at Raquette Lake in the Adirondack Mountains, and during the autumn of 1923, he decided to remain over the winter and cut timber for the host proprietor. There, on a Sunday afternoon, he literally bumped into one Dorothy Clark, an attractive young schoolteacher, locally employed, who, after their first date in a canoe, decided that she was going to marry, tame, and "make a success" out of this handsome barbarian.

Before that could be accomplished, Dorothy's parents, propertied, Protestant, Scots-English Yankees from the Thousand Islands region of New York, would have to consent. What appeared to be a formidable problem quickly dissipated as the alien suitor's hunting prowess impressed Dorothy's father, and his open, affectionate banter charmed the mother. Moreover, the young roustabout "must have some promise" considering his father's well-publicized status.

The wedding in Clayton's impressive, quarried granite Catholic church was a great social event for the village, and Father Ettinger deeded to the newlyweds the family house in suburban Haworth, New Jersey.

A promising career developed as Albert secured employment with the Thomas Publishing Company, selling advertising copy to manufacturing firms, but coincident with the stock market crash of 1929, the beautiful three-story house in Haworth burned to the ground, and the young family—there were now two children—moved first to a rental house on Long Island, then to an apartment in the Bronx.

To my mother, these residential moves were decidedly downhill, and I acutely recall the frequent arguments over money and my father's occasional penchant to visit Manhattan bars with his buddies after work.

A long-awaited raise and a veterans bonus enabled the family to rebuild in Haworth in 1938. But the following year, my mother met a charming railroad attorney, whose avocation as an umpire for the Eastern Lawn Tennis Association offered an irresistible alternative life style.

Red moved to Florida in 1939, and after a 1940 divorce, married Ardel Carrette, a strong-willed lady of French-Irish descent. With the attack on Pearl Harbor, he soon enlisted in the Marine Corps because of his fond memories of the Corps from World War I, and he probably could not get assurance of transfer to the 69th should he enlist in the Army.[5]

Following a back injury, incurred while wheeling a fighter

plane out of a flaming Navy hangar, Red was discharged, returned to Florida, and built the first motel and tavern along the sixteen-mile stretch of Tamiami Trail between Venice and Sarasota.

His clientele was a remarkably heterogeneous lot. Retired teachers hobnobbed with local commercial fishermen and airmen from a neighboring fighter squadron based at Venice. During infrequent visits as a student, I found the fishermen the most interesting. Excluded from most of the other bars along the Trail because of their exuberant behavior, they were no problem at "Al and Del's." Red would cash their checks and occasionally make small loans that were invariably repaid—and the "interest" consisted of frequent gifts of smoked mullet, scallops, and shrimp. He and Ardel would attend their funerals and weddings, and a mutual loyalty developed that was quite beautiful. This relationship extended to Red's leisure hours when he was often invited on hunting trips by native Floridians, some of whom might have qualified as professional poachers.

My father was often invited to run for this or that political office, but both he and Ardel knew that he would become too emotionally involved in the issues at stake. When Red Ettinger became "involved," an issue no longer had aspects, facets, or complexity. There was but one obvious solution, and soon a state of war was declared against those offending fools or knaves who believed otherwise.

Although not politically active in a partisan sense, in the early '50s, Al Ettinger organized and served on the Sarasota County Veterans Commission to accommodate the needs of Korean War vets who, he believed, were being denied legitimate benefits.

During our military action in Vietnam, my father was appalled by civilian opposition to that effort. He reacted by organizing a project in support of American servicemen in Vietnam that operated out of a shed in his Florida backyard. From conversations with returning veterans, he identified those articles of greatest need to "grunts" in the field and obtained a list of the names and addresses of all Sarasota County servicemen in Vietnam. Then, every month, beginning in 1966, he and Ardel mailed each of them a five-pound box containing such items as strong plastic tape to mend rifle stocks, boots, and shelter halfs; WD-40 lubricant to prevent the jamming of M-16 receivers; beef jerky to supplement canned rations; bubble gum (prized by GIs and Vietnamese children alike); and single-edge razor blades. These were articles he had succeeded in badgering from local businessmen and large companies.

The response was amazing. Hundreds of servicemen replied with letters of appreciation. Dad would answer as many of these letters as possible, and an informal information network developed that extended far beyond the boys of Sarasota County. Eventually, old Red was writing to generals at Saigon Headquarters, recommending promotions or transfers—and several times he got action!

Sergeant Jimmy Parks, an aerial rescue medic from Venice, Florida, brought my father's attention to a Vietnamese nun who ran orphanages for children in the Delta and the Highlands, and after Red stormed the local church societies and women's clubs, "Project Vietnam" extended its support to include donations of money and clothing for Sister Anicette's orphans. At Dad's request, General Creighton Abrams dispatched engineers to her village to repair a school and a dispensary that had been shelled by the Viet Cong. That good general also donated a jeep to the orphanage to replace one that had been expropriated by an ARVN colonel. Project Vietnam was brought to the attention of the Freedom Foundation, and the "Old Doughboy" was honored by a presentation from Omar Bradley, the "Soldiers' General" of World War II.

My father was devastated by the fall of Saigon. How could the United States desert an ally in a life and death crisis? How could we permit the waste of so much blood and sacrifice? He, along with the thousands of American GIs, and hundreds of thousands of South Vietnamese with whom he identified, had fallen victim to that struggle. The emotional strain was too great. A physical powerhouse for his age, he became weaker and his eyesight began to fail, as if to shut out the world that had rejected values he considered elementary. He began to retreat more and more into the past, to a time when American servicemen had popular support, when a commitment was just that, when retreat was rare, defeat unthinkable, and college students enlisted during wartime as a matter of course. It was during this period of psychic withdrawal that he began to discuss World War I—the genesis of this book.

★   ★   ★

Taps

Albert M. Ettinger died of cancer at his home in Sarasota on November 13, 1984, attended by his wife, myself, and a deeply caring granddaughter.

The Vietnam Veterans of Sarasota/Manatee Counties had previously orchestrated a delightful ceremony at which their old champion had been presented Honorary Membership Card No. 1. Now they became the pallbearers at his funeral, while the Veterans of Foreign Wars officiated at the chapel service, and the American Legion presided at the grave site.

His dear friends, Lieutenant-Colonel Harriet Knarr, post commander of the Legion, and the Reverend J. D. Hamel, V.F.W. chaplain, followed Red's wishes and organized that funeral to a perfection that rivaled Arlington. The multi-talented Reverend Hamel played taps and, in closing, read the following passage from Joyce Kilmer's "Rouge Bouquet" that Dad himself had often recited at veterans' funerals as the flag was folded from the casket:

> *And up to Heaven's doorway floats,*
> *From the wood called Rouge Bouquet,*
> *A delicate cloud of buglenotes*
> *That softly say:*
> *"Farewell!*
> *Farewell!*
> *Comrade true, born anew, peace to you!*
> *Your soul shall be where the heroes are*
> *And your memory shine like the morning star.*
> *Brave and dear,*
> *Shield us here.*
> *Farewell!"*

★   ★   ★

Appendix A

The Genesis of
Doughboy with the Fighting 69th

Albert "Red" Ettinger was an accomplished raconteur. He told poignant stories about people that were often funny and tragic at the same time. He had an aversion for "jokes," ethnic or otherwise, and all his stories were true as he remembered them. He had lived most of them, and his multifaceted life reflected their variety and humanity.

During the '30s, as New York State sales representative for the Thomas Publishing Company, Red made an annual tour of manufacturing firms. An admiring son, my greatest pleasure was to accompany him on some of these trips and listen, fascinated, while he would describe the background of the region through which we drove. A history buff, with a particular interest in the French and Indian and Revolutionary wars, he could evoke the imagery of us tramping together with Rogers' Rangers or Anthony Wayne. Then he would tell me about his life as a lumberjack in the Adirondacks, where he wooed a young schoolteacher, later my mother, in a canoe—he was an expert canoeist. Or about his experience as a crew boss working on roads or building bridges. Or as an overseer on a North Carolina hog ranch. Or as a young man "adjusting" to peacetime through parties and excursions in prohibition era New York.

Inevitably, I would implore: "Tell me about the War, Dad," and he never would. He would pause and, with a voice somewhat broken, change the subject.

Immediately upon our entry into World War II, my father enlisted in the Marine Corps at age 41, and after the war, we exchanged stories about our service experiences. He was not emotionally inhibited by that conflict because, much to his disgust, he had been restricted to state-side duty because of his age. And he had acquired new stories about the Gulf Coast commercial fishermen who frequented his tavern and the native Floridians with whom he hunted in the Everglades. Still, very little about World War I.

During a spring visit in 1976, old Red and I sat under a large blossoming cherry tree in my Arlington, Virginia, backyard. We had exhausted our critique of world events and were into our second can of beer when, apropos of nothing, he began to reminisce about Joyce Kilmer in France during World War I. As the minutes ticked by, it occurred to me that a precious slice of history was about to escape among the cherry blossoms that Kilmer so dearly loved. I dashed into the house to retrieve a tape recorder, placed it alongside his lounge chair and insisted that he repeat the story. That was the genesis of this book, although neither of us then realized it.

My father was an accomplished letter writer, so I urged him to write about his war experiences. He did so, and the *Rainbow Barrage,* a newsletter of the Father Duffy chapter of 42nd Division veterans, printed several episodes found in this book. When the old man's eyesight failed to the degree that he could no longer write, I began to record these conversations and persuaded Red to himself tape as much as he could recall about his World War I encounters. There resulted 19 cassette recordings, most initiated from his home in Sarasota, Florida.

It was as though old Red's mind had become a liberated motion picture projector. A full panoply of characters emerged associated with New York's "Fighting 69th" and the 42nd Rainbow Division of the First World War: Colonel/Brigadier General Douglas MacArthur; Majors/Colonels Frank McCoy, William Donovan, Timothy Moynahan, Charles Hine and Harry Mitchell; Captain/Major Alexander Anderson; the magnificently profane Lieutenants/Captains Herman Bootz and Mike Walsh; the remarkable chaplain, Francis Patrick Duffy; heroic sergeants Abram Blaustein and Tom FitzSimmons; and scores of unforgotten doughboys.

Red Ettinger knew these men because, as a headquarters company dispatch rider, he delivered messages from one to the other and, as a member of the Stokes mortar platoon, he observed and fought beside them in combat. However, scenes of battle horror were few. As my father put it: "You tend to remember the good times and the funny episodes. The stench of dead bodies and the screams of the wounded, we tried to leave in France." Thus, those aspects of fellowship unique to the time, place, and ethnicity of his National Guard regiment—New York's Irish "Fighting 69th"—predominate in this book.

It quickly became apparent that the seventeen-year-old Ettinger was not a model soldier. His ingenuity at going AWOL was exceeded only by his ability to survive such inconveniences as a determined German counterattack during the Battle of the Argonne; four intimate shell bursts; convalescence in two hospitals; strafing by a German pilot; driving into a stone wall, through a railroad crossing guard and off a bridge on his motorcycle; and a military stockade, where he was incarcerated after fighting with a sergeant and inadvertently striking a lieutenant—from which he was released by personal order of General MacArthur.

When, in May 1984, I learned that my father had cancer of the pancreas, what had been intended as a future retirement project took on the aspect of a crash program. I wanted Red to hear the results of his labors before he "passed over the rainbow," as the veterans of his division put it. Therefore, I took a leave of absence from employment, and with my wife's invaluable assistance in transcribing the tapes, this book is the result.

Fortunately, while my father still lived, he was able to review a partial draft, make some corrections, and fill some gaps. Finally, I embarked upon a study of World War I and several times traveled to France to visit the places he had described in order to acquire a feeling for the narrative. In so doing, I fell as deeply in love with that country as had my father seventy years ago.

My contribution to *Doughboy* involved providing background through a general "Introduction" and a "Reconnaissance" to each chapter, offering editorial comment and supplementary information via footnotes and appendices, organizing the episodes in chronological development of the events described, and, insofar as possible, subjecting a number of these stories to tests of verification.

I have held instructive, research, and executive positions of responsibility in which a consideration for objective fact was highly desirable. Consequently, I am aware that truth, in respect to one person's version of events, can be illusive, particularly when the episodes occurred years ago, holding the truth hostage to memory loss, compensated by imagination and invention. Indeed, under these circumstances, the problem of veracity is even more difficult, for what the author once might have acknowledged as invention could, over the years, have become so internalized that it became perceived as truth.

Thus it was that, having completed the organization and editing of this manuscript, I could not escape the question of authenticity. Some of the narrative might be considered too important to foist on a reader as historical fact if, indeed, it was the product of a fertile imagination. To resolve that problem, I tested my father's account against regimental and division records, interviews with a few surviving members of the regiment, conversation with elderly French residents of villages in which the regiment was billeted, and an examination of the terrain involved that would render his account either feasible or suspect.

I have read, heard, and seen enough to conclude that most of these stories are essentially true, a conclusion reinforced by my direct knowledge of persons described by my father in other stories of incidents that occurred subsequent to 1940.

In part, I ascribe the amazing detail of these vignettes to a diary that young Red maintained through most of the war. Although that diary was destroyed during the Meuse-Argonne Offensive, it would undoubtedly have aided his subsequent recollection of events.

His frequent retelling of these stories in postwar years to his veteran companions must also have assisted his recall. At first monthly, with his buddies from headquarters company, then annually, at division reunions, my father would rehash these events in an intimate setting. I would occasionally accompany him to programs at the regimental armory, which inevitably concluded in a torrent of stories at the veterans' bar.

Finally, I learned that my father's extraordinary recall was not unique among World War I servicemen. John

Keegan comments on this phenomenon in his superb analytic treatise, *The Face of Battle,* p. 293:

> While studying a large-scale trench map of the Western Front, I asked my father if his battery of 6-inch guns had not been positioned in the area it covered. He agreed that it was and at once began to point out on it, with that faculty of total topographical recall— undimmed by fifty years' absence—apparently possessed by all survivors of the First World War, its salient features.

The episodes in the book involving hearsay are, at this late date, almost impossible to verify, except through corroborative accounts, of which there are precious few. Concerning "Donovan's Last Charge," for example (Chap. X), it is doubtful that my father would have been sufficiently close to Donovan to overhear the latter's purported exchange with the military police captain. It is understandable why Donovan would not report such an incident, but it is surprising that none of his men did not gleefully relate it to a highly receptive press, unless they all feared adverse repercussions. Initially, therefore, one is inclined to dismiss this magnificent tale as the ultimate serviceman fantasy— dispersing military police at bayonet point. Other sources, however, lend plausibility to the story. First is the documented experience of the 15th New York Guard at Brest the previous week. As footnoted, the aggressive military police captain there involved would have been just the kind of person to confront Donovan on an incident of the nature described. The second is Charles MacArthur's reference in his book, *War Bugs,* to a sanguinary evening in Brest, when his artillery outfit, which often buddied with 69th boyos, beat up a group of military police. Most of the other stories concerning Donovan, McCoy, Kilmer, MacArthur, Duffy, and Anderson, while impossible to verify, are vintage in character, mannerism, and expression.

Unfortunately, the written word cannot possibly express old Red's emotive force. I have sought to accomplish that through liberal use of the exclamation point and even fully

capitalized words, when epithets were hurled across battlefield and barrack ground. But my father's frequent accompanying laughter and occasional subdued sob are lost to the
written page. And how does one catch a tear in print?

A Doughboy with the Fighting 69th has little to say about
military strategy or tactics, although it has many implica-
tions concerning morale and leadership. It is essentially a
series of related vignettes about a kind of love known as
comradeship; about young men who relished strong drink
and laughter, cherished women and children, and generally
believed that what they were doing was necessary and
sanctioned in the eyes of God. In the beginning, most of
them also enjoyed the prospect of battle. It is a book about a
remarkable breed of two generations past, many of whom
were truly heroic.

—A. Churchill Ettinger
November 1987

Appendix B

Moral Advice from "Big Brother" Bill, Age 20

In Camp
July 5, 1917

Dear Brother Al:

Well old kid Ma tells me that you go to camp tomorrow. Thats what you have been waiting for and I guess you are very happy as you should be.

About 50 people more or less have given you advice and wished you luck etc so I guess I may as well take a crack at you too as long as you are too far away to defend yourself.

This is the dope Al. First of all remember that you are a Catholic and a good one and train around as much as possible with the other fish-eaters in your company. Not that you ought to be biased at all but merely because by such association you will remember more

267

strongly your religous duties and your obligations which you should keep up as much as possible. you are a good hardworking kid and it is ridiculous for me to give you advice about taking seriously what your officers say and always staying with it.

But al being in camp and in the army dont mean that you should act any less the gentleman. your discipline will be lots stricter even than ours and when you get time off you will be tempted to let loose. I dont want you to be a saint or any other impossible thing but you can have a hell of a good time without figuring booze or fooling with the girls — and that leads me to the most important part of this boob letter.

Listen kid. Around your camp there will be a bunch of hangers on - camp followers - women

2. from all parts of the country ~~who~~ who come there merely to vampire around with the soldiers. ~~Keep~~ away from them! This cannot be emphasized too ~~strongly~~. These women are ill bad - and most of them are diseased. Now I know you ~~twice~~ enough guts to do it for this reason if no other. If you have a scratch on your old hand and hold hands with one of those bums you will catch one of two diseases either one of which will affect your whole ~~so~~ life. It would be a whole lot better for you to be killed in action than slowly rot with any filthy disease that would make Mother and Father ashamed instead of proud of you even if it was not your fault. There are 20 men in one camp now who will never see action but who have a fine mental

picture of the inside of the guard-house.
I hate to talk this way but straight
talk is the best.

well ol old truck I'd like to
be with you to see you entrain
and ship you the nit but never
mind I'll get I have if I
can and drop down and
give the once over to you. You
are brave and I know you
will make out all right. You
know I'm with you and I'll
see you "in France" but
I hope on furlough. We
are going over very soon I
think as the camp here is filled
to overflowing and they are
assembling the ambulances very
quickly. We have a song here
that goes like this – maybe you've
heard it.

> " Where do we go from here boys?
> Where do we go from here?
> Ship a pill to Kaiser Bill
> and make him shed a tear.
> and when we see the enemy
> We'll shoot him in the rear.
> Oh joy Oh Boy where do we go from here?"

270

3.

Well old sloppy seventh I have to turn out for lecture now — we just finished our morning drill so I will have to cut it short.

It a great life and I never felt happier. Do your duty al and <u>keep clean</u> and when you hear the old Taps blow you can thank God that you spent one part of your life for your country and in the right way. Write to mama often al and to Pop's too. It will keep them from getting lonesome. Your big (?) brother who used to pull your hair and poke you in the nose (and then run) is proud of you.

           lovingly

             Bill.

P. S. Write to me ~~once in a while too~~ .

     U. S. ARMY Ambulance Corp
     Section 52 Co # 6
     Allentown Pa.

March 5, 1919
Wacht am Rhein
Alsace
(near Mulhouse).

Dear old Al:

Well convict #666
wots the good word? Am
hoping and praying that
by the time you git this,
most of your troubles will
be but an unpleasant memory
and that you will be bound
back for the Fightin Irish.

Miss Vivian the lady I
spoke of in my other
letters has just written me

and assured me that Morgan
Harges her bankers have
already sent you a draft
for 200 francs and I
will certainly tell the world
that I hope you get it as
that will put at least a
paper lining the the dark
yellow cloud if not a silver
one. She also says that
she has it on the authority
of her nephew — a Colonel
in the U. S. army that you
will not be put in the

Labour Batt. and she has it on the authority of Casey her nephews chauffer that "Father Banahan will be gettin the bye out of it all right for Father Banahan do be a foine man and if the Sairjint made war sigutin remark about the byes goin to Mass Father Banahan will be gettin the bye out uv ut all together." So I conclude from that that if Heaven and Father B. can do anything to help you they sure will.

The Section is cantoned at Sausheim near (3 kilos) Mulhouse but Jim my Synch (of the White Sox) and myself are holding down a post on the Rhine carrein injuries from the receiving station ut the rink near to the railroad station 5 mins away.

Mama + Bups + the kid are all well but Aunt Kate is pretty sick.

Keep a stiff upper lip old soldier and write soon to Your loving brother
Bill

Appendix C

The 15th New York National Guard

Colonel William Hayward, organizer and commanding officer of the 15th New York National Guard, had initially tried to have his regiment made part of the New York 27th Guard Division, but its commanding officer rejected his overture. Then he sought affiliation with the Rainbow Division, but again his offer was refused, allegedly with the comment that "black is not part of the Rainbow." Sent to Spartanburg, South Carolina, for training, men of the 15th had to put up with unaccustomed indignities. Local stores and restaurants would not serve the black troops. It so happened that three white regiments from New York City were also training at Spartanburg as part of the New York 27th Division. Men from two of these, the 12th and 71st New York, boycotted the offending stores.

Captain Marshall, a black Harvard alumnus and member of the New York bar, was thrown off a streetcar; Drum Major Sissle was knocked down and kicked by the hotel manager as he tried to buy a newspaper in the hotel lobby; and black soldiers were routinely pushed off the sidewalks. On one such occasion, Whites of the 7th New York rescued a black trooper who was under assault by local bullies. It reached a point where all the troops, white and black, were ready to take that town apart, so the 15th was ordered to Camp Mills.

When the 15th New York (which became the 369th U.S. Infantry as the 69th had been redesignated the 165th) arrived in France, it was technically part of the 93rd Division, along with three other black infantry regiments, but the other regiments didn't arrive in France until five months later. The French were crying for American troops to beef up their army and they didn't particularly care about the color of the rifles. A.E.F. HQ, on the other hand, professed to have reservations as to the value of black troops in a combat capacity (in spite of their demonstrated competence in the Civil War, the Spanish-American War, and on the American frontier) but really feared the post-war consequences at home of Blacks, experienced with weapons, who had also experienced a taste of French freedom and hospitality.

Immediately upon disembarking in France, the 15th was put to work laying railroad track alongside troops of the Service of Supply. Colonel Hayward, commander of the 15th, was furious. Moreover, other officers of the 15th, half of them Black, were gentlemen of considerable influence back home. With support from Secretary of War Baker, they pressured Pershing to assign their regiment to the French Army. New York's "Men of Bronze" were in combat longer (191 days) than most regiments of the A.E.F. During that time, they suffered 1500 casualties, never lost a foot of ground or had a man taken prisoner, and failed in only one attack (as had the 69th) when required to go against barbed wire and concrete fortifications without artillery support.

Another excellent black regiment, the old 8th Illinois National Guard (redesignated the 370th U.S. Infantry) joined the 15th in time for the Champagne Defensive. All but three of its officers were Black, and these Chicago doughboys compiled an enviable record as well.

—Arthur Little, *From Harlem to the Rhine*
(New York: Covici-Friede, 1936), pp. 52–71 ff.

Appendix D

Pre-War Background of William J. Donovan

William J. Donovan was a native of Buffalo, New York, of first generation Irish Catholic parentage, who from early adulthood, revealed a driving ambition for fame combined with almost fanatic courage, intelligence, and a wide-ranging curiosity.

At Columbia University, Donovan studied political philosophy. He was also the school's star quarterback, and it was in this latter capacity that he acquired the sobriquet, "Wild Bill," although why is a mystery, since there was never anything in his behavior to suggest lack of control.

Although he graduated from Columbia Law School with mediocre grades, Donovan soon became "well connected" with a prestigious Buffalo law firm and in 1914 married Ruth Rumsey, a beautiful Protestant heiress. Before this marriage, he and other members of an exclusive Buffalo social club organized a cavalry troop as part of the New York Guard's 1st Cavalry Regiment, and he was soon elected its commanding officer.

Early in 1916, the Rockefeller Commission dispatched Donovan to Europe on famine relief work behind German lines. In late June of 1916, he was recalled from Europe by the War Department to command his cavalry troop on the Mexican border. There he quickly established a reputation as a demanding taskmaster, and in his mid-thirties, led the pack in their strenuous field maneuvers.

Donovan was a major on brigade staff of the 27th New York National Guard Division when word was received that the 69th was to be first overseas from the state, whereupon he immediately sought and received transfer as commander of its First Battalion. The evidence suggests that William J. Donovan left New York City a "glory hunter," and it was not until the Battle of the Ourcq River, where over half his men were killed or wounded, including the death of his two dearest friends, that this drive for military fame appears to have been tempered through traumatic recognition of its human cost. At the Argonne and in latter life, Donovan revealed a profound recognition of the value of human life in the defense of freedom and this country's national interest.

—See Anthony Cave Brown, *The Last Hero*
(New York: Vintage Books, 1982), pp. 1–72.

Appendix E

Sergeant Blaustein
and Jewish Members of the 69th

While Sergeant Blaustein's popularity among men of the pioneer platoon was constrained by reason of his difficult position vis-a-vis Lieutenant Quirt, and the misconception that he had testified against O'Day, the officers of the regiment had only unqualified praise for "Blaustein of the Irish." Father Duffy applied the benedictus in his regimental history, p. 106:

> By the way, I cannot remember anything that delighted me more than when I heard Sergeant Abe Blaustein was to get the *Croix de Guerre*—he was recommended for it by Major Donovan and Major Stacom (the pride of our parish) and Lt. Kavanaugh. He is a good man, Abe, and the 69th appreciates a good man when it sees him. John O'Keef's poem made a hit with all of us.

> *You talk about your melting pot,*
> *The crucible of man—*
> *Where Celt and Saxon, Slav and Scot*
> *Are made American.*
> *But oh! 'tis war makes strangers one*
> *To face a foe defiant*
> *Like Sergeant Abey Blaustein,*
> *The scrappy, happy Blaustein,*
> *The hustlin', bustlin' Blaustein in*
> *The Irish Sixty-Ninth.*
> *Sure, foolish prejudice some took*
> *At first in racial pride,*
> *When Danny's pug and Solly's hook*
> *In line ranged side by side.*
> *But what's a nose when, mid the din,*

> *Its owner is reliant*
> *Like Sergeant Abey Blaustein,*
> *The scootin', shootin' Blaustein,*
> *The mighty, fighty Blaustein in*
> *The Irish Sixty-Ninth.*
> *O'Connell, here's a slainthe lad*
> *And Donovan, here's two.*
> *I wish an open tube I had*
> *To share the drink with you.*
> *And next I lift a Yiddish boak,*
> *Far bigger than a pint,*
> *To Sergeant Abey Blaustein,*
> *Untirin', firin' Blaustein,*
> *To Abey Blaustein, one in soul*
> *With all the Sixty-Ninth.*

From records obtained through the Jewish War Veterans, I learned that, prior to the war's end, Abram Blaustein was commissioned a second lieutenant, and in 1944 he was promoted to captain of infantry with the New York Guard. His heroic behavior at the Rouge Bouquet was reported in full in the *Brooklyn Eagle* of March 25, 1918.

According to Father Duffy (*op. cit.*, p. 379) about seventy Jews left New York with the regiment. Burr Finkle, a corporal with K Company, was awarded the *Croix de Guerre*, the Distinguished Service Cross and the *Medaille Militaire*. That last decoration, the most cherished of the French Army, was received by only three other members of the regiment. Burr Finkle became one of the two color sergeants of the 69th and was entrusted with the regimental colors, perhaps the most honored position an enlisted man could aspire to.

The 69th's treatment of its Jewish volunteers was probably more favorable than that found in southern and midwestern regiments. This assessment is based on anti-Semitic comments found in two of the regimental histories that I perused. However, I was unable to locate a single reference work on the subject. Considering the bitter experience of Jews from Russia and the relative tolerance accorded by the Imperial German Government of that day, it is surprising that so many Jews volunteered for service with the American Expeditionary Force. Although only 3.3% of the population at that time, 5.7% of American servicemen were Jews, and they received 1,132 decorations, including three Congressional Medals of Honor and 147 Distinguished Service Medals and Crosses. In essence, we find a replication of the Irish and German immigrant experience. Loyalty to their newly adopted country exceeded their animosity for one or another of America's allies.

—See Fredman and Falk, *Jews in American Wars,* 1942.

Appendix F

Father Duffy: Biographical Sketch

Francis Duffy was born in Cobourg, Ontario, on May 2, 1871 of first generation Irish parents. At age ten, young Duffy was employed in a local factory to augment family income, while also attending a small Catholic parochial school. One of his teachers recognized the boy's potential, encouraged him, and gave him considerable personal attention. He received a scholarship to St. Michael's College in Toronto and further studied and taught at St. Francis Xavier College in New York City. Duffy was admitted to St. Joseph's Seminary in 1894 and, upon ordination, took postgraduate studies at Catholic University in Washington, D.C. After receiving his Doctor of Divinity in 1896, "Prof Duff" became a highly popular instructor of logic and psychology at St. Joseph's in Dunwoodie, New York.

During the early twentieth century, as revolutionary movements swept Europe and democratic socialism made its debut on the American scene, its theological counterpart in the Catholic Church was the emergence of "Modernism," an intellectual movement which essentially concluded that the Church should "open" its dogmatic structure to scientific data, particularly from the fields of archaeology, anthropology and psychology. Between 1905–08, Father Duffy was an editor of the Catholic *New York Review,* a monthly review which addressed modernist thought. Both a theologian and a psychologist, he was uniquely qualified to comment on such issues. He also wrote widely for other Catholic publications. In 1907, after traumatic dispute, the Holy Office stigmatized modernist thought as "the summation and essence of every heresy." The *New York Review* ceased publication.

In 1912, Duffy was tasked with organizing a new parish in an economically depressed section of the Bronx. He did so superbly, demonstrating an administrative skill commensurate with his intellectual gifts, and the Church of the Savior flourished.

When the 69th was mobilized for duty on the Mexican border, Captain Duffy became senior chaplain of the regiment. In France, he was soon promoted to major as senior chaplain of the Rainbow Division, and he left France a lieutenant colonel. The World War I military success of the "Fighting 69th" was due, at least as much to the men's bed-rock confidence in this inspirational priest, as it was to the talents of its combat officers.

Upon return to the States, Father Duffy became pastor of the Church of the Holy Cross near the center of the theater district. According to my father, "many actors and actresses attended mass there. They all loved Father Duffy, because he understood theatrical people and their problems. In those days, entertainers and artists were often criticized as having loose morals and so forth; but not by Father Duffy because, in them, he saw the future of American culture."

In the presidential campaign of 1928, Father Duffy drafted Governor Al Smith's reply to Charles Marshall's inflammatory aspersions on the loyalty of American Catholics.

Concerning his personal philosophy and politics, Father Duffy wrote:

> For myself, I cannot claim any special attribute except that of being fond of people—just people. The object of civilization, it seems to me, is to cultivate a set of human beings who are at least tolerant of each other in everything that is not destructive and at the same time leave room for the cultivation of particular interests or enthusiasms. . . . While I do not take any definite color politically, still in economic questions I stand with the class of people that by birth and association I belong to and love in the direction of organized labor and social reform.

> —Ella Flick, *Chaplain Duffy of the Sixty-Ninth Regiment* (Philadelphia: Dolphin Press, 1935), p. 153.

The death of Father Duffy on June 26, 1932, brought an outpouring of tribute from persons high and low, from the

President of the United States, to thousands of clerks and blue collar workers who thronged the route of his funeral procession. And what a procession that was! Perhaps the most impressive of any in New York's history. Church and State combined forces to accord the fullest honors to this extraordinary parish priest. As the cortege, accompanied by his National Guard regiment, its veterans, and delegations from other units of the Rainbow, escorted the purple-draped caisson, generals of the Army preceded it with shrouded swords, and Army planes flew overhead in tribute. But the best tribute was written by Alexander Woollcott:

> This city is too large for most of us. But not for Father Duffy. Not too large, I mean, for him to invest it with the homeliness of a neighborhood. When he walked down the street—any street—he was like a cure striding through his own village. Everyone knew him. I have walked beside him and thought I had never before seen so many pleased faces. The beaming cop would stop all traffic to make a path from curb to curb for Father Duffy. Both the proud-stomached banker who stopped to speak with him on the corner and the check-room boy who took his hat at the restaurant would grin transcendentally at the sight of him. He would call them both by their first names, and you could see how proud they were on that account. Father Duffy was of such dimensions that he made New York into a small town.

> —Alexander Woollcott, *While Rome Burns* (New York: Grosset & Dunlap, 1936), pp. 49–50.

—See p. 260, n. 11.

Appendix G

The Court-Martial of Tom Shannon

One of the problems of hearsay, refined over the years, is that another horror story, the court-martial of William O'Day, makes this one seem credible. The actual event, obtained from official records, is less appalling than my father's version because, this time, the regimental miscarriage of justice was corrected after division review.

During January and the first half of February 1918, the men of the 3rd Battalion were billeted in the hamlet of Baissey, a few miles west of Longeau. Baissey was distinguished by a distillery, which was off limits to the men, but its produce was occasionally made available, for a fee, by a priest who lived in an adjacent house.

On January 20, Shannon and his buddy, Private Francis Hays, had been drinking in their billet, just across the street from the distillery. To replenish their supply, Shannon gave Hays a twenty-franc note to buy another bottle from the priest, but the priest didn't have change for the note, so wouldn't sell it. When Hays returned without the desired lubricant, Shannon became upset, put a clip in his rifle, stepped out of the billet, confronted the priest and allegedly said: "You son of a bitch; you won't give me anything; I'll blow your fucking head off."

A sentry guarding the still, and another doughboy who witnessed this confrontation, hustled the priest into his house. A few minutes later, the three of them heard a shot, but since all three were inside the house, they didn't see who shot or at what. Thirty seconds after the shot, the sentry peeked out of the door and saw Shannon head back for his billet. There he relieved Shannon of his rifle, ejected the clip and discovered one round missing. At this point, Shannon returned to the priest who gave him a bottle of liquor. Shannon was court-martialed on the charge of having feloniously shot a .30 caliber ball cartridge at one E. Gieneros, with intent to do him bodily harm. All witnesses testified that Shannon was blind drunk, no one had seen him fire the rifle, and E. Gieneros was not within his vision. Nevertheless, he was found guilty and sentenced to be dishonorably discharged and to be confined at hard labor for six years. Fortunately, the findings and sentence were disapproved at division level, but Shannon may well have suffered "up keep platoon" punishment of the sort adopted by Colonel Bennett of the 168th Ohio regiment for summary court offenders.

That punishment is described in a June 11, 1918 memorandum from Colonel Bennett to Major General Menoher.

> Attention is particularly invited to that clause which provides that, while the prisoner is kept in the front line trenches continually during the term of his sentence, he is available for regular duty with his company when it occupies front line position and subject to extra fatigue for upkeep of his own particular G.C.

> —WWI Organization Records, 42nd Division,
> HDQRS—Dec. File 253, Box #90.

Such punishment today would be considered overzealous, but it was common in the Rainbow, and possibly, in the rest of the A.E.F. For example, the same file folder reveals that a sentinel of the 167th Alabama found sleeping at his post was dishonorably discharged and sentenced to five years at hard labor; and a private from the 117th Ammunition Train, who stole two hams and two shoulders from a French civilian, suffered the same penalty, as did another private from that same outfit, for having refused to leave a cafe, while cursing the corporals who had ordered him to do so. One speculates that had such offenders been systematically apprehended, and uniformly convicted and sentenced, the A.E.F. might have been decimated.

Appendix H

Major General Charles P. Summerall's Impact on the 69th, the Rainbow Division, and the Advance on Sedan

On the evening of October 15, Major General Charles P. Summerall criticized and subsequently relieved the 83rd Brigade commander, General Lenihan, and the 69th's colonel, Harry Mitchell, as well as two of the 69th's staff officers, for having failed to break through the wire at Landres-St. Georges. All of these officers were well liked and highly respected by men of the regiment.

Both General Lenihan and Colonel Mitchell were replaced by artillery officers, Lenihan by Colonel Henry Reilly, the effective commander of the 149 Illinois Field Artillery, and Mitchell by Lieutenant Colonel Charles Dravo, the division's machine gun officer.

General Summerall was an artillery officer who often proclaimed the determinate effect of overwhelming, selectively directed artillery fire in advance of an attack. But during the Meuse-Argonne offensive, he was Pershing's "hatchet-man" and had developed a penchant for concluding orders with such expressions as ". . . at all costs," ". . . or the division must show at least 6,000 casualties to indicate the extent of its efforts," or "You will give us the Cote-de-Chatillon tomorrow or turn in a report of 5,000 casualties."

Colonel Mitchell had tried to cope with Summerall's demands with calm reason, to no avail. MacArthur did so through dramatics. "General Summerall," he postured, ". . . if this Brigade does not capture Chatillon, you can publish a casualty list of the entire Brigade with the Brigade Commander's name at the top." It is reported that "tears sprang into General Summerall's eyes."

While MacArthur was a consummate actor, not averse to using grandiose remarks crafted to the situation, there is evidence that on this occasion he might have matched deed to the word, for shortly later he ordered the Iowa and Alabama regiments to take the Cote by night attack using only bayonets. This would have been a suicidal venture. Fortunately, he was persuaded to desist. [See Reilly, pp. 659–682 and Tabor, Vol. 2, p. 186.]

Father Duffy, ever temperate in his published remarks, took issue with Summerall in his regimental history:

> I think his decision was wrong. It was a question of whether our Colonel was a man to get out of his regiment all it was capable of. No person who knows him could ever accuse Harry D. Mitchell of losing his nerve in a battle. He liked a fight. He would have been happier out on the line as Lieutenant Colonel than back in his P.C., but he knew that there was nobody who could handle an attack and put courage and dash into it better than Colonel Donovan . . . Colonel Mitchell's spirit was equally resolute and his orders crisp and strong. The whole regiment was devoted to him, and anxious to do their very best under his command . . . The worst blow to our morale that we ever received was inflicted by the order relieving our Colonel. (pp. 276–278)

Apprised of the circumstances of Summerall's action, Lieutenant General Liggett, commanding the First American Army, soon returned these men to active status, General Lenihan commanding a brigade with New York's 77th Division.

A few weeks after this incident, the Rainbow was proceeding toward Sedan, their ultimate objective. Freely interpreting an order from Pershing, and in Liggett's absence, General Summerall instructed the 1st Division, which he had previously commanded, and which also was a favorite of Pershing, to make a race for Sedan and capture it. (To the Rainbow, the 1st Division was often referred to as "Pershing's Pets.") This necessarily involved cutting through the line of advance of both the New York 77th Division and the Rainbow at night, in the midst of combat —an extraordinarily irresponsible action (perhaps the biggest American command boner of the war), which caused considerable disruption among the divisions affected before the order was countermanded by General Liggett. Said Liggett:

> This was the only occasion in the war when I lost my temper completely . . . The movement had thrown the I Corps front and the adjoining French front into such confusion that had the enemy chosen to counter-attack in force at the moment, a catastrophe might have resulted.

Indeed, the situation had become so confused that Mac-Arthur, uniquely attired in riding britches and turtleneck sweater, was mistaken as a German officer and taken prisoner, at the point of a pistol, by an enterprising First Division lieutenant. MacArthur did not protest this *snafu* and was later given command of the Rainbow on Summerall's recommendation.

As an alternative to court-martial, General Summerall later became Chief of Staff of the United States Army.

—Liggett, p. 229–230; James, pp. 30–37; and Coffman, pp. 348–354. See also memorandum from Colonel Reilly, C.O. 83rd Brig., to General Menoher, C.O. 42nd Div. "Subject: A. Interference of the 1st Division with our lines; B. Complaint of the French 40th Infantry Division as to our sector limits." WWI Organ. Records, 42nd Div., 165th Inf., 242-33.6, "Special Reports of Operations," RG 120, NA.

Endnotes

Endnotes to Introduction

1. Fully 1.6 million volunteers served in the armed forces of the United States between April 1, 1917 and Nov. 11, 1918, of whom 606,000 were sailors and marines. An additional 2.8 million men were drafted. Thus, 36% of all forces were raised through voluntary enlistment. Two million Americans served in France. Of the 1.25 million who experienced combat, probably over half were volunteers. Volunteering was prohibited on August 8, 1918 to retain skilled workers at home.
> —*Encyclopaedia Britannica*, 1967 ed., "Conscription."
> Bach & Hall, *The Fourth Division* (Pub. by Div., 1920), p. 261.

2. See Clara Eve Schieber, *The Transformation of American Sentiment Toward Germany* (Boston: Cornhill Pub. Co., 1923), for a pioneering example of content analysis.

3. The German Army shot hostages and destroyed villages in retaliation for Belgian civilian resistance, and its policy was publicly proclaimed as attempted deterrence.
> —See Barbara Tuchman, *The Guns of August* (New York: Macmillan, 1962), pp. 225–228, 310–322.

4. This conclusion is based chiefly on Barbara Tuchman's *The Zimmermann Telegram* (New York: Macmillan Co., 1958). It is also in general accord with Samuel Morison, *History of the American People* (New York: Oxford University Press, 1965), pp. 848–860; Newton D. Baker's *Why we Went to War* (New York: Harper, 1936); and Patrick Devlin's *Too Proud to Fight, Woodrow Wilson's Neutrality* (New York: Oxford University Press, 1975).

5. A further perspective of the relative human cost involved in these conflicts for American servicemen is seen below:

	W.W. I	W.W. II	Korea	Vietnam
Combat deaths	52,513	292,131	33,629	47,356
Other causes	63,195	115,185	20,617	10,795
Total deaths	115,708	407,316	54,246	58,151
Non-mortal wounds	204,002	670,846	103,284	153,303
Total casualties	320,710	1,078,162	157,530	211,454

	W.W. I	W.W. II	Korea	Vietnam
Death as % of casual.	36%	38%	34%	27%
Number serving	4,743,826	16,353,659	5,764,143	8,744,000
Casual. as % serving	6.7%	6.6%	2.7%	2.4%

—Source: *World Almanac and Book of Facts,* 1990.

6. Laurence Stallings, *The Doughboys* (New York: Harper & Row, 1963, pp. 26–27, Stallings, a Marine with the 2nd Division, who lost a leg at Belleau Wood, probably wrote the best book on the A.E.F. from the perspective of an American combatant.

7. The American First Army, at this time, comprised over 550,000 men, but the nine divisions that were committed to combat at St. Mihiel totaled about 230,000 Doughboys, while an additional 128,000 stood by in reserve. The remainder of forces were involved with supply, aviation, special Corps artillery, Patton's tank brigade, the staff of three Army Corps, etc.

— Sources for this and most other American battles that are not Rainbow specific are primarily derived from The American Battle Monuments Commission, *American Armies and Battlefields in Europe* (U.S. Government Printing Office, 1938); Hunter Liggett, *A.E.F.* (New York: Dodd, Mead & Co., 1928); and Stallings, *op. cit.*

8. In the initial phase of the Meuse-Argonne offensive, 200,000 Doughboys moved out along a twenty-four mile front against five German divisions (61,500 men). In so doing, Pershing achieved complete surprise, not only through strategic feints and misinformation leaked to the enemy, but also because it was assumed that this sector was virtually impregnable. Of course, the Germans quickly reinforced their troops in the Argonne and both they and their Doughboy protagonists fought with extraordinary tenacity.

9. This "Square Division" turned out to be too large and unwieldy and was in the process of reduction and reorganization as the war came to an end.

10. Information on the organization of the division, including letters from Secretary of War Baker and Douglas MacArthur, is found in Henry J. Reilly's *Americans All: The Rainbow at War* (Columbus, Ohio: The F. J. Heer Printing Co., 1936), pp. 25–54.

11. Background information on the 69th was derived from a pamphlet prepared by its regimental historian, Lieutenant Colonel Kenneth Powers, Ret.

For World War I data, personnel, and narrative of the regiment, nothing can surpass Francis P. Duffy's *Father Duffy's Story* (New York: George H. Dorn Co., 1919), with its appendix by Joyce Kilmer. Valuable supplemental regimental information is found in Reilly, *op. cit.*

12. According to Colonel Powers, MacArthur confided to one of the regiment's veterans that he had selected the 69th for service with the Rainbow because it had the best list of battle honors of any regiment in New York State, and its service record on the Mexican Border had been superior.

Endnotes to Chapter One

1. It was Secretary of War Baker's recollection, and generally believed among the men of the "Rainbow," that MacArthur had so named their division; but MacArthur, in an interview with Brigadier General Henry J. Reilly, ascribed its initial naming to a newspaper reporter. "I shall call it the Rainbow in my dispatch," the reporter said, after MacArthur had declared that "In the make up and promise of the future of this division it resembles a rainbow." Major MacArthur immediately seized upon this brilliant happenstance, and he and General Mann officially proposed to the War Department that the new National Guard Division, which had not yet been even numbered, be called the Rainbow Division. See Reilly, *op. cit.*, pp. 25–27.

2. Colonel Powers notes: "And apparently the only group that was escorted to the 69th by their parent regiment, all because of the great affection that had existed for years between both regiments." A unique relationship appears to have existed between these two New York regiments, so dissimilar in composition, yet so affectionate of each other. Some of the most popular officers of the 69th in World War I had transferred from the "Kid Gloves" 7th, namely, William Cavanaugh, "Big Tom" Reilley, and the McKenna brothers. According to Colonel Powers, the genesis of this relationship derived from their Civil War experience. I would further conjecture that it was during the New York City Draft Riots of 1863, when the 69th arrived from Gettysburg to relieve the 7th Regiment beleaguered in its armory by the rioters.

3. Hereinafter, the abbreviation for Headquarters.

4. See Appendix C: "The 15th New York National Guard."

5. Nowhere in the division, regimental, or inspector general

records could I find reference to this alleged fatality, and none of the few surviving vets whom I questioned recalls it. The official Alabama account of this initially strained relationship between the regiments follows:

> Something went wrong and [the Alabamians] were quarantined because of a few cases of mumps and meningitis. It was considered a rotten deal. While the entire organization was confined to the limits of the camp, several ugly rumors were maliciously circulated to the effect that the men were undisciplined and out creating trouble. The ban was not lifted for six weeks. Too, a very insignificant scrap of a personal nature, between small groups of Alabamians and New Yorkers, started a lot of baseless criticism against the former.
>
> It is said the men of the 165th Infantry (old 69th New York) would tell incoming organizations: "The Alabamas are coming over to clean you out." A specific case is cited that when the negroes of the 15th New York arrived, whites from the same state ran out and embraced the blacks, repeating to the latter the warning: "The Alabamas are coming over to clean you out," which caused the 15th that night to have a call to arms, though the men of the 167th at the time were all sleeping soundly.
>
> —William Amerine, *Alabama's Own in France*
> (New York: Eaton Gettinger, 1919), pp. 55–56.

On April 25, 1990, I interviewed 95-year-old veteran Paul Jarrett at his home in Palm Springs, California. At Camp Mills, Jarrett had been a lieutenant with the 166th Ohio. He said that the first night of the 15th New York's arrival in camp, his regiment was mustered out to bodily interpose itself between the Alabamas and the black 15th, because the former had mobilized to dislodge the latter.

> The Alabama regiment was camped right next to us. One night there was an awful ruckus over there, and the next thing we knew we were called out to emergency duty with arms. We went over there, and here were the Alabama guys and Negro troops, standing there, faced off, getting ready to fight. They marched us right down between them to separate them. We were kind of nervous about that, because they all had guns and bayonets and were glaring at each other. But they finally settled down, and we could go back to our tents.

In reference to a later confrontation, former Congressman Hamilton Fish, then a captain with the 15th New York, verified that his officers had obtained ammunition from men of the 69th prior to an anticipated raid by the Alabamians, and he described how that raid was prevented at the last minute. [See Henry Berry, *Make the Kaiser Dance* (New York: Arbor House, 1978), p. 417.]

A reasonable scenario that might be inferred from these accounts suggests that sporadic fist fights in the local bars among men of the three units resulted in the 15th New York being relieved of their ammunition, and the Alabamians being confined to camp, using mumps and meningitis as a pretext, while the men of the 69th continued to get passes. Naturally, the Alabamians were furious, indelicate language was exchanged, and a group of Alabamians advanced on the 69th camp. They were repulsed by the division's MP unit from Virginia. The black 15th suffered the most from these antagonisms, being transferred to Camp Merritt in New Jersey, which had been deserted for years and was in deplorable condition.

6. Colonel Powers writes: "I always thought Cavanaugh was originally from Boston. A bachelor and lawyer, he lived in the New York Athletic Club. In World War II, he was executive officer of the 69th and later its commanding officer."

7. Which raises the question concerning my father's subsequent stories about Quirt. To Red Ettinger, danger from the German Army palled to insignificance compared to the menace posed by Lieutenant Quirt. Donald Adair believed that Quirt had been a competent officer. "Remember," he told me in an interview shortly before his death, "Quirt had to deal with a pretty rough group." Then, I ask myself, why did he subject the most helpless member of the group to a general court-martial? [See "The O'Day Incident," Chapter 3.] Adair had no knowledge of that incident, and his transfer to the intelligence section had been facilitated by Quirt.

8. See Appendix D for pre-war background of Donovan.

Endnotes to Chapter Two

1. Paul Jarrett, a 95-year-old veteran of the Ohio regiment, had been lounging on the forward deck of the *Agamemnon* when all this happened. In my April 1990 interview, he said he was terrified as he saw the bow of the *Von Steuben* loom from the foggy darkness, and he was catapulted across the deck by the collision. His fellow

doughboy, who dropped to the deck of the *Von Steuben,* had been sleeping in a lifeboat.

2. Martin Hogan (*The Shamrock Battalion of the Rainbow,* p. 25) saw only fog after the *America* put into Brest Harbor. It was difficult for Hogan to see beauty anywhere, which is understandable in view of the hell he went through. But it is questionable that my father saw green trees and fields in November.

3. Naives-en-Blois is located in the southeastern part of the old duchy of Lorraine, 30 miles west of Nancy, and is populated by 95 hospitable people and 500 cows.

4. In late May of 1987, my wife and I met several people in Naives who had known the Dumanois, showed us where they had lived, and provided us with Madame Dumanois' first name, Eugenie.

The other regiments of the Rainbow were billeted under similar conditions; this from Tabor, *op. cit.,* pp. 46–47:

> The winter of 1917–1918 was one of the severest on record, and weather toward the latter part of December sent the mercury below zero and held it there. . . . The enlisted men of the regiment were still wearing the light garrison shoes issued in September at Camp Mills; many of them had only summer underwear and no gloves; and half of them had but one pair of socks. Some had knit helmets, but regulations and orders from higher up forbade their wearing them.
>
> And the billets! The troops were distributed in sundry barns and attics whose chief claim to merit was an unobstructed ventilation, so exposed to the wind and weather that often snow sifted in through the crevices and covered the men as they slept on their beds of straw. . . . The French appreciated the difficulties of the Iowans and were anxious to do anything that would make it easier. These were the first Americans that Rimaucourt had ever seen, and it opened its heart to them. In the evenings, the soldiers could usually find some hospitable French fireplace to huddle around until the call to quarters, and the cafes were open and popular. Given a piano, a warm fire, a little wine served by a smiling mademoiselle, and they could forget all about the polar accommodations to which they must return in an hour or so.

5. Grand is 22 miles south of Naives-en-Blois. The regiment arrived there on December 13, 1917, thus completing the first stage

of a six-day march to Longeau, which was to be the division's base
for more advanced weapons training and maneuvers. A picturesque
and relatively prosperous village of 600 souls, Grand is located on a
high plateau that separates the valley of the Meuse in the northeast
from the Haute Marne that lies to the southwest. Once a religious
center for the ancient Gauls, the Romans built a temple and an
amphitheater here in an effort to control hostile Gaulic tribes. The
regiment spent two weeks in Grand girding itself for the next 60
mile leg of the journey.

Warner Bros.' movie, *The Fighting 69th*, depicts the regiment
arriving in Grand by railroad, without a trace of snow on the
ground. It was but one of many caricatures of reality perpetrated by
that film. There is, and was, no railroad in Grand.

6. General Pershing was not particularly loved by his troops.
Donald Adair wrote to his family from Remagen, Germany, on
March 5, 1919, and included the following:

> We expect our beloved (?) Commander-in-Chief, Gen. Per-
> shing to come here soon to review the division. I hope he will
> make it snappy and shoot us along to the docks soon after.
> Most of the A.E.F. is hoping that Pershing will run for
> President on the Republican ticket next term so that we can
> show what good Democrats we are.

Although popular affection was not the General's first, second, or
even third priority of business, he truly loved his army; and for
many years after the war he spent summers at a cottage adjacent to
the St. Mihiel American Military Cemetery at Thiaucourt, France.
One suspects that, through grief, he there came to terms with the
awful responsibility he had borne.

7. As in Naives-en-Blois, so too in Grand, my wife and I met a
gentleman in the local cafe who, as a child, had known Madame
Bouvier of the village butcher shop. Madame Bouvier is, of
course, deceased, and the butcher shop was demolished years ago.

Endnotes to Chapter Three

1. Had there been five fatalities in one regiment, one might
conjecture 25 for the entire division. Nowhere in the records did I
find explicit reference to these fatalities, but they are implied by
Hogan, *op. cit.*, p. 43:

It had caused the officers great concern to see the men dropping here and there in the snow from hunger, weakness and from disease. Some of these men, they knew, might lie in the snow for hours before being picked up, and this exposure could well result in fatal pneumonia on this march.

Further evidence is found in a 12/29/17 memo from Colonel Hough to General Lenihan, in which he reported that 38 of the Ohio men were taken to a hospital; and in a 1/2/18 memo from Colonel Hine to Lenihan reporting that 181 men from the 69th were moved by ambulance to their station because they were unable to march.

—"Misc. March Reports & Correspondence." WWI
   Organization Records, 42nd Div., Historical, 83rd Inf. Brig.,
   56.2-65.1, Record Group 120, National Archives,
   Washington, D.C.

Whether bad luck or negligence of command, certain hard facts need be considered: (1) The division was required to consolidate south of Langres for advanced training, while a French division was scheduled to replace them for defense of the region. (2) Marching the 80-mile distance would be a normal means of attaining the objective, while further conditioning the troops. (3) The weather was unanticipated and unprecedented. (4) It developed that the chief problem was criminally deficient boots, which should have been discovered and remedied at Naives-en-Blois.

2. After the march was completed, General Lenihan required a report from all company commanders on their experience with the field boot then in use. Most of the reports were devastating, some highly articulate. The 69th's Captain Tom Reilley wrote a memorandum calculated to require the supplier of these boots to wear them in hell. Following detailed specification— scrap leather pressed with paper composition, not wet proof, shrinks one to two sizes across instep, etc.—Ohio's Colonel Hough concluded that "the shoe is inferior in quality, faulty in construction, and unsatisfactory for this sort of service."
   —*Ibid.*, 1/1/18, and 1/4/18.

General Menoher then had orthopaedic surgeons attached to the division examine all the men. They, too, specified the inferior quality of the boots, and further noted that "only ten percent (10%) of the enlisted men are wearing correctly fitted shoes."

3. The 69th's regimental adjutant at the time, Captain Walter

Powers (later division adjutant), concluded his report on the march as follows:

> The entire march of the command, for the four days, has been excellent in every respect, under the most trying conditions. The health of the command, aside from bad feet [due to criminally inferior boots] has been fine. The morale has been that of veteran troops—any commander who knows and appreciates pluck and endurance in men little used to the rigors of winter marching can appreciate the standard attained. . . . I have yet to see or serve with troops that I consider the superior of the troops that I now serve with.
>
> —*Op. Cit.*, memorandum from Powers to Lenihan, 12/29/17.

4. Not so. James Collintine knew what of he spoke. World War I occurred during the heyday of the British Empire, when that *empire* was represented by the *British Crown*, not the English Parliament. There were many Irish, Scots, Welsh, Punjabis, etc., fighting with him under that same Crown, simply because it was a more reliable provider than their local squires, satraps, or nabobs.

5. A regimental training memorandum identifies the ridge just north of Versailles-le-Haut, only one mile from Longeau.
   —"To Battalion Commanders and C.O. Hq. Co. 165th Infantry," in folder "165th Inf.—Training (1918)," WWI Organ. Records, 42nd Div., 165th Inf., R.G. 120, Box 28.

6. I am advised by the German Embassy that there was no official German national anthem until August 1922, when, under the Weimar government, it became "Deutschland uber Alles." Until then, "Heidi im Siegerkranz," sung to the tune of "God Save the King" and "America the Beautiful," had long been regarded as an unofficial anthem.

7. According to Mr. Jean Morrisot, whom I interviewed during the summer of 1987, and who was twelve years old during the regiment's sojourn in his village, there was no convent in Longeau in 1917–18, although there was the church property described, and there may have been teaching or nursing sisters on the premises. However, Donovan, in a 2/1/18 training memo to company commanders, *op. cit.*, instructed: ". . . drill in the field south of the Convent."

8. I reviewed the court-martial proceedings, which are a matter of

public record. My father and the other men of the platoon had been misinformed. Sergeant Blaustein was not a witness at the court-martial of William O'Day, and the latter did not die en route to Leavenworth, although he twice tried to escape during the journey and was once shot in the attempt. [See follow-up on O'Day in the *Epilogue.*]

9. See Appendix E, "Sergeant Blaustein and Jewish Members of the 69th."

10. In his regimental diary, pp. 32–33, Father Duffy commented about John Mangan:

> Everybody likes Mangan: half-rebellious prisoners and sodjering details and grasping civilians and grouchy division quartermasters. For "he has a way wid him." At bottom it is humor and justness, with appreciation of the other fellow's difficulties and states of mind. With his fairness and balance, he carries such an atmosphere of geniality and joy of life that everybody begins to feel a new interest in the game and a new willingness to play a decent part in it.

Following the war, John Mangan became Deputy Police Commissioner of the City of New York.

11. Jean Morrisot, a local resident, told us that when the fire alarm sounded on that cold winter night in 1918, he got out of bed and made a beeline for the door, but his mother told him he couldn't leave the house and to go back to bed. But Jean never missed a fire, so he sneaked out of the bedroom window and joined our men on the bucket brigade. According to Jean, the old fire chief referred to by my father did indeed have a pronounced limp, the result of a war wound, but was not equipped with a wooden leg. In later years, Jean Morrisot, himself, became the village fire chief.

12. Indeed, so obvious was the solution, and so convenient the replacement buttons, some have speculated that the whole affair had been anticipated by General Pershing, and was a ploy designed to convince the Allies that American troops would be a considerable problem if dispersed among the French and British armies, as they constantly advocated. Pershing and President Wilson were determined that American soldiers fight under American command as a national army. More likely, the regimental quartermaster had simply tried to avoid the onerous task of replacing the buttons.

Endnotes to Chapter Four

1. Luneville, with a population of 23,000, was a medieval walled city, formerly part of the Duchy of Lorraine, in northeastern France. It is on the Meurthe River, 18 miles southeast of Nancy.

2. According to M. Jules Legras, an elderly gentleman from the village of Croismare, Camp New York was located 2.5 kilometers north of Croismare on Route D-160. His immediate reaction to our inquiry was: "The soldiers from New York, Oui. We have all heard about them and Camp New York." Nothing remains of the old barracks, and the area is still farmland abutting the Forest of Parroy.

3. Elderly residents of neighboring villages call them "the American Trenches." Though eroded by the rains of seventy years, they are still visible in the gloom of the Forest of Parroy, along with mounds that used to be dugouts. Sub-Sector Rouge Bouquet and strong point Sorbiers are found alongside the road between Mouacourt and Laneuveville-aux-Bois just north of the Route du Haut de Faite in the Bois de Chaussaille. [See *Carte Topographique,* #3515 ouest]

4. American aggressiveness was a double edged sword for both our French ally and the enemy. For several years, there had been a gentlemen's agreement between the latter parties that, insofar as possible, peace would reign in the Lorraine Sector. Each side knew the exact location of the other's positions, which would have made an artillery duel extremely damaging, and since both sides needed a rest area, this had been it. French officers took heart at this display of Yankee vigor, but the veteran poilus initially despaired of those "crazy Americans" and tried to distance themselves from the lightning they knew would inevitably follow the cursed thunder.

5. Yes he was. The reports of Lieutenant Oscar Buck and two sergeants identify Quirt as the first officer at the scene of the tragedy, directing the pioneer platoon. Strangely, however, unlike Buck, Donovan, Lieutenant Cunningham, and five sergeants, Quirt was not cited for his rescue/reorganization efforts, and he is not even mentioned in Father Duffy's account, where Sergeant Blaustein is credited with leading the pioneers.

　　　　—File: "Report of Events in CR Rouge Bouquet," *op. cit.,* 11.5-33.7; and Duffy, p. 63.

6. Bodies from the dugout were disinterred after the war and, if not claimed for shipment home, were transferred to the Meuse-

Argonne American Military Cemetery at Romagne, where I verified some of their identities from the cemetery roster. They lie there cheek by jowl with black troops of the 92d and 93d Divisions. These awesome cemeteries are the only integrated memorials of World War I, simply because, after the war, remains were buried as they were received from battlefield grave sites in the region, without regard to race, rank or religion. Troops from black labor battalions had the onerous task of exhuming and reinterring the bodies.

The German WWI military cemeteries in France are also impressive. Less visible than their Allied or American counterparts (most lie tucked away in wooded areas), and devoid of monuments, they are meticulously groomed, and one occasionally is shocked to find a newly potted plant under an iron cross dating to 1914. They, too, are integrated, with Jewish tablets made of stone interspersed among the crosses.

7. Kilmer, *op. cit.*, vol. 1, pp. 105–107.

8. See Appendix F: "Biographical Sketch of Father Duffy."

9. One must remember that O'Day's court-martial and conviction was a regimental action. From a review of this and other 69th general court-martials, I am convinced that the sentences were disproportionate to the offense, probably because officers of the regiment were fearful that Army HQ would perceive the regiment to be undisciplined. Father Duffy knew this and his intercessions were motivated by both mercy and justice.

10. This excellent memory was enhanced by the fact that virtually the entire age-eligible male population of Duffy's former parish in the Bronx, a parish that he personally had founded, had enlisted in the 69th. In addition to his several qualifications as a saint, Father Duffy was also an astute politician. He quickly perceived in the character of William Donovan a potential future president who could establish the status of Irish Catholics in the United States, and he did everything legitimately possible to promote Donovan's career, both within the regiment and after the war.

11. From a cast of extraordinary characters, the most impressive and intriguing to this writer was Francis Patrick Duffy: superb teacher, peerless chaplain and parish priest, advocate of secular and religious liberty, and champion of mankind against its own intolerance and bigotry. Of all the period war literature that I perused in research for this book, Duffy's was one of the few that eschewed an obligatory hatred for the enemy.

Father (Lieutenant Colonel) Duffy was a recipient of the Distinguished Service Cross, Distinguished Service Medal, Legion of Honor, and the Croix de Guerre with palm—and from his book we find:

> I trust that my appreciation of patriotism or courage or any other attractive human trait is not limited in any degree by racial or religious or sectional prejudice. That was the spirit of our Army. May it always be the spirit of our Republic.

Unfortunately, racial segregation and discrimination was so entrenched in American society and the Army of that day, that even Father Duffy apparently saw nothing prejudicial about it. See Appendix F—Father Duffy: Biographical Sketch.

12. In his report on the raid, Lieutenant Bootz stated that the leg of the soldier in question had been shattered by artillery shrapnel.

—For a detailed report on the raid, see Lieutenant's Bootz report in file: "Raids—Report Coup de Main, March 21/18," *op. cit.,* Box 28.

13. This is a case of mistaken identity. Three Minogues served with the regiment, but Jim, who read the manuscript of this book before he died in late 1988, was not related to the other two and did not participate in the raid. Tom Minogue was killed in the raid's aftermath, but I do not know if Roger Minogue (who was killed at the Ourcq River) was Tom's brother, or whether he participated in the raid.

14. Indeed, he already had many thousand "Herman Bootzs" in his command, particularly with the 32nd National Guard Division from Wisconsin and Michigan. The prejudice evidenced against Herman Bootz and other German surnamed Americans was fairly common during the war and was almost as intense as that displayed against U.S. citizens of Japanese descent during World War II. When the 32nd Division first arrived in France, an initial attempt was made to break it up by using the men of its 128th Infantry Regiment as replacements for other units. Then seven thousand of their troops were detailed as helpers in the Service of Supply. Nevertheless, the 32nd survived these indignities to earn the sobriquet "Les Terribles" from the French, and they effectively fought with the Rainbow at the bloody Ourcq River and in the hell of the Argonne.

—See Stallings, *op. cit.,* pp. 166 ff.

Endnotes to Chapter Five

1. The small city of Baccarat (pop. 5,500) straddles the beautiful Meurthe River 20 miles southeast of Luneville and is world-famous for its crystal glass. Immediately abutting Baccarat, on the high ground to the southeast, perches the ancient walled village of Deneuvre, initially settled by the Gauls, then fortified by the Romans as a sanctuary for the worship of Hercules.

2. Father Duffy described Colonel McCoy as "a man of good height, of spare athletic figure, with a lean, strongly formed face, nose Roman and dominating, brows capacious, eyes and mouth that can be humorous, quizzical or stern, as I learned by watching him, in the first five minutes. He has dignity of bearing, charm of manner, and an alert and wide-ranging intelligence that embraces men, books, art, nature." —*Op. cit.,* p. 92.

3. The location of this misadventure was probably 2 km SE of Bertrichamps at *Noires Terres,* where a secondary road crosses the Meurthe River alongside a railway, both en route to St. Die, then French Division HQ.

4. My father has confused Reherrey, which was regimental HQ, with battalion HQ at Ancerviller. The latter, not the former, had been half-destroyed.

5. There is a shortcut between Reherrey and Ancerviller (battalion HQ at the front) that conforms to my father's description, and another between Reherrey and Deneuvre. However, both are only 2 km long, and he would have had to be traveling from Reherrey. Today, only the grove of trees on the latter route would afford sufficient concealment, and it is to the side of, not across from, the intersection.

6. "By the time the first elements of the American Expeditionary reached France, the American Field Service had grown to approximately 2,000 men. . . . It did not serve with American troops but remained with the French Army until the termination of hostilities." —A.B.M.C., *op. cit.,* p. 503.

7. Bill's son, Kevin Ettinger, received from his father one Croix de Guerre, with citation, and a Purple Heart with citation.

8. See Appendix C: "The 15th New York National Guard."

9. The Meurthe River flows between Deneuvre and Reherrey, but there is no village along it on what would have been my father's

route, according to this description. Again, I think he has confused Deneuvre with Ancerviller, because there is a stream that passes Montigny between Ancerviller and Reherrey.

10. On our second visit to Reherrey in 1988, my wife and I found an elderly gentleman sitting next door to the barn/watering trough location described by my father, the focus of several of these stories. He identified himself as M. Litaize, who was 12 years old when the 1st Division entered Reherrey in 1917, followed by the 69th in 1918. When I asked him about the second group of American soldiers, particularly those on motorcycles who may have been billeted next door, he said: "I certainly do remember them, Oui! They were the kings of the road. They just zoomed by. Everyone else had to march."

11. There is a railroad crossing on Route D-935, two km South of Merviller between Reherrey and Baccarat. Warning lights have replaced crossing guards.

12. A French regiment held a position in the Vosges Mountains to the immediate right of the 168th Iowa, which was within the 42nd Division perimeter. On June 10, the French were relieved by two companies of Donovan's 1st Battalion, plus a company of the Division's Virginia MPs. In so doing, this unit of the 69th leap-frogged both the Alabama and Iowa regiments in the Baccarat sector. My father's dispatch probably addressed this pending transfer. The road he likely travelled (D-992) extends southeast from Badonviller, a beautiful village of 2,000, although then half-destroyed and defended by the Iowans, into the Vosges Mountains. It is a challenge to drive during the day. At night, without lights, it must have been a riveting experience.

Donovan's post of command in the Vosges was called the *Rendezvous des Chasseurs*. In September of 1989, I travelled to Badonviller to photograph the precise location of the command post, as well as the view from the promontory, described by Father Duffy on p. 111 of his book. Both the mayor of Badonviller and my local host, Antoine Humbert, assisted me in this project, to no avail, although I was able to inspect several trenches and bunkers, including a three-level concrete German bunker confronting Donovan's position that could do service today. Finally, we went to the home of retired captain, Marcel Gruber, local historian and newsletter publisher. Amazingly, he was then in the process of writing an article about the history of the *Rendezvous des Chasseurs,* and he graciously provided me with copies of old photographs and maps, as well as the former location of the elaborate wood and stone bunker. After the war, the local forester needed material to rebuild his home, demolished by German shell fire. Since he could make no impression on the concrete German bunkers, he went to the *Rendezvous des Chasseurs* and transported it timber-by-timber and stone-by-stone to the village, where he rebuilt his home. My host drove me to the forester's house, pointed to its beautiful stonework and said: "La, la est le *Rendezvous des Chasseurs."*

In August of 1989, the village of Neuviller, just north of Badonviller, honored 95-year-old former doughboy Paul Jarrett of the Ohio regiment with an elaborate ceremony, which included renaming a village street. It is now *la rue Paul Jarrett.*

Endnotes to Chapter Six

1. I identified the foundation of a chalkstone wall 11 kil. south of Breuvey on Rte. D-281 where it dead ends into Rte. D-81.

2. The fork in the road was probably at St. Etienne, ten kilometers north of Chalons. Vadenay was the immediate destination, thence into Camp Mourmelon. The left fork was by way of Dampierre and St. Hillaire; the right fork via Cuperly. According to regimental records, the 69th made this march in one night, and Father Duffy reported excellent weather. It may be that the 84th brigade, with MacArthur, followed or preceded the 83rd brigade by one night.

3. I was not able to locate this ravine on either of the two possible routes involved. There is a fall-off in grade on the north side of the most probable route, but it hardly constitutes a ravine. I did not have access to Camp de Chalons, in which there was much shifting of division forces prior to the battle, but the map topography therein does not suggest a ravine.

4. For years, my father used a coat of this description while duck hunting, and I recall his having told me that he brought it back from France. How he retained it through all the vicissitudes subsequently experienced boggles the mind.

5. The actual message follows:

"To the French and American Soldiers of the Fourth Army Headquarters Fourth French Army, July 7, 1918

We may be attacked at any moment.

You all know that a defensive battle was never engaged under more favorable conditions.

We are awake and on our guard. We are powerfully reinforced with infantry and artillery.

You will fight on terrain that you have transformed by your work and your perseverance into a redoubtable fortress.

This invincible fortress and all its passages are well guarded.

The bombardment will be terrible. You will stand it without weakness.

The assault will be fierce, in a cloud of smoke, dust and gas.

But your positions and your armament are formidable.

In your breasts beat the brave and strong hearts of free men.

None shall look to the rear; none shall yield a step.

Each shall have put one thought: to kill, to kill, until they have had their fill.

Therefore, your General says to you: You will break this assault and it will be a happy day.*

(Signed) GOURAUD

*According to Father Duffy, "And it will be a happy day" became a popular refrain among the officers of the regiment. Any prognostication of future events invariably led to a chorus of . . . "And - it - will - be - a - happy - day."

6. The Ohio regiment manned one of these sacrificial posts, as did a unit from the black 15th New York Guard, the 369th, a few miles to the east.

7. Excellent eyewitness accounts of the battle are found in *Father Duffy's Story*, pp. 129–145; Hogan, *op. cit.*, pp. 126–135; and Reilly, *op. cit.*, pp. 241–304.

When I asked veteran Paul Jarrett, then a lieutenant with the Ohio regiment of his most vivid recollection of the war, he said it was the sight and stench of the hundreds of German bodies that lay in front of their lines after the second day of the Champagne battle. "It was over a hundred degrees out there, and I still dream of those bloated bodies."

During part of the battle, Jarrett had been ordered to observe and report on particularly heavy fighting in the 69th sector, where his superiors anticipated a possible German breakthrough. He said that, through his binoculars, he could see vicious hand-to-hand combat through swirls of dust, as 69th men poured out of their trenches to engage the enemy. "For a while, it was touch and go," he said.

8. Usually, only the right ear was severed. In so doing, it was presumed that the victor would incorporate the strengths and virtues of his adversary.

9. The boy's loss was particularly grieved by a distinguished uncle. This from Frederick Palmer's biography of Secretary of War Newton D. Baker, vol. 2, p. 59:

> After reading scores of pages recording Baker's three days on the national witness-stand, I cannot refrain from a word about Senator Wadsworth, Republican, of New York, who did not ask questions for questions' sake, or to score a point, but apparently only on subjects that he knew, and with a constructive object. . . . His conduct as a member of the Senate Committee on Military Affairs had a thoroughbred quality from beginning to end. . . .

10. Blighty: "A wound or furlough permitting a soldier to be sent back to England from the front during World War I." *Random House Dictionary*.

Endnotes to Chapter Seven

1. The Rainbow's final casualties from that battle were 6,500 men, most occurring the first three days. Casualties for the 69th were 238 killed, 1,180 wounded, and 153 missing—out of 3,000 effectives—50% for the regiment as a whole.

2. Action reports indicate that William McKenna was regimental adjutant at least until September 11, 1918. He was replaced by Martin Meaney on September 27. It is possible that McKenna was on leave when my father rejoined the regiment and that his replacement was acting.

3. Kilmer, *op. cit.*, vol. 1, p. 108.

4. See Appendix G: "The Court-Martial of Tom Shannon."

5. Father Duffy (*op. cit.*, p. 218) notes that "Tom Shannon, being carried in, got off his stretcher and wanted to give his place to another man who, he said, was worse wounded than himself. An officer ordered him back on the stretcher and he was carried in, and since then I have heard he has died of his wounds."

6. That platoon action is described by Father Duffy, *op. cit.*, pp. 186–187.

"It's task was to cover the left flank as the line advanced, which brought the men along the top of the hill, where they suffered severely. Sergeant Crittenden was killed and Louis Torrey, a pious lad; Charles Geary also, and Carlton Ellis and R.J. Schwartz. Sergeant Dan Garvey, Frank Daley, John J. Murphy, Patrick Cronin and one of the Gordon brothers were fatally wounded and carried off the field. Harry McAllister was badly wounded. Big, impulsive Mike Cooney carried him down through a rain of fire to the bottom and then went back through it to get his rifle. James Allen lay out on the hill moaning. Harry Horgan started up to get him but was killed before reaching him. Thomas O'Connor crept up cautiously and coolly. He was stooping to pick him up when a bullet struck him and he fell on the body of his comrade. Nothing daunted, Michael Ruane and William McCarthy made their way up that hill of death and carried down their wounded comrade. Both Allen and McAllister afterwards died of their wounds."

Of such stuff are heroes made, and this action of the 1st platoon, Company C, 69th New York Infantry, was not untypical of other deadly encounters on that morning of July 29, 1918, above the Ourcq River.

7. Among the survivors of the battle recommended for regimental citation, five are featured in this narrative. They were Sergeants Jack Ryan and Tom FitzSimmons, and Privates Spencer Sully, James Collintine, and John Mahon. According to Father Duffy, Mahon, the only avowed atheist of Headquarters Company, "always has some special reason why he should be selected as a member of every gun crew sent to the front line."

8. Because the enemy, considering the sector to be excessively vulnerable, had already begun to evacuate it. For an excellent description and analysis of the battle, see Liddle Hart, *History of the First World War*, Chapter 8.

Others might ascribe the ease of advance to a rainbow:

"Halfway across the bog the sun sailed out from behind a cloud. Bayonets flashed for twenty miles. In the same moment a rainbow ran across the sky, and the division for which it was named let out a yell that rang high above the roaring barrage. Obviously it meant

308

Gott Mit Uns. Supernatural or not, that rainbow was the big thrill of the war."

  —Charles MacArthur, *War Bugs* (Garden City: Doubleday,
   Doran & Co., 1929), p. 143.

  9. While compelling in detail, "The Colonel's Equerry" is probably either fictitious or occurred in a different time frame, because Harry Mitchell commanded the 69th during the St. Mihiel Offensive. Frank McCoy had been promoted to brigadier general in command of the 63rd Brigade of the 32nd Division in late August, and there is nothing in Duffy's book to indicate that he visited the regiment following the battle.

  10. Charles MacArthur, by turn, was winsome, brash, morose, insightful, and infuriating to the pompous, whose egoes he loved to puncture. He is the only Doughboy I heard of who refused promotion to private first class. His book, *War Bugs,* describes through sardonic humor how men survive imminent destruction, discomfort, and unreason. Veterans of the 69th who read the book immediately identified with it because, for most, humor was also their means of coping with war's calamities. To appreciate the genius of its author, read *Charlie,* by Ben Hecht.

  When MacArthur's artillery outfit arrived at the Argonne a few days earlier, but in the same area as the 69th, this was their view:

  "The sun appeared, and we gave our new surroundings the once-over. It was hardly a garden of roses. The woods were splintered into small bits, green with mustard gas. There wasn't a live leaf in twenty miles. Thousands of dead men sprawled in the ulcerated fields. Horses, their legs awkwardly pointing up, and a general litter of junk. . . . Everything pointed to panic and massacre. . . .

  "One of the kids lay on the ground dying with a bullet in his guts. He had been yanked from a stenographer's job in New York, trained (as they say), and exposed to his first fire—all in thirty-seven days. . . .

  "The doughboys told of being marched in a column of fours right down to the trenches in full sight of the German gunners. More Sears-Roebuck officers. One gang of artillerymen told us of firing for thirty-six hours without effect. It turned out that they hadn't used fuses. Apparently their officers thought shells went off by themselves and had been pegging iron cucumbers through the entire battle."

> —Charles MacArthur, *War Bugs* (New York: Doubleday, Doran & Co., 1929), pp. 173–74.

11. Apparently the admiration was mutual. In *War Bugs*, p. 214, Charles MacArthur describes his outfit overtaking the 69th at Brieulles on their push to Sedan:

"New York unbelted with food and coffee, and we swapped opinions of the war, as always. Our opinions proved that (a) New York was the best regiment of infantry in the world, and (b) Illinois was the best artillery. A great comfort derived from these exchanges, however dark the day. Throughout the war it was New York and Illinois—against the world."

12. The favorite non-scatological marching song of the regiment was "In the Good Old Summertime."

Endnotes to Chapter Eight

1. Prior to initiating the attack, Donovan issued instructions that revealed a tactical initiative rare in the annals of the A.E.F.

> Another matter I took up at this time was to remind the battalion and company commanders that the standard attack formation was not the best one to use, but that we should profit by our experience in the Ourcq and St. Mihiel battles to gain ground forward by moving a few men at a time, and infiltration, rather than attempting a continuous simultaneous advance.　　　　—Reilly, *op. cit.*, p. 691.

Yet Donovan had not revolutionized small unit tactics. The German Army had fully developed the concept of dispersal, infiltration, and envelopment with squads of storm troops in late 1917. Moreover, soon after the Ourcq River battle, Captain Van S. Merle-Smith issued a remarkable memorandum (intended recipients unspecified), under the direction of Colonel McCoy, that proposed radical changes in battle tactics for the regiment. While there is no evidence that the Division adopted these recommendations, it is a prime example of initiative developing from experience, and Donovan's instruction at the Argonne implemented one of the conclusions of the Merle-Smith memorandum.

—"Tactical Points Observed During Recent Action," August 10,

1918, WWI Organ. Rec., Hist., 42nd Div., 165th Inf., RG 120, Box 27, NA.

2. These estimates of distance are most puzzling. According to the battle map prepared for Reilly's division history, as well as my "Carte Touristique," the regiment never advanced more than one mile beyond its line of departure along the Sommerance-Romagne road, although Duffy, himself (*op. cit.,* p. 268) affirms a two-mile distance. However, since the entire area between the German wire and the regiment's starting point was vulnerable to almost continuous artillery fire from both the front and its right flank, the battlefield may have seemed larger to my father and others than it actually was. My father may also have overstated the number of German prisoners taken. I find no reference to prisoners taken by the 69th in other accounts of the battle. On the other hand, the Germans took a number of our bravest men prisoner—those very few who survived after penetrating the first belt of defensive wire.

3. My father was of the impression that Mike Walsh was wounded the following day, and that he and his runner were killed by a shell burst soon after being directed to the rear by Colonel Donovan, but the actual event is found in Major Reilly's book, *op. cit.,* pp. 698–9.

". . . de Lacour reported to me that Captain Walsh had been hit. I went over to the sunken road, where I found him. I said, 'What is the matter? Are you hit?' 'Yes, I'm hit in the arm,' he answered." Major Reilly told Mike to get back to the hospital, but Walsh replied, "I can't leave my men up front." Reilly assured Mike that there would be no further advance that day. He then repeated his instruction as a direct order and Mike headed back. That night, Corporal Fielder of I Company advised the Major that "as we were coming up just at dusk tonight we saw the body of Captain Walsh on the right of the road about a hundred and fifty yards in the rear of the sunken road. The whole back of his head is caved in. We would like to go out and bring his body in." They did so, and the word spread like wildfire. According to my father, "There wasn't a dry eye in the 3rd Battalion that evening."

4. Mike Donaldson, a former sparring partner of middleweight champion, Stanley Ketchel, received the Congressional Medal of Honor for his heroism that day. See Reconnaissance No. 10.

5. "The German main line of defense, the Kriemhilde Stellung

... was a well prepared and strongly wired position consisting of three lines of wire and trenches. The first rows of wire were breast high and as much as twenty feet wide, all bound together in small squares by iron supports so that it was almost impossible for artillery to destroy it unless the whole ground were beaten flat. Back of this were good trenches about four feet deep with machine gun shelters carefully prepared. Behind this front line at thirty yard intervals they had two other lines with lower wire and shallower trenches."   —*Father Duffy's Story*, p. 265.

6. To the right of the 69th, the Alabamas and Iowans of General MacArthur's 84th Brigade incurred even greater losses in their attempt to capture the Cote-de-Chatillon. Concluding the first day's action, they had managed to secure a toehold on its southern approach, only to be driven back the second day. In the process, however, Major Lloyd Ross' battalion of Iowans took fiercely defended Hills 288 and 242, capturing over one hundred prisoners. Lieutenant Taber of that regiment described the landscape as follows:

> The terrain was as forbidding as any the 168th had ever seen. Thick woods, tangled underbrush, scarred trees, gaping shell holes, deep ravines, and lofty ridges united to make a country already desolate and difficult still more forbidding. . . . Dead bodies, some of them in a bad state of decomposition, littered the woods and slopes.
>   —Taber, *Story of the 168th Infantry*, Vol. 2, p. 160.

7. Most American troops did not have tank support until the Battle of St. Mihiel. There, under Lieutenant Colonel George S. Patton's command, 174 French Renault light tanks acquitted themselves reasonably well, although during the first day's action, 40 became stuck in ditches or trenches, and 30 ran out of gas by early afternoon.
            —Martin Blumenson, *The Patton Papers*, pp. 567–600.

The action cited by my father, *was the last American tank action of World War I.* Patton's information, as reported by Blumenson, smacks of fantasy, perhaps because he had been wounded and was in a hospital at the time and did not bother to verify a report of one of his captains, who claimed that ten tanks had reached their objectives, but "the infantry did not follow and the tanks returned. Large bodies of the enemy were dispersed during this advance."
            —*Ibid.*, p. 620.

At that time, surviving veteran Paul H. Jarrett was a lieutenant commanding the 2nd platoon of Ohio's M Company. He told this author that one of those tanks attached itself to his platoon and began to draw heavy fire, so he yelled at the tanker to either move out or get lost.

The number and disposition of tanks actually involved is confusing. The 83rd Brigade Operations Report includes the following entries:

> 8:40   It is reported that 9 tanks are at 0.1-8.8. Other 7 tanks are out of action on account of mechanical trouble.
>
> 10:05   C.O. tanks reports that he went into action with 10 tanks and has now withdrawn 7. Many casualties among personnel and mechanical trouble.
>
> —WWI Organ. Records, 42nd Div., Historical, 83rd Inf. Brig., 242-33.6, "Report of Operations," p. 7. For additional versions of this action, see Reilly, pp. 694–695, 708; Duffy, p. 273; and Cheseldine, p. 252.

From these accounts, it appears that sixteen tanks arrived too late to spearhead the 83rd Brigade's attack, ten were committed to action, and one may have reached the enemy wire. At least one tank was destroyed; others suffered an unspecified degree of damage and retired. However far the tanks advanced, it is clear from an on scene intelligence report of the Ohio regiment (quoted in Cheseldine) that 69th men were fighting in the wire. According to Reilly (p. 657), their bodies were recovered two weeks later. It is also clear that large bodies of the enemy were not dispersed.

8. Colonel Donovan's description of the scene is found in a letter to his wife, quoted from Brown, *The Last Hero,* 62–63:

> —Smash! I felt as if somebody had hit me on the back of the leg with a spiked club. I fell like a log but . . . managed to crawl into my little telephone hole. A machine gun lieutenant ripped open my breeches and put on the first aid. The leg hurt but there were many things to be done. . . . The situation was bad. . . . Messengers I sent through were killed or wounded and messages remained undelivered. We were shelled heavily. Beside me three men were blown up and I was showered with the remnants of their bodies. . . . The telephone was still out. . . . Gas was thrown at us thick and nasty. Five hours passed. I was getting very groggy but

managed to get a message through withdrawing the unit on
the line and putting another in its place.

9. MacArthur commented on the event as follows: "Officers fell
and sergeants leaped to command. Companies dwindled to platoons and corporals took over. At the end, Major Ross had only 300
men and 6 officers left out of 1,450 men and 25 officers. That is the
way the Cote-de-Chatillon fell."

—MacArthur, *Reminiscences* (NY: McGraw Hill, 1964), p. 67.

While the courage and sacrifice of Major Ross' Iowans is indis-
putable, much credit is also due a Major Ravee Norris of the
Alabama regiment. He successfully urged the infiltration of a
company of his men through a chicane in the left flank of the enemy
wire that had been identified from an aerial photograph. This
infiltration, made possible by a massive and highly effective machine gun barrage, and followed by an overall assault, provided the
key to success.   —See Reilly, *op. cit.*, p. 680–687.

Today, sans the debris of war and a new growth of trees (old,
dead ones lean askew, riddled by bullets) the Cote-de-Chatillon remains much as it was on that fateful day in October of 1918. As
hills go, it is not particularly high, steep or large and could barely
accommodate an American size company of men. Heavy artillery should have been able to pulverize it, yet only a few large
craters are visible on its peak, and there were no hardened positions. (French farmers do not remove them from unproductive
land.) Yet, for three days, entrenched small German units with
machine guns, mortars, and telephone links to artillery had used
it to give particular hell to one of the best infantry divisions in
the AEF.

10. My father was not alone in reporting casualties from "friendly
fire." In *Alabama's Own in France*, pp. 191–193, William Amerine
writes:

> The 12th and 13th passed quietly except for considerable
> shelling on the support positions. There our own artillery
> fired short, unfortunately, and on the evening of October 13,
> killed two men in Company K. Others were wounded, and in
> spite of repeated flares and telephonic reports, the gunners
> showed no improvement. . . . On the night of October 13–14
> . . . the supporting artillery was still falling short, with the
> result that more casualties were suffered. This not only

continued all night, but also during the barrage preceding the attack.

Major Ross of the Iowa regiment reported the same problem:

During the night, long range artillery fire from south of Gesnes fell just in front of our assault lines . . . as to cause casualties from shell splinters. Efforts were made all . . . night to get this artillery fire raised . . .   —Reilly, p. 670.

But these casualties were as nothing compared to the havoc wreaked on the 4th Division by "friendly fire" the day before. The 4th was attacking a sector six miles east of the 42nd. On the afternoon of October 12, it was subjected to "a heavy and sustained artillery barrage [coming from the southwest] . . . which caused harrowing losses. More than two hundred men were killed or wounded by this artillery fire."

—Christian Back & Henry Hall, *The Fourth Division*
(Published by the division, 1920), p. 195.

11. But the worst blow to regimental morale was inflicted, neither by the enemy, nor by the weather, but by Major General Charles P. Summerall, commanding the Fifth Army Corps.

See Appendix H—"Major General Charles P. Summerall's Impact on the 69th, The Rainbow Division, and the Advance on Sedan."

12. MacArthur's genius of command is here encapsulated. The typical officer would have taken umbrage at this kind of prank and thus place himself in an untenable position. The almost inevitable response to such a wisecrack is that made by Major Anderson: "Who said that!" Such a response never fails to delight the ranks because it generates a contest that the officer never wins. The culprit rarely confesses, and to penalize the group guarantees dislike and disrespect for the officer. MacArthur, by his delightful retort, not only defused a minor crisis but enhanced his popularity.

But if MacArthur was one-of-a-kind, McGuire was another. This irrepressible young Irishman may have been the only subordinate ever to have made a wisecrack involving MacArthur within hearing of that proud patrician.

13. Beginning with the slaughter they had experienced in taking Belleau Wood, the 2nd Division suffered 37% more casualties during the course of the war than the Rainbows. They thus deserved the Landres walkover.

Endnotes

This from the 42nd Division history, pp. 752–754:

> The 42d Division had had a total of 144 guns of calibers [in its earlier effort]. In the attack of November 1st, the 2d division had a total of 284 guns of all calibers. The 89th Division to its right had a total of 252 guns. . . . In addition, the 5th Corps had 72 155-mm. guns for use on the combined fronts of the 2d and 89th Divisions. . . . The assault was preceded by a two hours fire of destruction. Then the "Summerall Barrage" began covering the entire front of the attack. It had a depth of 1200 meters. For the first eight kilometers of the infantry advance, they walked behind this . . . wall of moving fire. This barrage was a mixture of bands of high explosives and shrapnel, and for the first part of the advance, a machine gun barrage as well. . . . There was not a tree lining the road between Landres-St. Georges and St. George which did not have several machine gun bullet holes in it.

14. Records of the American Battle Monuments' Commission reveal that Horace Baker died on November 7, 1918 and was buried in the Meuse-Argonne cemetery at Romagne. He there rests with 14,246 comrades, almost all killed in the Argonne.

15. At this point we leave the regiment, which, soon after my father was evacuated, took off in pursuit of its military protagonists, echeloned to the left of the 2nd Division.

On November 5, 1918, the Rainbow relieved the 78th Division and, together with elements of the 77th New York Division, were the first American troops to reach the Meuse River overlooking Sedan when the Armistice was signed. A congratulatory order pertinent to the 69th included the following:

> "The dash and elan of the 2nd Battalion under the command of Captain H.A. Bootz when, their ammunition exhausted, they charged Hill 346 and cleared it of machine gun nests with their bayonets; the coolness and courage of the 1st Battalion under Captain Van Merle-Smith in clearing the east edge of the Bois de la Marfee, making possible the advance of the 2nd Battalion; the advance of the 3rd Battalion under Major T.F. Reilley, from Hill 346 against increasing resistance, to Hill 252. Wadelincourt and the banks of the Meuse east of Sedan add another brilliant page to the already glorious history of this regiment."

Father Duffy sums it up (p. 305):

> The cost of victory was high. There were 4,309 casualties for the 42nd Division in the Argonne. Of these, 758 were killed or died of wounds, and 3,551 were wounded. The 69th suffered 1,321 casualties, 44% of its overall complement. Of the survivors, not many more than 600 were men who had left New York with the regiment a little over a year ago. . . . In the line companies, there are about twenty-five rifle men to each company who are oldtimers, and nearly all of these have wound stripes earned in earlier engagements. The great bulk of the old regiment is in hospitals, convalescent and casual camps; some of them promoted, some transferred, hundreds of them invalided home, a great many, alas! buried on battlefields or in hospital cemeteries.

Following the Armistice, the Rainbow took up occupation duty in Germany, the 69th based at Remagen.

Endnotes to Chapter Nine

1. Colonel Robert Joy, professor of the Uniformed Services University of the Health Sciences in Bethesda, noted as follows: "As we *now* know, this is the worst thing you can do to a patient with pulmonary impairment. Restricting respiratory movement increases vascular stasis, infection and so on. This is why we no longer "strap up" the cracked rib patient."

2. The Allerey Hospital Complex was enormous. According to Mr. Antonin Guillot, a teacher in the neighboring village of Verdun-sur-Doubs and the best living authority on the history of this medical complex, its location was dictated by the juncture of two strategic railroad lines, which together, serviced all the fighting fronts. Spread across 160 acres of land, over 600 structures, most of them barracks, had been hastily built by American and French engineers with civilian assistance, including a large number of women. The complex consisted of several base hospitals, field hospitals, and evacuation hospitals. It was a reflection of the American mentality of the day that bigger is necessarily better and more efficient.

At least forty-five thousand casualties went through these hospitals during the six months of their operation. Over a thousand patients who didn't survive were buried in a military cemetery on the hospital grounds. Before completion of the Allerey complex, American troops had been scattered among seven base hospitals around Paris and southern France, and many had been sent to French and British military hospitals, which had become over-crowded, and it was readily predicted that the coming offensive would require added facilities.

For a complete official description of the Allerey complex, see Joseph H. Ford, "Volume II, Administration American Expeditionary Forces," *The Medical department of the United States Army in the World War* (United States Government Printing Office, 1927), Chap. 22.

3. The "sad result" imputed to the 92d Division actually involved only one battalion of one regiment in its initial engagement during the Argonne offensive, but may have had less to do with inadequate experience in the lines than lack of wirecutters, no artillery support, no maps, and no food for two days prior to its attack. The fundamental problem was prejudiced white general officer organization and leadership. Moreover, during this same time frame, elements of several white divisions also broke under German counterattack. [See Barbeau and Henri, *The Unknown Soldiers*, pp. 145–163.]

4. This kind of complaint about the American Red Cross and the Y.M.C.A. was common among the doughboys of World War I, and the reputations of these estimable organizations suffered from it for a generation. [See "That Damn Y" in Henry Berry's, *Make the Kaiser Dance*, pp. 84–86. But, see also p. 81.]

Actually, on the matter of charging for various sundries, it was General Pershing who was responsible, lest the men become "objects of charity." They were not to be "pauperized." [Pershing letter to Newton D. Baker, Nov. 13, 1917, cited in Frederick Palmer's, *Newton D. Baker: America at War*, Vol. 2, p. 4.]

But if white doughboys were inconvenienced, the experience of black troops with the "Y" was devastating. They were either rigidly segregated in an inferior section of the hut or excluded altogether. According to Barbeau and Henri, p. 41, "The Knights of Columbus and the Salvation Army had a much more liberal racial policy and did a good job . . . of providing recreation for black soldiers" in integrated huts.

5. Having twice been in a guard house, my father had begun to acquire such esoteric knowledge.

6. The Federal Records Center at Suitland, Maryland, was unable to locate a record of this court-martial proceeding. It would have been fascinating. When, tongue in cheek, I suggested to my father that a court-martial was long overdue, and that it simply had been convened for the wrong reasons, he did not think the comment amusing.

The "Colonel Forbes" referred to by my father was probably Colonel Joseph H. Ford, then commander of the Allerey hospital center.

7. Assuming its authenticity, this is a fascinating example of "the world turned upside down," in which Blacks dominated the informal social structure of the stockade. Presumably, northern white boys went along with the arrangement as a lark, but for southern Whites the experience must have been traumatic.

We thus find three places in France of 1917–19 under Army control that were not racially segregated: hospitals, stockades, and cemeteries.

8. Such was the conversion of a son of the 69th who, only the day before, fully shared his comrades' view that the "Fighting Few" were unseemly in their contest for headlines of glory. The dislike was mutual. While passing a Marine contingent, some leatherneck was bound to shout: "WHAT COMES OUT *AFTER* THE STORM?" And a hundred Marines would yell: "THE RAINBOW!" The immediate response to such lese majesty was: "GO HOME AND TELL YER MOTHER YOU SEEN A SOLDIER!" But the worst leatherneck cut was: "WHAT'S THE BRIGHTEST COLOR IN THE RAINBOW?" "YELLOW!" The Rainbow's answer to this incitement was too obscene to print. Suffice to say, when applied, it ensured that the Marines *had* to be the "First to Fight."

—Berry, *op. cit.,* pp. 114–117; and Charles MacArthur, *op. cit.,* pp. 75–76.

9. Donovan, at this time, was the Colonel of the 69th, and MacArthur had been promoted to command the Rainbow.

10. Today, all that remains of the American Military Hospital at Allerey, once the largest medical complex in France, is the brick remnants of a cistern. The small village of Allerey continues much as at the turn of the century.

Fortunately, I there met Monsieur and Mme Albert Dorey who vividly recall those hectic weeks of 1918–19, when hospital trains disgorged thousands of wounded into this monstrous complex.

Endnotes

Albert Dorey was then 13 years old, and almost every day, after school, he would hasten to the camp to visit an "adopted" American doughboy patient. He showed our party more than a dozen period postcards that portrayed the camp as it functioned, and personally conducted us over the now deserted fields, indicating where this and that building had made an indelible impression on his young mind. He then guided us to the village cemetery. There among the meticulously maintained graves of Allerey's past generations, stood a unique granite column, on one side of which was inscribed:

PAUL E. BURTON, Private, Base Hospital No. 25, U.S.A. Died July 15, 1918. HE VENTURED FAR TO PRESERVE THE LIBERTIES OF MANKIND.

And on the other side:

ERECTED BY THE CITIZENS OF ALLEREY OVER THE FIRST AMERICAN GRAVE IN THEIR COMMUNE.

The ruins of a cistern and the grave of Private Burton are the sole vestiges of a mighty American presence in a community where once generals and high-ranking civilian officials paid their respects. Private Burton died and was adopted by the village before the hospital cemetery had been developed. The remains of hundreds of other patients who died at Allerey were disinterred after the war, either to be returned to the States, or consolidated in one of the large American World War I cemeteries in France. If the latter, they repose in largely forgotten splendor. Few Americans visit those cemeteries today (although I have seen busloads of French school-children). Private Burton is fortunate in having frequent visitors and is often remembered by the citizens of Allerey.

Due to the efforts of M. Antonin Guillot, a teacher in the neighboring village of Verdun-sur-Doubs, there has been a resurgent interest in the history of the American hospital camp. In 1975, Mr. Guillot arranged an exposition of old photographs of the camp for the museum of Nicephore Niepce in Chalons-sur-Saone.

Endnotes to Chapter Ten

1. I would have added: "During this period of engagement, he countermanded an order from superior officers to attack, when he

had every reason to believe the result would have been both ineffectual and disastrous for the regiment, taking full responsibility for his action."

——WWI Organ. Records, 42nd Div., HQ 333, "Inspections and Investigations," Box 94.

2. At this time, Smedley Butler was already a Marine *nonpareil*, having twice received the Congressional Medal of Honor for acts of extraordinary heroism at Vera Cruz and in Haiti. Although a highly acclaimed leader and organizer, and immensely popular within the Corps, he was never appointed its Commandant, presumably because of his occasional criticism of this country's Latin American interventions.

3. What a remarkable expression! What was Duffy referring to? My father died before I could reflect and quiz him in greater detail on this event. Possibly, the enjoinder was directed at the court-martial board and was uniquely tailored to the immediate need, as Duffy perceived it, to displace the young doughboy's guilt and to restore his self-confidence. Father Duffy was no monk and took the secular world far too seriously to summarily dispatch its inhabitants to hell, and elsewhere, he ascribed greater virtue to the Army hierarchy of the day, particularly in matters of race, than it deserved. On the other hand, this expression succinctly expresses the irreverence toward secular authority in general so characteristic of the Irish-American Doughboy.

4. Amazingly, my father had remembered the name of his brother's buddy, presumably a person he had never met. *The Fordham Monthly* (Vol. 36, Oct. 1917) contains a roster of the 140 members of the Fordham Ambulance Unit that sailed for France. Included in the listing is a Charles J. Dolan from Pennsylvania. Although, the story involving Dolan is improbable on its face, Bill Ettinger was cited for two medals, a *Croix de Guerre* and a Purple Heart. Both repose in the custody of his son, Kevin Ettinger.

5. Although I have seen no other account of this incident, Charles MacArthur, in *War Bugs* (p. 300), refers to "a glorious night out [prior to departure] in which we beat the hell out of the brass-knuckle boys stationed in Brest to guard morals and enforce saluting. . . ." MacArthur's Illinois gunners frequently buddied with men of the 69th.

The story also gains credibility through a documented experience of New York's 15th Guard. A week earlier, they, too, had arrived in Brest, homeward bound. Shortly after detraining, two MPs split the skull of one of the black doughboys because he had dared to interrupt their conversation with an inquiry. Upon arriving at the explosive scene that ensued, Major Arthur Little of the 15th demanded an explanation, and his confrontation with the captain of MPs involved was characteristic of Donovan's alleged encounter.

—See Arthur Little, *From Harlem to the Rhine*, pp. 350–356.

6. Actually, Camp Dix, New Jersey.

Endnotes to Epilogue

1. Peter Grace was a good friend of Donovan, and both Donovan and Father Duffy often found employment for the hard-pressed former members of the regiment. It was a sustained operation of the "Old Boy Network." In all probability, that is how FitzSimmons was hired by Peter Grace.

2. See Appendix F: "Father Duffy: Biographical Sketch."

3. Dorothy Clark, my father's first wife, and my mother.

4. Don Adair passed over the rainbow four months after my father's death. Only a few weeks before his coronary, I had spent a delightful weekend with Don, his sister, and brother-in-law in Essex, Connecticut.

5. On December 7, 1941, the 69th was encamped at Ft. Polk, La., having been activated for over a year. The following is from a letter provided by Bernard Kelly, Commander of the 69th Veteran Corps:

"The . . . regiment was called to active duty with the 27th (New York) Division on 15 Oct 40 and sent to Ft. McClellan, Alabama. It participated in [three maneuvers in the South]. . . . On 10 Dec 41, the troops [entrained to Los Angeles] . . . and the regiment proceeded to Burbank, where they performed security for Burbank Airport and the Lockheed Aircraft Company. In Jan 41, they were sent to Ft. Ord, where the regiment was brought up to full strength . . . and in April 41, they embarked . . . [for] Honolulu, [arriving] on Easter Sunday '41. They marched across the pier to another troop ship which took them to Kauai. They and the rest of the 27th Division established the defense of the Hawaiian Islands. (This was a couple of months before Midway and an invasion of Hawaii was seen as a distinct possibility.) The 27th Division was the first U.S. Division to deploy overseas in WWII.

"While on Kauai, two cadres were taken from the Regiment . . . to help form the 10th (Mountain) and 11th (Airborne) Divisions.

. . . Many others left for the Air Corps and Officers Training. Members of the regiment fought in just about every major army engagement in both theaters of operation.

"The Regiment saw action on Makin, Saipan and Okinawa. They were a part of the occupation of Japan. A Medal of Honor was awarded on Okinawa, and "F" Co. was awarded a Presidential Citation. 473 men made the supreme sacrifice and thousands were wounded. It was the only war in which the Regiment lost both a Regimental Commander (Colonel Conroy on Makin) and a Chaplain (Father Lynch on Okinawa).

"The Regiment was mustered out in Japan in Nov 45 after almost four years overseas and over five years duration of service."

Selected Bibliography

*American Battle Monuments Commission. *American Armies and Battlefields in Europe*. United States Government Printing Office, 1938.

Amerine, William H. *Alabama's Own in France*. New York: Eaton & Gettinger, 1919.

Army Times. *The Daring Regiments: Adventures of the AEF in World War I*. New York: Dodd, Mead, 1967.

Bach, Christian and Hall, Henry. *The Fourth Division*. The Division, 1920.

Baker, Newton D. *Why We Went to War*. New York: Harper, 1936.

*Barbeau, Arthur E. and Henri, Florette. *The Unknown Soldiers*. Philadelphia: Temple University Press, 1974.

Barnes, Harry Elmer. *The Genesis of the World War*. New York: Alfred A. Knopf, 1929.

*Berry, Henry. *Make the Kaiser Dance: Living Memories of the Doughboy*. New York: Arbor House, 1978.

*Brown, Anthony Cave. *The Last Hero*. New York: Vintage Books, 1982.

Cheseldine, R. M. *Ohio In The Rainbow*. Columbus, Ohio: F. J. Heer, 1924.

*Coffman, Edward M. *The War to End All Wars: The American Experience in World War I*. New York: Oxford University Press, 1968.

Devlin, Patrick. *Too Proud to Fight, Woodrow Wilson's Neutrality*. Oxford University Press, 1975.

*Duffy, Francis P. *Father Duffy's Story*. New York: George H. Doran, 1919.

Flick, Ella. *Chaplain Duffy of the Sixty-Ninth Regiment*. Philadelphia: Dolphin Press, 1935.

Fredman, George & Falk, Louis, *Jews in American Wars*. Hoboken, N.J.: Terminal Printing & Publishing Co., 1942.

Flanagan, Thomas. *Year of the French*. New York: Holt, Rinehart & Winston, 1979.

---

*Particularly recommended in the context of this book.

Grattan, Hartley. *Why We Fought*. New York: Vanguard, 1929.

Hart, Liddell. *History of the First World War*. London: Pan Books Ltd., 1982.

Hogan, Martin J. *The Shamrock Battalion of the Rainbow: A Story of the "Fighting Sixty-Ninth."* New York: D. Appelton, 1919.

Holiday, Robert Cortes, Ed. *Joyce Kilmer*. New York: George H. Doran, 1918.

*Horne, Alistair. *The Price of Glory: Verdun*. New York: St. Martin's, 1963.

*James, D. Clayton. *The Years of MacArthur,* Vol. 1, Boston: Houghton Mifflin Co., 1970.

Keegan, John. *The Face of Battle*. New York: Viking Press, 1976.

Liggett, Hunter. *A.E.F.* New York: Dodd, Mead, 1928.

*Little, Arthur W. *From Harlem to the Rhine*. New York: Covici-Friede, 1936.

Manchester, William. *American Caesar*. Boston: Little, Brown & Co., 1978.

*MacArthur, Charles. *War Bugs*. New York: Doubleday, Doran, 1929.

MacArthur, Douglas. *Reminiscences*. New York: McGraw Hill, 1964.

MacDonald, Lyn. *Somme*. London: Michael Joseph, 1983.

Marshall, S.L.A. *World War I*. New York: American Heritage, 1985.

Palmer, Frederick. *Newton D. Baker*. 2 vols. New York: Dodd, Mead, 1931.

*Paschall, Rod. *The Defeat of Imperial Germany,* 1917–1918. Chapel Hill: Algonquin Books, 1989.

Pershing, John J. *My Experiences in the World War*. New York: Frederick A. Stokes Co., 1931.

*Reilly, Henry J. *Americans All—The Rainbow at War*. Columbus, Ohio: The F. J. Heer Printing Co., 1936.

Schieber, Clara Eve. *The Transformation of American Sentiment Toward Germany*. Boston: Cornhill Publishing Co., 1923.

*Stallings, Laurence. *The Doughboys*. New York: Harper & Row, 1963.

Taber, John H. *The Story of The 168th Infantry*. Iowa City: State Historical Society of Iowa, 1925.

Bibliography

Toland, John. *No Man's Land*. New York: Ballantine Books, 1980.

*Tuchman, Barbara. *The Zimmermann Telegram*. New York: Macmillan, 1958.

Tuchman, B. *The Guns of August*. New York: Macmillan, 1962.

*Watt, Richard M. *Dare Call it Treason*. New York: Simon and Schuster, 1936.

Wolf, Walter. *The Story of the Rainbow Division*. New York: Rand McNally, 1919.

Index

GENERAL

PERSONS

POEMS